SAS BRAVO THREE ZERO

Des Powell
and
Damien Lewis

SAS
BRAVO
THREE ZERO

QUERCUS

First published in Great Britain in 2021 by Quercus.
This paperback edition published in 2022 by

QUERCUS

Quercus Editions Ltd
Carmelite House
50 Victoria Embankment
London EC4Y 0DZ

An Hachette UK company

A CIP catalogue record for this book is available
from the British Library

MMP ISBN 978 1 52941 416 5
Ebook ISBN 978 1 52941 414 1

PICTURE CREDITS

All images are © and courtesy of the author Des Powell except, in order of appearance:
18, 20, 28 – Cameron Spence's *Sabre Squadron*; 19 – AP/ISNA/Ruhollah Vahdati;
21 – Wikimedia/Vitaly V Kuzmin; 22 – Peter de la Billière's *Storm Command*;
26, 27 – US Department of Defence

10 9 8 7 6 5 4 3 2 1

Typeset by CC Book Production Ltd
Printed and bound in Great Britain by Clays Ltd, Elcograf S.p.A.

Papers used by Quercus Editions Ltd are from well-managed forests and other responsible sources.

For Jake, Sam and Jessica (The Acorns).
From small acorns grow big Oak trees.

Des Powell

For Mark Bradley and Jeff Allum.
Warriors, mavericks, true friends.

Damien Lewis

We are the pilgrims, master; we shall go
Always a little further; it may be
Beyond that last blue mountain barred with snow
Across that angry or that glimmering sea.

James Elroy Flecker
(the unofficial regimental collect of the SAS)

CONTENTS

FIRST AUTHOR'S NOTE

For reasons of national security and/or confidentiality, it has been necessary to change some details of events, including names, places and dates, when writing this book.

This book has been written from my memory and from conversations with those fellow soldiers who were able to talk with me about the events portrayed. No one recorded the conversations that took place and few written reports were produced. I have therefore re-created conversations as accurately as I can and as I, and others, remember them.

I have been fortunate in that several other accounts of the SAS's 1991 war in Iraq have been published, and I have been able to cross-check many of the events portrayed. These include first-hand accounts of the activities of various patrols, plus more general books giving a wider sense of the UK special forces campaign in Iraq. I have included a full bibliography at the end of this book, for those who wish to read more on the subject.

In the 1980s, a covert force was formed to better respond to the nature of modern-day conflict. Only experienced veterans were selected and each was exhaustively vetted. The name of this force remains classified, but the kind of missions undertaken were those our government might wish to deny. This outfit still exists, and it carries out some of the Regiment's most interesting operations. For the purposes of this book it is referred to simply as 'The Unit'.

Des Powell, July 2021

PREFACE

A while ago I drove north to the city of Bath, to meet up with a former Special Air Service operator called Derek 'Des' Powell, together with his close friend Paul Hughes, who is also ex-military. Paul had reached out to me via mutual friends, to tell me a little about Des's remarkable career in the SAS, particularly the time he spent deep behind the lines in Iraq, in 1991, during the First Gulf War.

We met at the very well-appointed Francis Hotel, in Bath's Queen Square, and spent several hours over tea and cakes, talking through the nineteen years Des had spent serving at the apex of Britain's armed forces and in all imaginable theatres of war. But what really stood out for me was that 1991 Iraq mission, one that I could not quite believe I had never heard about, especially as I have read and written extensively about special forces missions.

A great deal of what the man on the street tends to know about SAS operations during the First Gulf War generally arises from the clutch of books that were published soon after by former SAS operators, most notably Andy McNab's *Bravo Two Zero* and Chris

Ryan's *The One That Got Away*. Both concern the eight-man SAS patrol codenamed Bravo Two Zero and the hellish fate that befell all on that team, after they were compromised by the enemy and forced to go on the run in Iraq.

The First Gulf War involved a UN-mandated coalition of armed forces from the world's foremost military nations, who went to war in the Middle East to evict the Iraqi dictator Saddam Hussein's military from Kuwait, a sovereign nation lying to the south of Iraq, which had been invaded, looted and comprehensively taken over. Saddam had sent his armed forces into the oil-rich country seeking territorial and financial gain – nothing more. All special forces sent into Iraq were warned that if they were captured, they should expect to face the direst of fates at the hands of their captors.

Consequently, the men of the Bravo Two Zero patrol did all in their power to escape and evade the enemy, but, moving on foot through terrible conditions, all but one were killed or captured. Chris Ryan was the exception, and his book tells the story of his epic escape to safety. As the story of the First Gulf War played out on the world's TV screens, the fate of the Bravo Two Zero patrol became known to the world's public, and even more so after the books were published.

I had read those accounts at the time, and the stories concerning the Bravo Two Zero patrol were undoubtedly compelling. Unsurprisingly, they captured the imagination of the British people. But what I hadn't realized until sitting down to talk to Des Powell was that there were *three* Bravo patrols sent into Iraq in January 1991: Bravo One Zero, Bravo Two Zero and Bravo Three Zero. Bravo One's story proved short-lived and this book explains why. With Bravo Two Zero, the British and international public all know the tale of what befell their patrol.

Until now, no one but those few hailing from the special forces community has been any the wiser as to the fate that befell the third patrol, Bravo Three Zero. Des served as its second-in-command, and what he was able to outline to me during our chat at the Francis Hotel proved utterly riveting. Des opened the door on an epic of untold action, heroism, courage and fortitude against all odds, while also telling of a series of significant failures and shortcomings suffered by all three Bravo patrols, underlining why the men of Bravo Two Zero may have suffered the dire fate that they did. He also spoke of the very significant achievements scored by the Special Air Service in Iraq, which seem to have been overshadowed by the spectacularly dark and fearful fate that befell that one patrol.

As 2021 marks the thirtieth anniversary of the 1991 Gulf War, it strikes me as being only right and proper that Des and his wider patrol finally get to tell their story. It is one that will not only grip from the very start, being a chronicle of immense personal courage and fortitude, but should also prove historically significant, offering up insight and lessons to be learned, ones that remain highly relevant today.

Damien Lewis, July 2021

CHAPTER ONE

BIG DOGS DON'T BARK

As we headed through the dusty, sun-baked, one-horse town of a place, I could sense the suspicion and hostility hanging heavy in the air.

Our vehicles – civvie-looking Toyota Land Cruisers – were perfect for crossing rough desert terrain, but not so great for keeping a low profile and making like locals. We were a two-vehicle convoy, but the Land Cruisers were just too damn modern and functional, and not beaten about enough, stained with oil and caked in dust to blend in. We were dressed in civvies, with Arab-style shemaghs – headscarves – wrapped around our faces, but that didn't hide the fact that we were outsiders.

Targets.

This area was notorious – barren, featureless, waterless mostly, and known to be a hotbed of extremism. Foreigners – Westerners in particular – were not always welcome in this part of the Middle East. I just had to hope my mucker, Steve Jones, riding in the rear vehicle, would prove himself as switched on and as clued in as I hoped he was, for I figured trouble was brewing big time.

1

There was a squelch of static in my radio earpiece. 'Lots of locals clocking us there, Des.'

'Yeah, seen that, mate,' I replied to Steve. Good to see that he was on the ball. 'Keep your eyes peeled.'

I could feel my adrenaline spiking and that weird, wired, hyper-alert feeling that takes over your senses whenever you feel combat might be imminent, or your life to be in mortal danger. Instinctively, I reached down with my left hand and felt for the reassuring shape of the M16 assault rifle I had jammed into the space beside my seat.

I am a left-handed shooter. In the Regiment, I was forever being slated for it. 'Des, you should've been drowned at birth. All lefties should have. You're an awkward cuss.'

In truth, there are significant drawbacks to being a leftie. As I'd learned to my cost, most weapons are designed for right-handed operators. Years back I'd been in Northern Ireland, on a covert recce where I needed to blend in. Dressed like a regular squaddie in green Army kit and tin lid, I'd been carrying an SA80, the British Army's standard assault rifle. But when it came to putting down some fire, all of a sudden I'd got smacked in the teeth while operating it left-handed. At first I thought I'd been shot, the blow was so powerful. It turned out the SA80's cocking handle was designed only for a right-handed operator: it had shot back while ejecting a spent round and cracked me full in the mouth. I still have the scars to show for it.

But there is one significant advantage to being a leftie, especially when serving alongside a right-handed operator, like Steve. A few days back we'd practised our anti-ambush drills out on the ranges. I had exited my vehicle first, putting down the initial burst of rounds, allowing Steve time to exit and make the first move, or 'bound' as we call it in the trade. With my weapon on my left shoulder, I could see Steve in my peripheral vision, and when he went static and started hammering out the rounds, I was up on my feet and moving like lightning. Fire-and-manoeuvre is the bread and butter of countering hostile enemy action, for which a left–right pairing is the perfect combination.

Steve and I pulled away from that hellhole of a town, fully aware that we had been clocked by the bad guys. We headed south, moving into a vast stretch of burned-brown, undulating desert terrain, which unrolled before us under wide, furnace skies. The horizon shimmered. Rivulets of sweat dripped down my back. There seemed little the vehicle's aircon could do to counter such suffocating heat. I could see my driver – Mo, a local and a real solid kind of a guy – glancing nervously in his rear-view mirror, his armpits dark pits of sweat.

He knew just as well as we did that trouble was coming.

All of a sudden Steve was on the radio again. 'Third party approaching from behind, Des.'

I glanced in my wing mirror. Sure enough, we had some kind of 4x4 motoring up towards us, trailing a thick cloud of dust. In this part of the world everyone drove like a bat out of hell and everyone carried a weapon. You couldn't just go blasting apart any vehicle that looked like it might be a drive-by shooting waiting to happen. More to the point, in the unit I hailed from it was all about winning hearts and minds, as much as it was about who dares wins. That was a lesson learned first during the SAS's earliest operations in World War Two, and we'd taken it with us into all conflicts ever since.

The 4x4 bearing down on us could just conceivably be some innocent locals, in a hurry to get somewhere . . . although I really didn't think so. If we acted first and took out what we feared was the threat, it could be a total disaster hearts-and-minds wise.

Hence my orders to Steve. 'Slow down. Let 'em pass. That way, we get eyes-on and we can suss out their intentions.'

'Got it.'

I motioned to Mo to ease off the gas. He'd been my driver for some weeks now, and as far as I was concerned he was as good as it gets. Tough, measured, loyal, brave, he was one of our prime sources of intel, as well as being more than half-decent behind the wheel. By now, few words needed to be said between us whenever I wanted something doing.

As the suspect 4x4 thundered past Steve's wagon and approached ours, I patted my bumbag, which I always wore on my front when riding in a vehicle. It contained my Glock pistol, plus a few very handy grenades: great for when you wanted to crack open your door and roll one out under a nearby vehicle, before accelerating away from the danger.

When riding in an armoured vehicle you can't open fire without cracking a window, or opening the door and bailing out – otherwise the bullets will ricochet off the armour or bullet-proof glass and most likely kill or wound you and whoever else is with you. That was the beauty of the grenades. If you slipped open the door and tossed one out, it would detonate under the hostile vehicle while doing you very little harm, because you were encased within a shell of protective armour. That was why I always kept a couple to hand, in case of the kind of threat I feared we were about to face now.

The 4x4 slowed its speed to match our own, and I swear I could feel the hostility of the stares drilling into the side of my head. They were two-up, a driver and a passenger, and both were very, very unfriendly looking. No sign of any weaponry yet, but that didn't mean a thing. They wouldn't be able to see my arsenal, either, or Steve's for that matter. A second 4x4 emerged from out of the dust and accelerated to pass us, the air crawling with danger and evil intent. That vehicle was also two-up.

So there were four of them versus the two of us shooters, for neither Steve's driver nor mine was armed.

The 4x4s pulled in ahead of us and slowed, throwing up a thick cloud of dust in our path, making for perfect ambush conditions: ideal for forcing us to a halt, guns blazing. I could feel every fibre of my body tensing with the knife-edge, pulse-pounding anticipation of imminent combat, my teeth grinding against each other as I psyched myself up for what I knew was coming. But finally, the dust cloud began to dissipate a little, and I could just make out the vehicles haring away at speed.

Gone to seek reinforcements, no doubt, I told myself, grimly.

'Mate, let's pull up for a chinwag,' I announced into my headset.

My voice had gone noticeably gravelly and deep, the result of all the adrenaline that was pumping though my veins. I rarely get like this, and only when true danger is threatening. I have been blessed with an acute kind of sixth sense. A threat radar. A gut instinct. I've learned never to ignore it.

We pulled over onto the side of the track. 'Right, those fuckers are up to no good,' I announced. I just knew – *knew* – we were in trouble, and my voice was laced with tension and raw aggression. This far from friendly territory, we had only two options – fight or flight – and it was one hell of a long way to head back through the badlands to reach friendly lines. 'I don't feel like being dead today.'

Steve locked eyes with mine. He was a man of few words, but bulletproof reliable, or so I hoped. He breathed not a word, waiting for me to set the tone for our next move.

'If they show their hand, let's knock those fuckers on their arses,' I announced, my finger punching the air in the direction the 4x4s had disappeared. 'And before they get the chance to do one on us.' Now to pop the million-dollar question. We were bound to be outnumbered and very possibly outgunned. Easy to opt to run in such a situation. But as far as I was concerned, there was no running from this one. 'Mate, are you fucking up for it?'

Forgive me for the cussing. In normal civilized society I rarely if ever swear. But using such language is a natural – unavoid-able – corollary to the aggression that is crucial to winning such a firefight as I felt sure was coming. It's also a simple fact of such situations that whether you choose to stand and fight or run depends to a great extent on the calibre – the raw warrior spirit – of those on your shoulder. I'd never been in action with Steve before. Right now was when the rubber would hit the road.

Steve's gaze remained steady, unwavering. 'Yes, mate, I fucking am. They show their hand, we take the fuckers on.'

Steve was former Parachute Regiment like me. I'd never really doubted him, but it was still good to hear those words and the rock-steady tone in which they were delivered. Even better to see the flinty determination in Steve's eyes.

'Right, this is what I want you to do. As soon as they make their move against us, I'll stop our vehicle and exit right. I'll put down rounds immediately to cover you. You exit as fast as you can and take the first bound forward. Once I see you putting down rounds, I'll make the next bound, stop, down on one knee and fire. Soon as you see that, you make the next bound, and we'll pepperpot right up to the target. You okay with that?'

I needed to double-check with Steve that he'd got it, as this is actually the *reverse* of how you normally train for such a scenario. Normally, when riding in a vehicle and facing an ambush, you make your bounds – 'pepperpotting' – *backwards*, away from the threat, to disengage from the source of the danger. But right here and now, I sensed that we had to do the opposite. We had to go forward, taking the fight to the enemy with raw aggression and deadly accurate firepower. It was the last thing they'd ever be expecting.

'Roger that,' Steve confirmed. 'We take the fight right to 'em.'

'Any questions?'

'None.'

'Listen, let's nail these fuckers. No one is going to tell us what we can and can't do around here, okay?'

'Got it,' Steve confirmed.

This wasn't any kind of vacuous pep talk. As team leader, I was revving us up for what I knew in my bones was coming. The smallest number you'd ever deploy with is two-up – a two-person team. I needed to get Steve – and myself – worked up into a fever pitch of self-belief and our blood well up, so we'd take the fight right down the enemy's gun barrels.

'Keep in contact via the body-sets. Control your firepower. Keep it tight and accurate and let's bound all the way up to the fuckers' eyeballs.'

'Got it.'

'And remember, no one ever dies from a loud bang.'

He smiled. No further words necessary.

No one ever dies from a loud bang – one of the oldest sayings in the Regiment. It's the corollary to: *Controlled and accurate shooting wins the day.* Most adversaries we tended to come up against had a habit of unleashing massive amounts of fire, but making precious little attempt to aim. Lots of noise and dramatic pyrotechnics, but not the best way to go about killing your adversary. Hence the saying: *No one ever dies from a loud bang.*

We had to presume these guys were carrying AK-47 assault rifles. In the Regiment we were trained to use just about every weapon imaginable, our own and the enemy's. With the AK's safety catch mechanism, the first click takes it off 'safe' mode and into automatic, the second to single-fire. That reflects the mindset of the Russian military, for which the AK-47 was initially designed: it was all about putting down as much hot lead as quickly as possible. By contrast, British and US assault rifles tend to have the opposite settings: first to single-fire, then to auto.

As sure as eggs is eggs, the bad guys would flick their AKs onto automatic, especially when faced with our gleaming Toyotas, which were just too tempting a target. The AK-47 is a big, heavy grunt of a weapon, and in auto mode it has a massive kick, which makes it slam back into your shoulder, forcing the barrel to rise into the air. That would play into our hands, or so I hoped, causing our adversaries to shoot high.

Plan sorted, Steve and I got back into the wagons and got underway again.

There was one other reason I was convinced we had no choice but to stand and fight: if we turned tail, we'd be in a car chase, which would automatically give the bad guys the upper hand. On tarmac, their 4x4s would very likely be able to keep pace with ours. If we ventured off road, experience had proven we'd risk getting bogged. Deprived of the vehicles – of our all-important mobility – we'd be finished.

On foot, they'd hunt us down in the desert like dogs.

We had a saying about this in Air Troop, the SAS unit I hailed from. Going off road was like sticking with a bad parachute during a jump: if it hadn't opened properly, it never would, and the ground was rushing up to meet you very, very fast. Likewise, leaving the road amidst such terrain was not a smart idea, especially as the locals were sure to know the area like the back of their hand.

Before joining Air Troop, I'd done a year with Mobility Troop – those who specialize in using vehicles as the means to enter hostile lands, as opposed to airborne (parachute) insertions with Air Troop, waterborne means with Boat Troop, or high-altitude means with Mountain Troop. In Mobility Troop, we'd had drilled into us this one vital lesson: lose your vehicles – your chief means of mobility – and you were finished. That was the key takeaway.

We had another saying in the Regiment that to me was like a universal mantra: *Always be cautious of people who talk loudly and brag – a lion never has to tell you it's a lion.* Those who mouth off and pose and swagger don't tend to have the fight in them, at least not when push comes to shove. Likewise, I'd sensed from the bad guys' posture and attitude that they wouldn't be able to meet fire with fire for long, and certainly not when faced with two maniacs – Steve and myself – charging down their very eyeballs.

A few klicks further along the road we reached our intended destination – a disused power station that we had to give the once-over. So far, there had been no further signs of the bad guys, but that didn't mean shit. Steve and I walked around the deserted buildings and sorted out our routes into and out of the complex, for when we had to return here with a far larger force, to execute the main mission. Today was just a recce. Before returning to the vehicles to head back to base, I reminded Steve to keep hyper-alert, for I didn't think for one minute that the danger had gone away.

Sure enough, we'd been underway for less than ten minutes when I clocked two vehicles in the distance up ahead, more or less blocking the road. Curiously, these weren't the 4x4s that we'd seen earlier. They were standard Nissan-type saloon cars. But that didn't mean a thing. It was the way they were parked up – in a V-shape and mostly barring the route ahead – that raised my suspicions.

Standard anti-ambush drills are to keep driving and to smash a way through any roadblock. But I didn't think for one moment that would work here. Fast and all-terrain friendly, the 4x4s were likely the recce force, while the Nissan guys would be the raw firepower. If we tried to ram our way through, there were bound to be further hostiles mustering up ahead. If we turned and ran that would be like a massive come-on, and they'd come tearing after us, so we'd be taking rounds up our backsides.

In elite forces circles, we always try to fight at a time and place of our own choosing. This was far from ideal, but it was better than all the alternatives I could think of. We needed to deal with this here and now, with swift, decisive and deadly firepower. That way, no one else would have the inclination to try to take us on.

I reached across to Mo, and gestured for him to slow the vehicle to a crawl.

'Steve: stand by, stand by,' I breathed into my radio.

'Roger that.' Calm, collected, but pumped with adrenaline – it was just the kind of response I was hoping for.

We crept forward at around 20 mph. Three hundred yards, two-fifty, two hundred – my mind was kicking off in all directions, my senses working overtime, heart racing as the tension kept building and building. I saw the doors crack open in the Nissans up ahead, as figures tumbled out into the dust and the fierce afternoon sunlight. I could see already that they were armed. But like I said, every man and his dog carries an AK-47 in this part of the world. We still needed them to show their hand.

Instinctively, it was now that I reached inside my shirt and grabbed hold of what I had slung around my neck. They were a bog-standard set of Army-issue dog tags, but to me they had become like a talisman. I wore them everywhere I went, no matter how secret or deniable the mission and bugger the rules. They had become my touchstone. At 25,000 feet and about to hurl myself off the ramp of a C-130 Hercules; at 30 feet and about to leap off the ramp of a Chinook into a raging, night-dark sea; anywhere heading into imminent combat – I'd grab hold of my dog tags, take a grip on my inner core and say these few words to myself: *Let's get the job done, Des, and let's fuck off home.*

Nothing more, nothing less; just those few simple words. It served to ground me and calm me and give me focus and self-belief. *Let's get this done and let's get home for tea and medals.*

I was once training with a bunch of Delta Force guys, and we were about to blow our way through the target house door. I put my hand to my chest, and one of the Delta guys – Delta Force is the nearest US equivalent to the SAS – saw me whisper my time-honoured mantra. After the exercise was over, he picked a quiet moment to come and have a word with me.

'Des, I saw you going through your ritual earlier. Heard you talking to yourself. But who were you speaking to really, Des?'

I smiled. 'Any sod who's listening.'

'Are you religious?' he pushed.

'Don't think so.'

'Are you spiritual? What type of faith d'you follow?'

'Not sure. My mam was a Methodist, my dad a spiritualist.'

'What does that make you?'

I paused for effect. 'A methylated spirit.'

The other SAS guys on the team dissolved into laughter. The Delta guy didn't get it, for methylated spirits is known as 'denatured alcohol' in the US, so the joke just didn't make any sense to him. He stared at me, head on one side. 'That your Brit sense of humour?'

I told him that it was.

And right now, as I put my hand on my dog tags and went through my revered ritual, I reminded myself of just why Steve and I were here. If you aspired to serve in the SAS – wearing the beige beret and the winged dagger – there would be times when you'd have to put your life on the line. If you weren't up for that, you should never have sought to join in the first place. It came with the territory.

I was proud to have served in the Parachute Regiment and even more to have made it into the Special Air Service. One of the favourite sayings we had at Hereford – hometown of the SAS – was *Big dogs don't bark*. That is a motto fit to live by. It was one that I figured Steve and I were going to have to embody right now, as we took the fight to the enemy.

Moments after finishing my ritual with my tags, I saw the figures up ahead start jockeying for position. Seconds later, the first guy brought his weapon to his shoulder and opened fire, spraying a long burst of rounds into the desert to the front and to either side of us.

I thrust out my right hand and slammed my palm across Mo's chest: 'Stop! Stop! Stop!'

As he came to a halt, I put my shoulder to my door, barged it open and hit the deck, running, running. I'd already configured my mags, slotting them into my chest pouches for ease of access, and I'd moved my M16 from beside me onto my lap. I dashed a good 20 feet ahead of the Toyota, moving forward and covering the first ground.

Then I went static, down on one knee, while bringing the M16 into my shoulder in one fluid movement. I could see four gunmen at the front of the roadblock, each brandishing an AK-47. There could be more of them, waiting in the vehicles. No way of knowing. Bullets were spitting and snarling all around as I opened fire, putting down controlled double taps – aimed, two-round bursts. I saw bullets spark off the flank of the nearest Nissan, and its headlamps shatter in a shower of glittering glass.

Blanking my mind to the fact that I was alone out here and in zero cover, I adjusted my fire, walking my rounds onto the human targets.

It was them that we needed to kill.

The gunmen shifted their aim, realizing that one of their targets had broken free from his vehicle. I saw the first spurts of dirt kicking up to the left and right of me as they let rip in my direction, the desert sand darting and spurting all around. While it was one hell of a lot of incoming, the fire was all over the place, but that didn't mean a stray round wouldn't kill. The AK-47 is a 7.62 mm weapon, as opposed to the 5.56 mm calibre of the M16, so it packs a considerably greater punch, and its bullets are decidedly lethal.

'MOVE NOW!' I yelled.

It was now that I needed Steve to make his first bound forward, to unsettle and confound the enemy. Conversely, if he didn't show, I was as good as finished, with little cover, nowhere to hide and no backup or covering fire. For the barest instant I wondered if I had misjudged him, before I saw a figure flash through my peripheral vision. Steve was around forty paces away from me on the far side of the lead wagon, dashing towards the enemy like Usain Bolt on speed.

Go, Steve, go.

I saw him come to a halt and go down on one knee. His weapon came up and he squeezed off the first rounds. Fast, fluid, instinctive, controlled, he was moving like a true professional. We might be outnumbered, but we were far more exhaustively trained, infinitely more resourceful and armed with better weaponry, I reminded myself.

Now, to win this.

'MOVE NOW!' Steve yelled.

As I rose to my feet, my left hand flipped out the first empty mag from the M16, reached for a replacement and slotted it into the weapon, even as my legs powered forward. I tore past Steve, advancing a good 30 feet, before dropping onto one knee and opening fire again.

I made sure Steve had spied my position, before yelling: 'MOVE NOW!'

In a carbon copy of my own dash, Steve raced ahead, changing his mag as he went. I kept hammering out the rounds – *bang-bang*; double tap, *bang-bang*; double tap – all the while reminding myself just what kind of psychological impact this had to be having on the enemy. Here we were in the depths of their territory, outnumbered and basically outgunned, but instead of fleeing or retreating we were racing down their very guns.

Unnerving, to say the least.

Soul-destroying and life-ending was what I fully intended.

I could see massive amounts of bursts erupting around Steve and myself, as fierce volleys of AK fire kicked up the dirt, blasted sand ripping into exposed skin and eyes. I could hear the distinctive, deafening *dzzzzzzzzztttt* made by several AKs unleashing on automatic. We might well be facing a wall of fire, but those long, greedy bursts would prove less accurate, and it would mean that they were burning through their ammo big time.

No one carries an unlimited amount of bullets. As I tried to comfort myself with that thought, rounds tore past like a swarm of angry hornets, the air juddering with the impact of deadly projectiles travelling at twice the speed of sound. Some were so close that I could feel the air snap and tear, as they ripped past just inches away from my head.

Then I saw myself drop the first guy. One moment he was unleashing in our general direction, his muzzle sparking fire, the next I had him nailed in my sights and let rip with a double tap. He folded into a bloodied heap on the sand. *Pleased with that*, I told myself. We were far from out of the woods yet, but the psychology of this truly had to be getting to the enemy.

'Go!' Steve yelled.

As I launched into a repeat of the previous bound, I noticed how with each leg Steve and I were converging on each other, closing the gap on the enemy. We were less than 75 feet away from them now, and as I dashed forward, moving in still further, I saw Steve drop a second of the gunmen. The figure collapsed onto his knees, as a pall of red bloomed on his chest, before another of Steve's rounds tore into him, flipping him around and down.

'Go!' I yelled, as my right knee hit the sand and my trigger finger let rip.

Steve leapfrogged ahead of me, and he was no more than thirty paces from the nearest gunmen by the time he went static. On his command, I raced ahead again, and we were close enough now to see the whites of their eyes. Faced with a couple of bullet-proof lunatics like the two of us, the bad guy made a dash for his vehicle, inside of which there could well be piles of extra ammo, grenade-launchers or other weaponry. Or the Nissan might even be wired as a gigantic bomb – a vehicle-born improvised explosive device; a VBIED. Before he could reach it, Steve and I had nailed him.

I was 20 feet from the enemy, as the last of the figures turned and ran. Or rather, he tried to. As he stumbled and then crawled towards his vehicle, I followed him in my sights, but I could tell that he was already badly – possibly terminally – injured. He wrenched open the driver's door and collapsed inside.

I'd already exhausted three mags, each packed with twenty-eight rounds of 5.56 mm. You never put in all thirty bullets, for it tends to over-stress the magazine's spring and can lead to stoppages. Either way, Steve and I had peppered the bad guys, plus their vehicles, with around 180 bullets. I had no idea if the Nissan was drivable, or how badly injured the figure slumped in the driver's seat might be, but as he tried to reverse away from us, the vehicle limped up the road at barely above walking pace, kangarooing and coughing as it went.

'You okay?' I yelled across at Steve. He nodded a terse affirmative. 'Leave the vehicle!' I added, gesturing at the crippled Nissan. 'Check the guys on the ground. I'll cover you.'

Of the three figures we'd dropped, I could tell that one at least was still alive. We needed to disarm any who might still have any fight left in them. That was our key priority right now – not brassing up a vehicle that was already shot to shreds and a driver who I doubted was going to live. Plus we had no idea if there were other hostiles lurking in the one remaining Nissan, and we needed to clear it fast.

Of course, I knew I could put an entire magazine into that fleeing – crippled – vehicle. I had more than enough ammo to do so. But we were SAS, not SS, we liked to remind ourselves. We were professionals and that wasn't our modus operandi, plus there simply wasn't the need.

The injured driver didn't have a dog in the fight any more. He might even live to see another day, although I doubted it. His vehicle had taken an enormous amount of punishment. It was down on its rims, the windscreen and side windows were completely blown away and the bodywork was peppered with bullet holes, which spread like a series of macabre spiders' webs across the flanks and the bonnet.

We had other priorities than being that man's executioners.

I saw Steve dart forward and kick the weapon away from the nearest wounded guy, as I covered him with my sights. After the deafening noise of the gunfight, it had fallen deathly quiet. The silence was ringing in my ears. I was suddenly aware how soaked in sweat I was, and how heavily I was breathing, sucking in the hot air and dust in great, searing gasps.

I saw Steve step back so he could cover the injured man and the other figures lying on the deck. 'One injured!' he yelled. 'Rest KIA.'

KIA – killed in action.

I acknowledged him, got to my feet and moved forward to join him. I headed past Steve to check out the remaining vehicle, my weapon firmly in the aim, just in case it still contained any enemy who were up for the fight. As I glanced through the windows, I saw upholstery riddled with bullet holes and piles of shattered glass. No sign of any bodies – living or dead.

I turned back to Steve. 'Vehicle clear! You okay, mate?'

'Yeah.'

I glanced from Steve to the bodies and the pools of thick blood congealing on the hot sand. I felt a momentary tinge of remorse, before reminding myself that they had forced us to do this. It was either kill or be killed. I checked on our Toyotas, positioned 150 feet back up the road. That was the amount of terrain that Steve and I had covered, in our full-on charge down the enemy guns. True to form, Mo and the other driver had turned the wagons around, ready to execute a swift getaway.

I ran an eye over the dead and the injured one final time. Correction. There were no injured any more. The last living bad guy had just breathed his last.

I eyed Steve. 'Right, let's get the hell out of here.'

We began the walk, moving back across the bullet-scarred terrain towards our vehicles. 'Good drills, mate,' I remarked to Steve. I meant it. To do what he had done took real cojones. Just as I'd suspected, Steve had what it takes in spadefuls.

'Fuck, mate,' Steve replied, still breathing heavily from the firefight.

He was younger than me and I didn't doubt he was less combat-experienced, so this may well have been his first full-on contact. He'd done us both proud.

'Right, let's get the hell out of here. Let's get back to camp. You know this place better than I do, so figure out a route. And just be aware, there may well be a follow-up.'

'Got it. You okay, Des?'

'Yeah, let's get the fuck out of here.'

Steve had been in-country for longer than me, hence my asking him to set the quickest route back to base. But more than that, I just needed a moment. Though we'd won the firefight and neither Steve nor I had a scratch on us, I was seething with anger. There had been long moments when it could have gone either way. A little less noise and a little more accuracy on behalf of the bad guys and we'd have been toast.

19

My overriding thought was this: *How dare they. How dare they want to take us on and take our lives. What had we ever done to them? How dare they.*

I took a moment to reconfigure my kit, reminding Steve to do the same – reloading, checking mags, that kind of thing. But more than that, I just wanted a few seconds to get my emotions back under control. Running through the well-honed military procedures gave me something to focus on, other than the sheer depraved murderous malevolence of what those guys had tried to unleash upon us today.

What had they been intending to do? Wound us? Disable us? Hold us to ransom, decked out in orange boiler suits? Or just rob us and our vehicles and leave us for dead?

I breathed deeply, pushing the anger and rage away. Time to get moving.

'Okay, mate, lead off,' I radioed Steve.

As we got underway, I scanned the desert to all sides. I wondered if the gunmen had got a call through to any of their backup, before we'd taken the fight to them. Either way, if we hadn't shown the steely resolve and sheer professionalism that we had done, I didn't doubt that would have been the last of us. I'd known that I had a good right-hand man in Steve. I'd known he was up for it. If not, I'd have ordered us to make an about turn and run.

Don't get me wrong: every time I've faced such situations I have been shit scared. Every single time. The answer is to channel the fear. My dog tags – they are my means to channel it. They reboot me, giving me the inner focus to face whatever is coming. At such moments I tell myself several things, which are my ground truths: there is no getting out of this situation unless I face it head-on; I've chosen to be here, so best get on with it; I'll doubtless find myself in such situations again, as they come with the territory.

So, let's get the job done, and let's get home for tea and medals.

CHAPTER TWO

SCRAMBLED

As with so many life-changing events, I heard about our Iraq deployment like a bolt out of the blue.

It was mid-December 1990, and with not a hint of anything special or remotely earth-shattering being in the offing, we were called together by Andy 'Geordie' Straker, the squadron sergeant major (SSM) who headed up B Squadron SAS. For months now the TV screens had been blaring out news regarding the war in the Middle East and how the conflict there was likely to escalate. In the summer of 1990, Iraqi dictator Saddam Hussein had sent his military forces to invade Kuwait, Iraq's southern neighbour, and the community of nations had reacted by giving him an ultimatum: withdraw, or a powerful military coalition would be assembled to evict him. No one believed that Saddam would comply, which meant the drums of war were beating.

Rumour had it that the SAS was going to be involved in the kind of deep desert raiding operations that had first been developed during the early years of World War Two, when SAS founders Colonels David Stirling and Blair 'Paddy' Mayne had perfected the art of jeep-borne hit-and-run attacks in North

Africa. Nothing remotely like this had been tried by the Regiment ever since, and for sure this was exciting, heady stuff.

Only, not for us it wasn't. Our chances of going to war in Iraq were just about zero.

Of the SAS's four Sabre – fighting – Squadrons, A, D and G had been dispatched to the Gulf, for acclimatization and desert mobility training, prior to deployment to Iraq. Us sorry lot in B Squadron had drawn the proverbial short straw. For months now we'd been consigned to counter-terrorism (CT) duties, as one squadron always needed to remain in the UK, in case of any terrorism, hostage-taking or similar incidents. In short, we weren't getting a look-in, in Iraq, and that was just how the cards had fallen.

Geordie Straker gathered us together in B Squadron's Interests Room, the nerve centre of our unit at its Hereford base. Each squadron has an Interests Room, and the plaques, flags, weaponry, war memorabilia, photos and other mementoes bedecking the walls encapsulate the history of the SAS stretching right back to World War Two. Of course, right now the walls of A, D and G Squadrons' Interests Rooms were plastered with maps, press cuttings, satellite imagery and related intelligence about Iraq and the coming Gulf War. By contrast, ours was displaying little of that, because none of us had a cat's chance in hell of getting there.

Or so we thought.

With little fanfare, Geordie stepped forward and made the following announcement. 'Right, lads, G Squadron is getting recalled to the UK to take over the SPT. Which means we're heading to the Gulf. Hand over your black kit to G and get your desert kit together, 'cause you'll be lucky if you get Christmas at home with the family.'

Not surprisingly, there was a ripple of merriment that pulsed around the room. Not a few of the guys were almost bent double with laughter. This just had to be some kind of Christmas wind-up.

A few piped up with comments like: 'Come on, Geordie, you can't be serious!' 'Yeah, and Santa Claus is real too!'

The SPT that Geordie had mentioned – the Special Projects Team – was another term for the CT squadron, those who would be decked out in 'black kit' – jet-black combats, respirator and the works – when on operations: the kind of gear those who had stormed the Iranian Embassy in London in 1980, had been wearing. The very idea that G Squadron might be pulled back from the Gulf, after spending months getting ready for desert warfare, to take our place on CT duties was just absurd. Likewise, there was less than four weeks to go before the deadline expired, so sending us lot to take G Squadron's place in the vanguard in Iraq was equally laughable.

Some figured Geordie was an anomaly for a sergeant major running an SAS Sabre Squadron. Men in his position tended to have a certain profile: hard as nails, blunt-spoken, daunting, unapproachable. One of the squadrons had a sergeant major who was known simply as 'Mad Dog', and he pretty much fitted the stereotype. But Geordie did things a little differently and he was unapologetic with it: he was a considerate, supportive, accessible kind of bloke, and I for one rated him highly. He also wasn't the sort to pull this kind of stunt; this kind of prize-winning wind-up.

'No, seriously, lads – you're headed for the Gulf,' he repeated, in that deadpan, matter-of-fact way of his. He took a moment to glance around the assembled men, letting the message sink in. His calm, no-nonsense attitude left no one in any doubt: *This is for real.*

A stunned silence settled over the room. No one was laughing any more. There wasn't so much as a stifled titter. Geordie had grabbed our attention alright.

'As I said, go prep all your CT kit for the handover to G, then grab as much Christmas leave as possible,' he continued. 'Get as much time as you can at home with the missus, girlfriend and the kids – whatever. Expect to be called back in a week, no more, when we'll head out to the UAE for prep. From UAE we'll move into Saudi, to forward mount from there, so we can get into the war proper.'

Geordie made it clear there wasn't a moment to lose, after which he had little more to tell us. We broke up and headed for the door. To say I was speechless was an understatement. It was less than ten days to go until Christmas, and I'd been winding down psychologically in preparation for the festive break. Being the CT – or 'standby' – squadron, we'd have remained on call even over Christmas, ready to race back to Hereford if needed, but not a man amongst us had been expecting anything remotely like this.

As we exited the Interests Room, a million thoughts crowded into my head. What was I to tell Emily, my wife? We were just about to complete on the purchase of our first house, and were moving in over the next few days. We'd been dreaming about having Christmas there. And now this: her husband of less than two years was about to shoot off to war. Plus this was no tinpot kind of conflict: Saddam's battle-hardened military was 900,000 strong, making it the fourth largest in the world. By contrast, the British military could muster less than a third of that number, reservists included.

Of course, we all knew the sketch about the war in the Gulf and what it had signified for the other squadrons. In a bloody eight-year conflict with Iran, Saddam Hussein had more or less bankrupted his country. On his southern border stood the oil-rich sheikhdom of Kuwait. On 2 August 1990 Saddam had sent his armed forces across the border, taking the country in a matter of hours. He saw it as the solution to all his woes. When world leaders had raised their objections, backed by threats of military action, Saddam had told them bluntly: 'Yours are societies that cannot accept 10,000 dead in one battle.'

In other words, you don't have the stomach for the fight.

Saddam's was no idle threat. Over half a million Iraqi and Iranian soldiers had died in the conflict between the two countries, which had lasted for most of the 1980s. So when it came to taking casualties, the Iraqi people were well seasoned. Even so, widespread international condemnation of the invasion of Kuwait led to the UN issuing a deadline for Iraq to withdraw: 15 January 1991. It was a dead cert that Saddam wouldn't comply, so A, D and G Squadrons had flown to the Gulf, executing months of build-up training based in friendly nations – the United Arab Emirates (UAE) first and foremost.

But now one of those squadrons, G, was being recalled, and we were slated to take their place.

What followed Geordie's bombshell briefing was utter chaos and pandemonium. We streamed outside into the winter sunshine

26

in something close to shock. It was a beautiful December day: cold, crisp, sunlit and clear. But that was mostly lost on us. Instead, we stared at each other in wide-eyed amazement: *Fuck, we're going to war.*

The next moment we were dashing for the Red and Blue Team hangars, where we'd spent the last several months on more or less permanent standby for any terrorist incident or similar kind of emergency. We gathered together all the black gear, plus the special-adapted CT Range Rovers, to shove into G Squadron's hot little hands. Understandably, those G Squadron guys were going to be utterly pissed off. But their loss was going to be our gain.

As we began to dump all the CT gear into the newly arrived guys' custody, there was more than a little slagging.

'Nice suntan. But what's with the long face?'

'Why don't you ask the CO for a transfer into B Squadron? There's still time.'

'Yeah. Join the best of the best.'

To which we got the standard response: dark scowls and a chorus of 'Piss off. Wankers.'

There was fierce competition between each of the four squadrons, especially when it came to getting the peachiest operations. Each squadron was seen as having its own distinct character and idiosyncrasies, which tended to influence the kind of tasks given out, as one of the old and the bold had once explained to me.

'Well now, Des, A Squadron are all funny buggers, aren't they?' he'd remarked. 'They don't even like each other, do they?'

'True,' I conceded. 'That lot don't seem to exactly get on.'

'Then there's G Squadron – the Wooden Tops,' he'd continued.

'Bunch of posh landed-gentry types. As long as they're inspecting each other's gleaming boots and buttons on parade, they're happy.'

G Squadron – often known as Guards Squadron – did strike me as being a lot like that: a good number of to-the-manor-born types in their ranks; hence the Wooden Tops nickname, after the BBC TV children's series about a farming family.

'Take a look at D Squadron,' he added, nodding to where a few of their guys were crossing the quadrangle. 'Good outfit, but a bunch of shy buggers – you'd never get them on the dance floor.'

I had to agree he had a point.

'And then there's B Squadron.' Pause. 'Come karaoke night they're first to make a move, getting the girls jigging and spinning, before getting totally shit-faced and making a right nuisance of themselves. That's why B Squadron is known as Disco Squadron, Des. They're loud and in your face. And that's why Disco Squadron tends to get a certain kind of op.'

Well, right now Disco Squadron were about to replace the Wooden Tops in the one theatre where war was imminent, which can't have gone down too well in some quarters. It struck me there must have been some serious infighting amongst the Regiment's senior command, and not a bit of bad blood. But all that was way above my pay grade.

Still, the more I thought about it the less sense it made. G Squadron would be at the very top of their game, after months of desert training; we were in rag order. Our deployment was going to be horribly rushed, and we'd doubtless be heading out ill equipped and ill prepared. But ours was not to reason why. We often joked that the letters 'SAS' really stood for 'Special Administration Shit'. At the same time we had that down-to-earth

Tommy attitude that despite the crap kit and the crap planning, we'd get the job done.

If you didn't expect anything much, anything you did get was a bonus.

It also struck me that this shock development – our sudden Iraq deployment – might offer a real opportunity. Maybe it was the chance that I'd been waiting for, to finally prove myself in the Regiment. To get truly accepted. It was four years since I'd passed Selection and I hadn't exactly covered myself in glory in the interim. I'd come from the Parachute Regiment, having joined up at age nineteen, and it was all down to my 'Para Reg attitude' that some at Hereford hadn't exactly warmed to me.

I'd spent eight years as a Para – the last few as a physical training (PT) instructor – and I'd loved every minute of being in the Maroon Machine, as we called it. But the Paras had an ethos and attitude that didn't always translate well into other units. If two blokes had an issue on a Monday, they tended to flare up on a Wednesday, have a punch-up on the Friday, and be the best of mates again come Monday morning. There was a man's-man's way of sorting things out, something that was actively encouraged. You were to work it out between you, bury the hatchet and make good. At first, I'd presumed the same would ring true at Hereford. Big mistake.

At 'H', you were supposed to be more mature and more able to be the 'grey man' – the individual who could fade into the background when on covert operations. Heading for weeks behind enemy lines in small, intimate teams, the four-man unit was often what we deployed in, especially on observation post (OP) spying-type or intel-gathering missions. It goes without saying that in such situations you can't go punching out the other blokes in your patrol. In short, when you made it into the SAS you had to put the man's-man's way of doing things very much behind you.

I'd found that somewhat challenging. Being a blunt-spoken northerner – I hail from the Steel City, Sheffield – I like to call a spade a spade. If I catch anyone talking behind my back, it's like a red rag to a bull. I flash. The first time it happened at H was when I attempted Selection, first time around. I'd made it through to the final days of the Jungle Phase – so all the tough hills, endurance and survival stuff was behind me – when I suffered an accident. I was airlifted out of the jungle and failed on medical grounds: it was seen as too risky for me to continue.

One of the handful of other blokes who'd made it through to that stage of Selection had made what I'd believed was a wise-arse comment. I'd flashed, and within seconds – *bam, bam* – I'd put the guy down on his knees. Of course, word got around and it was made crystal clear to me that the powers that be didn't approve. 'This isn't Para Reg,' I was warned. 'Up here, you don't take matters into your own hands. Those who do don't tend to last.'

I'm not a big guy. Far from it. I stand around five foot eight and I'm a shaven-headed whippet-slim slip of a bloke. But I'm fast as lightning and fit as a butcher's dog, plus I've done a great deal of martial arts training – so much so that I was made B Squadron's de facto unarmed combat instructor. While I weathered that first punch-up, and even got invited back to try for Selection again, I'd had a few further incidents since then. My final big flash at

Hereford very nearly got me binned – returned to unit (RTU'd). It was only when some of the senior NCOs opted to stand up for me and argue my case that I was given a second chance.

Was I the black sheep of B Squadron? Not quite. A round peg in a square hole? Maybe not that, either. But I'd earned a certain reputation. One of the things I had yet to fully appreciate was that the SAS was as much about saving lives as it was about taking them; as much about earning loyalties and allegiances as about making enemies. Winning hearts and minds was the bedrock of the SAS, whose founders had quickly realized that small-scale behind-the-lines missions were all but undoable without the support of the locals.

Local communities were the water within which the fish had to swim. Deprived of that, they would suffocate and drown. You won the allegiance of the locals by doing good in their communities; by showing them respect; by forging links and brotherhood. As a simple example, I was one of the most highly qualified medics in B Squadron. We trained extensively so we could deal with any casualties. But we were also trained to deal with all kinds of common ailments, and even to deliver babies, so that we could serve as makeshift doctors amongst those remote populations we came across.

Perfect for winning hearts and minds.

What many don't realize is that passing Selection is only the first step in being truly accepted into the Regiment. For the next few months – or years, even – you're basically on parole. The system is informal and unspoken, and mostly the senior ranks will engineer it so that those they don't want – those who don't fit in – end up RTU-ing themselves. No one can say how long a newbie stays on parole, but I had a distinct feeling mine was still up and running, four years into my time at H.

So it struck me that this shock development – B Squadron's sudden Iraq deployment – might be my chance to finally make good. That same 'Para Reg attitude' – the punchy, Maroon Machine, fight-our-way-through-anything viewpoint – could well prove an advantage where we were heading. No one doubted the seriousness of the threat we would face in the Iraqi desert, and raw aggression and a hunger to take the fight to the enemy might well pay dividends.

That was all underlined when our role was outlined to us. We were deploying in support of A and D Squadrons, as Battle Casualty Replacements, or BCRs. A BCR does exactly what it says on the tin: you're held in reserve, ready to be rushed in when any of the patrols suffer casualties. In that event, we'd fly out to rendezvous with either one of the squadrons, to be swapped for any wounded, or to slot into any unfilled places – seats on vehicles vacated by men who had been killed or were missing in action.

The fact that they intended half of B Squadron to serve as BCRs reflected the level of casualties the Regiment was anticipating. It was reinforced by a rumour that had done the rounds. Prior to us, A Squadron had been the last to deploy, and before they had left Hereford they'd been called to the gym, one of the few buildings on base that can accommodate squadron-size briefings. One of the senior officers had proceeded to deliver a pep talk, but his words hadn't exactly left the boys with a warm fluffy feeling.

'Lads, make no mistake – this is happening,' he'd stressed, having first outlined the chances of Saddam backing down, which were next to zero. 'When it does, we're going to be at the very forefront of operations.' It was then that he'd added, ominously: 'So, you need to prepare for the worst that might happen. You know the level of threat posed by Saddam's armed forces. If the shit hits the fan, some of you will not be coming home. Best face up to that now.'

A man of his standing – a colonel in the SAS – does not utter such momentous and frankly daunting sentiments without word getting around. We'd heard various versions of the colonel's speech. Only, before now we hadn't considered it anything much to do with us. Now, as BCRs, we were going to be very much in the thick of it.

We had seventy-two hours to get our shit together, before grabbing a few days' precious Christmas leave. In between sorting vital paperwork, weaponry, personal kit, specialist desert equipment, communications gear, mapping, satellite imagery, intelligence materials and the like, there was no end of briefings, covering the complex nature of the multi-national coalition being assembled, plus what we were to expect from Saddam's military, and what targets we might encounter on the ground.

With the UN deadline fast approaching, thousands of US, British, Australian, French, Polish, South Korean and Arab-nation troops were converging on the Gulf. Britain's 8,000-strong 7th Armoured Brigade had already deployed, plus we had helicopters, fighters, bombers and surveillance aircraft in theatre. By the end of the month some 30,000 British troops were slated to be there, but that would be dwarfed by the 700,000 American military personnel, along with all the kinds of lethal hardware they tend to deploy with.

We had a series of target-assessment briefings. Power stations, airfields, command bunkers, leadership hubs, hydro-electric dams in the mountains of northern Iraq – we were heading into a target-rich environment, as long as we could slip our patrols through the desert to hit them. That was what we specialized in, of course, and no one doubted that we'd be infiltrating by vehicles, as opposed to inserting by air, which was my personal speciality, along with the rest of the guys in my unit, Air Troop.

There are four troops within each SAS squadron – Mountain, Mobility, Boat and Air. I was serving as a corporal in Air Troop, those who specialize in making airborne insertions into hostile terrain, mostly by high-altitude freefall parachuting. I was determined to sort out my own personal gear, to give me the best possible chance of proving myself, when we got boots on the ground in Iraq. We Air Troop lads had privileged access to the one place on base where we could get our kit modified and bastardized, even at extremely short notice.

Stirling Lines – the SAS base – had its own dedicated seamstress. Beryl was in her early fifties, and she'd been around ever since anyone could remember. Her role was to adapt our kit to suit individual needs. Often she would have to attend to relatively mundane matters – like sewing wings onto a new recruit's uniform, or adding medal ribbons to 'number two' (formal) dress for an up-coming function. I'd paid my fair share of visits to Beryl, as much for a cup of tea and a motherly chat as anything. But she was always busy, and right now I didn't doubt she'd be snowed under.

So I made a beeline for the hangar that housed 'Big Kev' and 'Mo' Morris instead. Big Kev and Mo were the dedicated

Air Troop parachute packers. Whenever we were deployed on jump training, they would accompany us, performing the back-breaking work of gathering up and repacking our chutes after each and every jump. It was hard enough being a parachute packer at Stirling Lines, where they had long wooden benches specifically for the task of spreading out and painstakingly folding and repacking 200 square feet of parachute silk. Doing it on your hands and knees with freezing fingers in the middle of nowhere was exhausting, and often they'd have to pack a dozen chutes several times in one day.

Along with their packing benches, they also boasted state-of-the-art sewing machines for repairing damaged chutes, and they were wizards at fashioning hammocks from spare parachute silk. Right now, we had no need of such things, of course. We'd not be encountering many trees in Saddam's desert from which to sling a hammock and chill out. But Mo and Big Kev were also a dab hand at fashioning extra pouches for spare mags and ammo, plus bespoke chest webbing or belt kit.

As they hailed from the RAF, it was fully expected of us to slag off Mo and Big Kev – to us, all RAF types were 'rock apes' or 'slipper queens' – before settling down to a brew and a chinwag. Not to buck convention, I threw a few choice insults in their direction, and got the expected slagging in return – which for me tended to centre around flat caps and whippets – before outlining exactly what I had in mind this time.

At H, the kind of kit you wore to battle was more or less your own choice. Each operator tended to adapt, improvise and refine until he had a set of packs, pouches, webbing and the like that suited him. Whenever there was a new modification to a key piece of kit, you'd get curious glances from the blokes, and the comment: 'Fuck, where did you get that?'

As we were going to deploy to Iraq in vehicles – 'wagons', in SAS terminology – priority number one was reconfiguring my webbing kit. Serving in Air Troop, I had a series of pouches slung around my waist, which I'd stuff with spare mags of ammo, medical dressings, emergency rations, escape and evasion gear, water bottles, weapon cleaning kit and the like. But when seated in a wagon and moving over punishing terrain for hours on end, waist pouches tended to dig into your hips, lower back and stomach, causing no end of discomfort. More to the point, my chosen pouch configuration was chiefly about getting access to spare mags of ammo as quickly as possible. When wedged into the seat of a Land Rover, waist pouches tend to fail to open properly.

I explained to Mo and Big Kev what I had in mind. I wanted the pouches moving up, so they hung off my torso like a yoke, the weight sitting mostly on my chest and shoulders. I'd modified the spare mags for my M16, so each had a length of paracord attached to the bottom. I'd slot the mags in upside down, so I could grab the paracord, haul out the mag and slot it into my M16 in one smooth move. Without that, it was hard to grasp the mag's smooth metal, especially if you had cold hands.

Some people preferred a gaffer-tape pull system, but over time the tape can wear smooth and slippery. Some people tied a loop in the paracord 'handle', to make it easier to grab and pull. But a loop can also catch on things accidentally – for example, when you have to exit a vehicle fast, during a contact. Not good, if you leave your spare mags behind. My solution was to burn the ends of the paracord, leaving a gnarled black knob of melted nylon on each – perfect for grabbing hold of in a hurry.

You never take off your belt kit – your webbing – when on operations. You sleep in it, crap in it, eat in it – everything. It's designed to enable you to fight and survive for twenty-four hours, in case you become separated from your main backpack – your Bergen – in a firefight, ambush or accident. So my belt kit also included an aluminium survival blanket and a fluorescent orange signal panel, to attract the attention of any passing aircraft.

I explained to Mo and Big Kev that in shifting around my waist pouches I'd lose some, which meant I needed extra capacity. These guys were demons at bastardizing Claymore sacks – the standard canvas bags used for holding the curved anti-personnel mines so beloved of the Regiment – into handy shoulder bags. Perfect for housing extra kit. I ordered one for myself, while giving Mo and Big Kev a quiet warning: there were sure to be other guys from B Squadron asking for the same, and they'd best prioritize Air Troop if they knew what was good for them.

By the time Mo and Big Kev had got my order ready, I was pretty much sorted for Iraq – or as much as I'd ever be, in the time allowed. That just left the small matter of letting my wife know. Emily was a half-German, half-Mauritian lass – Mauritius is the tropical paradise island nation in the middle of the Indian Ocean – and she was truly the love of my life. Petite, lithe and super-smart, she ran her own business as a fitness instructor. In fact, she was striking enough to have graced the cover of the odd fitness magazine, much to my Hereford mates' irritation.

'How did an ugly Northern git like you land something like that?' they'd demand, in disbelief.

'Err . . . It's me northern charm that done it. That, plus the bread-and-dripping butties.'

Blessed with a very broad, inner-city Sheffield accent, I'd learned that it was best to play up to the stereotype. Trying to deny it was just an invitation to a whole world of slagging.

Emily and I had first met when she was not yet sixteen years old. I was twenty-two, and three years into my time in the Paras. A mutual friend had introduced us, and at five feet four, dark-skinned, with smoky eyes and long lashes, Emily took my breath away. Nothing much happened then, but a year later we bumped into each other again in a Wimpy bar in Milton Keynes, where she happened to be waitressing. In the time that had passed, she'd blossomed into a striking young woman. In fact, she'd changed so much that at first I didn't realize it was even her.

'You don't recognize me, do you?' she'd teased, as she served my order.

I did a double take and the penny finally dropped. 'Wow! I do now. Err, you've changed a bit.'

She laughed.

Tongue-tied, I left vowing to return and to ask her out. I made it back to the Wimpy a few weeks later, only to learn that she'd changed jobs. Luckily, someone was able to direct me to where she then worked – a coffee bar nearby. I hurried over and found her looking as beautiful as ever, and we struck up some chat.

'So, what're you doing this evening?' I finally plucked up the courage to ask.

'I'm heading down to Peaches.'

It was the local nightclub. I told her what a coincidence, 'cause I was going there too. That evening I dressed for the part – Para

Reg blazer, shiny shoes, grey slacks – and I even managed to stretch to a tie. She turned up looking a million dollars: tight, pencil-style dress, high heels, long, dark brown hair and almost zero make-up. She didn't need it, and she knew it.

I took her hand, led her to the bar, started to buy the drinks and before long we hit the dance floor. Even back then I was a natural for Disco Squadron, although I little knew it at the time. Being a PT instructor at Para Reg, I could put on a show on the dance floor – headstands, flick-flacks and even a few martial arts moves. I like to think I outdid myself that evening.

By the time we left Peaches, we were an item, and we'd never looked back since. But my dispatch to the Gulf could not have come at a worse time. Amidst the mad-crazy rush of the past few days, I'd just got confirmation that our house purchase had gone through, with no last-minute hitches. We were slated to move in just before Christmas Eve.

Now, I might well be in Iraq by the time Santa slipped his belly down our chimney.

CHAPTER THREE

THE SUN'S FITTEST COUPLE

As a married couple, Emily and I were entitled to Army accommodation – married quarters – in and around the base. Those who didn't opt for such quarters tended to rent or buy in Hereford, keeping close to Stirling Lines. The reasons why were obvious: we spent a good deal of time on call, which meant you needed to be able to get back to base at the drop of a hat.

And that made my choice of home something of an anomaly, to say the least.

Emily and I lived in Peterborough, a good three-hour drive from H. The reasons were simple. My father had died when I was a youngster, and my mum, my sister and brother and I had moved out of Sheffield. We'd ended up in Peterborough, where mum started a newsagent's business. She'd sadly passed away when I was twenty-two, and I'd taken over the house that she rented. That was where Emily and I had first set up home. It was where we'd put down roots and made friends. As a bonus, it was from there that Emily ran her fitness business. We saw no compelling reason to move. In fact, I liked the separation it afforded us.

Apart from attending the odd formal function, Emily was rarely in Hereford and she wasn't exactly plugged into the SAS side of my life, as some wives tended to be. In Peterborough, no one knew what I really did for a living, bar one or two carefully selected individuals. The most our friends were aware of was that I served as a PT instructor in the Paras.

The three-hour drive from Hereford to Peterborough served as my decompression time. I'd play *The Best of M People*, the dance band, over and over, on my Ford XR3i's stereo, and by the time I got home I was generally well chilled. I could keep home life and H life firmly decompartmentalized, which suited me down to the ground. In Peterborough, I could simply be me. I wasn't one of those secret black-clad assassins, as the uninitiated tended to view us. I liked that anonymity. It helped keep me sane.

One day a Peterborough mate had popped the inevitable question: 'Des, have you ever thought of joining the SAS?'

'No, mate,' I told him. 'They're those killer-ninja cloak-and-dagger weirdos, aren't they? Can you really see me fitting in? Doing that sort of thing?'

'You're right, Des, that really isn't you.'

Whenever I was on immediate standby I'd have to remain at camp, which generally meant I could get a lot of training, admin and fitness done. But when I was on less-urgent callout, I had a special arrangement with one of the B Squadron NCOs, a guy called Steve Roper. If something looked like it was cooking up, Steve would give me a ring.

'Des, there's an incident brewing – best get yourself back to H.' That was all that was needed – a quiet word.

It typified Steve's attitude. He knew that, residing in Peterborough, I was at the very limit of the time allowed to make it back to base. They could have pressurized me to move closer to H, but Steve appreciated that was where Emily and I had made our home. He was all about the blokes spending as much time as possible with their families, which was also a priority for the Regiment as a whole. Family mattered. It grounded and matured the men, knocking off the hard edges and making them more able to deal with the kind of missions the SAS would demand of them.

But that separation still didn't mean that Emily hadn't come to the attention of the Regiment. Quite the opposite, in fact. She just wasn't the sort of girl to hide her light under a bushel.

We'd married in 1988, in a wedding that had been kept a complete secret from yours truly – the groom. But even before that, Emily's bombshell persona had blown into Hereford like a whirlwind. As with my punchy, Para-Reg attitude, it hadn't exactly enamoured me to higher command – especially since I'd only just passed Selection when all of a sudden Emily and I graced the front pages of Britain's highest-selling newspaper.

One day Emily had made a passing comment that she was entering us into *The Sun*'s fittest couple competition. We were both forever at the gym, so I figured what was the harm? It was typical feisty Emily, and as we all know, happy wife equals happy life. A few weeks later she told me we'd been selected by *The Sun* as one of five couples to go head to head for the prize.

'Yeah, baby, great news,' I told her, still not quite realizing what I'd let myself in for.

Then she revealed that we had to be in London that Saturday, at a gym right next door to the famous Pineapple Dance Studios, in the trendy Covent Garden area. My alarm bells had started to ring just a little bit by now.

When she'd first told me she'd entered us, I'd figured I could squirm out of it if need be, by making sure I was on a training exercise – maybe freefalling in Florida, or something equally distant, which would make it impossible for me to attend. But she'd told me on a Wednesday about the Saturday callout, and I'd just got home for a few days' leave. There was no way I could wriggle out of this one.

In due course we caught the train to London. We pitched up at the Covent Garden gym, only to discover there was a raft of celebs there, including Eddie Kidd, the world record-winning stunt-rider and the face of the Levi jeans adverts on TV. There were also Maria Whittaker and Linda Lusardi, the famous Page 3 girls, plus one of the singers from Bananarama, the phenomenally successful girl band.

Trouble is, I am by nature a competitive bunny. The whole thing started off being just a bit of fun, but very quickly it turned serious. There was a rank of photographers capturing every moment, as the instructors began to beast us. We moved from the weights bars and dead lifts – pure strength tests – to what was mine and Emily's bread and butter: dips, pull-ups, press-ups, burpees and star jumps.

At one stage I leaned across to Emily and whispered: 'Babe, let's fucking win this.'

'Yeah,' she smiled. 'Let's win this.'

True to form, on the press-ups she out-performed even some of the guys. By the end of the day, we'd proved true to our pledge to each other. I was asked to hold Emily in my arms as she brandished the winner's cup, so the photographers could snap away.

'Well done, babe, for pulling us through,' I whispered, as we smiled for the cameras. In truth, by the end there hadn't been another couple that was able to keep up with us.

At some stage I'd been asked what I did for a living, and I'd just told them I was 'in the military'. Oddly, I hadn't quite connected all this with what was about to happen. Come Monday morning Emily and I were told we were going to be front-page news, the me-holding-her-with-the-cup photo taking pride of place.

By the time I'd driven back to Hereford I was seriously worried. I figured it was best to go and confess, before word got around. I went to see Steve Roper and told him exactly what had happened. Steve had the reputation of being a good if hard taskmaster, and most importantly he was known to give guys a fair hearing. But after I'd said my piece, to say his eyes were out on stalks would be an understatement.

'You – fucking – what?'

'Steve, it's not as bad as it sounds.'

'Hang on a minute, Des, you've entered a fucking fitness competition with your missus and you're going to be on the front page of *The Sun*. How is that not as bad as it fucking sounds?'

'Look, Steve, calm down a bit. Can I just explain some? They don't know I'm in the Regiment.'

'Oh, well that's alright then, isn't it, Des?' He had the proverbial steam coming out of his ears by now. 'Let me get this straight. You entered this competition with *The Sun*, they're running a front-page story, with photos, but it's all okay 'cause you didn't

44

tell them you were in the SAS. Is that really what you're trying to tell me?'

'Yeah.' I was convinced this was it: I was going to get booted out of the Regiment, and I'd only been in for a matter of months.

'Des, why the fuck did you enter this competition in the first place?'

'The missus. She entered us. I mean, I didn't think we'd ever actually do it.'

'But you did, didn't you, Des?'

'Yeah,' I conceded. 'We did.'

'Right. Right.' He took a few very deep breaths. 'I need to go speak to the adjutant. Are you sure they know nothing – diddly fucking squat – about you being in the SAS?'

'Yeah. Nothing.'

'Right. Leave it with me. Wait out.'

The adjutant is the officer who serves as the assistant to the Regiment's CO. Steve would go and argue my case with him, as a roundabout way of bringing it to the CO's attention.

A few days later the article did appear in *The Sun*, and thank heavens there was no mention of my elite military background. More importantly, I seemed to have gotten away with it at H. The worst I seemed to get was a shedload of slagging from the blokes, which was all about sneaky-beaky Des the SAS ninja lording it with the celebs on the front pages of the papers. But unbelievably, that wasn't the end of it. A year later, the story came back to haunt me with a vengeance.

Emily had backed me all the way when I'd told her I wanted to try for the SAS. That was over two back-to-back Selections, and no matter that the first one really knocked me for six. She'd done so on one condition – that we got hitched. Of course, I dragged my feet a little, as blokes tend to, but she found a way around that. With the help of one or two of my closest mates, she organized our wedding in complete and utter secrecy.

I arrived home one weekend, only to have it sprung upon me out of the blue. We got hitched on the Saturday, and truth be told I was over the moon. But some months later I was at H when I took a call from a worried-sounding Emily. Apparently, one of the wedding guests had phoned *The Sun*, to let them know the 'Fittest Couple' had just got married in secret. *The Sun* had called Emily, asking to come and take some photos for a follow-up story. She'd declined, but she felt sure they were going to run something anyway – '*Sun*'s Fittest Couple: Secret Wedding'.

Oh shit. In short order I found myself before the adjutant, trying to explain it all, and convinced that this was it: two strikes and you're done. Two stories in *The Sun* and you're finished in the SAS.

After I blurted it all out, the adjutant told me to calm down a little. 'Des, take a few deep breaths and tell me the facts.'

I repeated the entire story, a little more calmly this time.

'Right. Not good.' The adj took a long, hard look at me. 'Listen, Des, we can slap what they call a D-notice on *The Sun*, which might stop them from running the story. But that often draws more attention to your case, revealing that you – we – have something to hide. Now, are you absolutely certain they have no idea you serve in the Regiment?'

'As far as I know, no one in Peterborough has a clue what I do, so no – there's no way *The Sun* can know.'

'Right then, I think the best thing to do is to leave it and let it run and see what comes out.' He paused. 'Reckon you've just got to hope for the best, eh, Des?'

I spent several days on tenterhooks waiting for the story to appear. When it did, there was still no mention of the Hereford connection – so once again the axe failed to fall. But as you can imagine, the idea of Corporal Powell keeping a low profile – of adopting the easygoing laid-back attitude required of the Grey Warrior – hadn't quite hit home.

It was 19 December 1990 as I made the drive to Peterborough, knowing that at any moment I could be called back to H, to deploy. During the journey, I deliberated on how to break the news to Emily. I hated the idea of getting sent out early, and leaving her to move house alone. In the end, I decided I'd let her know only when I was absolutely sure I had to go. That way we could enjoy as best a Christmas as we could for as long as possible.

One of the first things I did when I got home was go and see my good friend Nick Tulip, who served as a firearms instructor in the local police. Nick was one of only two mates in Peterborough who knew what I did for a living. I told Nick I was off to Iraq, and asked him to help me get in shape. I wanted him to come running with me every day and to push me.

Nick asked if Emily knew about Iraq. I told him no, and it needed to stay that way. But smart cookie that she is, Emily soon began asking questions. Why all the training all of a sudden? Thinking on my feet, I told her that Nick was going on a special firearms course and that he needed to get in shape, and I'd agreed to help him do so. It was a white lie, and the best lies are always as close to the truth as you can make them.

By Christmas Eve I still hadn't got the call for Iraq, and Emily and I had managed to get all our stuff crammed into our new home. The place was complete and utter chaos, with piles of boxes everywhere. My other close friend in Peterborough was Steffan Cairns, an insurance broker. Steffan and Nick had helped us to move all our stuff in. As we surveyed the carnage, Steffan dangled a set of keys before our eyes.

'Lock the door,' he announced, "cause you guys are having Christmas at our place.'

I could have kissed him, I was so relieved. We drove around to Steffan's house, and there was a beautiful Christmas tree all lit up, complete with a living room boasting some wonderful decorations. Then Steffan really got us tearing up. 'Happy Christmas,' he announced, jingling those keys again. 'It's all yours.'

Steffan was the one other friend in Peterborough who knew that I was about to head for the Gulf. Without so much as breathing a word, he'd arranged to spend Christmas at his partner's place. That way, Emily and I could enjoy the last few days – or maybe hours – that we had together, before myself and the rest of Disco Squadron headed to war.

A few days later, I was ordered back to Hereford. It was then that I finally levelled with a tearful Emily about what was really happening. I asked her to get the house ship-shape, so we could try for a baby just as soon as I returned. I told her there was nothing to worry about. Nothing bad was going to happen in Iraq, because the mighty SAS would give Saddam's ragtag forces a good shinning – or at least, that was how I portrayed it to her.

'I'll be home before you know it,' I promised. 'We'll get to nest properly, just as soon as I get back.'

If the truth be told, I wouldn't have had it any other way with Emily and the saga over *The Sun*. It might well sound bat-shit-crazy, and indeed it was, but that was what I loved about her. She was strong-willed, go-getting, intelligent and gutsy, and she knew exactly what she wanted from life. She believed in living in the moment, in making the most from each and every day, in embracing each and every new experience with open-hearted gusto.

A few weeks back I'd been on a specialized CT training task. We'd driven our slick Range Rovers into the heart of an urban centre somewhere in the UK – the location of which remains classified – to rehearse counter-terrorism drills at the obvious targets: multi-storey skyscrapers, the sprawling labyrinths of the shopping malls, plus buildings with clear religious and political significance.

We'd taught ourselves to scale the tallest buildings, before descending again in a covert fashion – the details of which remain classified – so we could assault the floor the 'terrorists' had seized and take them by utter surprise.

The CT training took several days and it proved a real blast. At the end of it I figured I was close enough to Peterborough to maybe wangle a night or two at home, before heading back to H. B Squadron's staff sergeant on Mobility Troop was a guy called Jamie 'Minky' McIver, who I got along with really well. Upon passing Selection, I'd first been assigned to Mobility Troop, under Minky's expert stewardship. But being a Para, I figured I was always destined for Air Troop. After a year in Mobility, during which I'd learned a huge amount from Minky about vehicle operations, I'd asked him if he minded if I applied for a transfer, for I felt Air Troop was always going to be the place for me.

'Go for it,' he'd told me.

'You won't be upset?' I asked. It mattered to me what Minky thought.

'Des, lad, follow your heart. Tell you what, I'll have a chat with the Air Troop staffy and get it all squared away.'

At the end of our urban CT week I asked one of the senior NCOs if I could sneak off for a night or two in Peterborough.

'No problem,' he told me. 'Tell you what – take one of the Range Rovers, go see your missus, and we'll see you back in H on Monday.' He eyed me for a second. 'But if we do get a callout, you'd best head to Hereford super-quick. Blue-light it all the way.'

That agreed, I slid behind the wheel and set a course for home.

For a guy like me, hailing from a working-class background, it was some kind of a kick to bring a vehicle like this home. I reflected for a moment on the kind of places the Regiment can take you to. I reached the house, pulled up outside and went to fetch Emily to show off the wheels. That done, I realized there was some sensitive kit still in the vehicle: some fast-roping kit, plus some night-vision goggles, or NVG. I told myself: *Don't want to risk that little lot getting nicked, if I leave it in the car.*

I carried it inside. Emily eyed the NVG sets, her eyes wide with curiosity. 'Des, what are those? I mean, what do they do? They don't shoot people, do they?'

I glanced outside. It was well after nightfall, our small garden cloaked in darkness. I grinned. 'Come on, lass, I'll show you.'

Typically, Emily was up for it. In no time I had her decked out in the NVG, the flip-down lenses firmly clamped over her eyes. I led her out into the darkness and we stalked around the garden a bit, giggling to ourselves like schoolkids.

'Wow, I can see everything! But everything's got this weird green glow.'

'Yeah. That's the effect of the night-vision optics.'

We did a bit more stealth prowling, before turning in. *Soulmates.* As we drifted off to sleep, I told Emily about how we'd got to go to one of the main airports, to do some CT training on a jet airliner, as the grand finale.

'Guess what we got up to,' I murmured, sleepily, before relating some of the more extreme stuff we'd got to do while the aircraft was parked on the tarmac.

Come morning, she revealed to me what her last thoughts had been, before she'd dropped off to sleep: it was of me, doing all that kind of Spiderman stuff while that aeroplane *was in flight*. Bless. With most airliners having a cruise speed of 500 kph, I really didn't think even us lot – the Disco Squadron boys – would be capable of doing that any time soon.

But that's what I loved about Emily: she was full of life and up for just about anything. As I headed back to H to deploy to the Gulf, I felt sure she was going to be strong enough to cope, whatever might happen to me out there.

No sooner had I reached camp than I had a call from my big sister, Lorraine. Her son, Derren, was serving in the Royal Corps of Transport, and she was worried sick what might happen to him in the Gulf. I told her not to worry. All British soldiers were being sent to one central camp out there.

'I'll keep a close eye on him,' I promised her. 'I'll keep him safe.'

It was complete and utter bullshit, of course: another white lie. I didn't think I'd be running into my nephew where we were heading. But I'd needed a way to ease my sister's concerns and to comfort her, and to stop her from worrying my nephew sick. Needs must, as far as I was concerned.

I set about my last-minute preparations, one of which was spraying my green Bergen – rucksack – sandy yellow. I didn't like having to do it, especially since it was a civvie Berghaus that I'd paid for with my own money, preferring it to the Army-issue version. But that pretty much defined the state of our kit: *Spray your rucksack the colour of where you are heading*. As I was busy spray painting it, a familiar figure wandered in. It was Bob Consiglio; we shared the same accommodation block.

Bob was small and stocky, with dark curly hair, and he was known to be something of a livewire. He was a former Royal Marine – a Boot Neck – and he served in Mountain Troop, so he wasn't the obvious pal for a former Para like me who served with Air Troop. But we'd bonded over a shared love of music, especially the Blow Monkeys' classic, 'It Doesn't Have to Be This Way'. We used to blare it out over the speakers, as we boogied up and down the corridor.

Bob was of Italian heritage, and he could pull these slick Latino moves. I fancied myself as a bit of a dancer, and most likely due to her Mauritian heritage Emily could shake it like a diva, so I'd had to learn how to keep up with her on the dance floor.

For a while Bob and I chewed the fat over what the coming weeks might bring. 'We're off to war, Bob,' I declared. 'What d'you think of that?'

'Yeah, Des, it's all happening,' he replied, with his typical upbeat attitude. 'The Iraqi deserts, eh? Can't wait. Tell you what, time for a blast of the Blow Monkeys, you and me.'

We could just sneak in one more rendition of 'It Doesn't Have to Be This Way', Bob figured, as he cranked up the volume. Little did I know that this was to be one of the last times that I'd ever see Bob alive. That song never fails to remind me of him.

The day before departure, we lugged our gear down to the quadrangle and packed it onto a convoy of four-tonners – the ubiquitous Bedford Army trucks. It was mostly personal kit only, for we'd pick up just about everything else, weapons included, upon arrival at UAE.

That night we headed en masse to the Palud-R-Inn Club – named with tongue in cheek after the antimalarial drug Paludrine – and hit the beers. I'm a light drinker. Always have been. By the time we caught the early-morning coach to Brize Norton, many of the B Squadron lads were still half-pissed. Others were being dropped off by distraught wives, who were making tearful scenes at the gates. I sat on the coach and watched, reflecting upon how I'd done all that with Emily back in Peterborough. She was a strong girl. I felt certain she'd cope.

We flew out of RAF Brize Norton, the atmosphere on the ageing RAF VC10 being a blend of sadness at parting, mixed with excitement and uncertainty, and not a few monster hangovers. With three squadrons deploying – A, D and now B – this was the biggest thing the Regiment had been involved in since World War Two. With several coach-loads of blades – fighting SAS soldiers – heading to the Gulf, this was as real as it gets.

We jetted into the United Arab Emirates, moving into an

isolated region called Sweihan, in the far northeast of the country. A deal had been cut with one of the Emirates' sheikhs, Zayed bin Sultan Al Nahyan: If we trained his elite guard in CT tactics, he'd give us free reign at a UAE training camp and in the desert all around. A good number of the B Squadron lads were slated to deliver the sheikh's CT training package, and trust me, no one wanted that gig. The rest of us were to prepare to be Battle Casualty Replacements (BCRs) – to be flown in to replace A and D Squadron's dead and wounded, once they thundered into Iraq to create merry hell.

No one was kidding themselves that we wouldn't take casualties. The intelligence people had warned that Saddam's military was battle-hardened and his Republican Guard – his nearest equivalent to Special Forces – were well equipped, intensively trained and die-hard. For any of us who had been foolish enough to dismiss the Iraqi military as being a bunch of useless 'camel herders', any such misapprehensions had been well and truly quashed.

That UAE base was a brand-spanking-new facility designed to be that nation's airborne forces training school. It came equipped with a slick new runway, plus four vast hangars arranged in a square, with alleyways leading down the centre and branching off to the sides. Each hangar was big enough to house a couple of jumbo jets, and came complete with air-conditioning – permanently on – bright fluorescent lighting set in the ceiling – permanently on – plus a series of jump harnesses slung from the ceiling, with which to learn the craft of making a parachute jump, before graduating onto real-life aircraft. Toilet blocks and a shower unit completed the complex. The Regiment had given it the codename Camp Victor.

It was utterly clean and spotless; in fact, it was so new it had yet to be occupied by the UAE military. Apart from A, D and G Squadrons having passed through, it was unsullied by human hand. Of course, in the process of blowing through, those guys had scarfed up all the best weaponry, ammo and associated desert kit from the piles of stores flown out from Hereford. We didn't exactly blame them. We'd have done the same in their shoes. But just how dire the shortages might prove was about to become painfully obvious.

We took up residence in one corner of a giant hangar, our boots echoing around the bare and cavernous interior. Those lucky enough to have a US Army camp bed dossed down on those; the rest slung carry-mats on the floor. The US military cots – slotted-together metal frames holding a canvas 'mattress' – were infinitely more comfortable, but as with so much of the kit, you had to buy your own. Or, as in my case, being a typical scrounging northerner, I'd managed to cadge one of the prized cots off some American troops during a training exercise. We each made a hide out of a pile of our own kit, complete with walls fashioned from empty ration packs and ammo crates, to lend a modicum of privacy.

As always, there was one key factor that dictated where I established my doss-down quarters: the location of Dinger. Like me, Stan 'Dinger' Bell was in Air Troop, and over time we'd developed something of a love–hate relationship. Being the PT and unarmed combat instructor on B Squadron, I was tasked with getting the guys up to speed in those departments. Mine was an informal role, as it was largely up to the blokes to keep themselves in shape and handy, but I did take it seriously.

A non-smoking gym queen who rarely hit the beers, I was forever getting ribbed for my clean-living, my-body-is-a-temple ways. It was said I survived on workouts, muesli and natural yogurt, as opposed to six pints and twenty fags a day. In fact, being from Sheffield, I was more of a bread-and-dripping type, but the lads never used to let the truth get in the way of a good wind-up. First in the queue was Dinger. Rough and ready and tough as hell, Dinger was one of the heaviest smokers on camp.

Our typical greeting went like this.

Me: 'How you doing, mate?'

Dinger (pulling out a packet of cigarettes): 'Tops. Still investing heavily in B & H, Des. D'you fancy one?'

'I'm gonna die one day, 'cause of your smoking.'

'Rubbish. B & H – they're good for you.'

These days Dinger would never dream of offering me a ciggie, and for good reasons. Once he was blowing smoke in my general direction, just to wind me up, so I actually accepted one of his B & Hs, arguing you had to try everything once. I went as if to light it up and then crumpled the ciggie and chucked it over my shoulder. Dinger was utterly horrified, and he made it clear I'd never pull that trick again.

Whenever we deployed, I'd always ask Dinger where he intended to sling his hammock. Then I'd choose the furthest possible point away from him. We did exactly that upon arrival at Camp Victor.

'Right, then, Dinger, where are you dumping your cot, mate?'

'Next to you, naturally.'

'No you're not, Dinger. I'll be down the far end.'

Off one of the corridors lay the officers' domain, a side-room with ranks of metal desks and plastic chairs arranged in a semi-circle, where the CO and his command, intelligence and signals cells – the head shed – would congregate. Bedecking the walls were giant maps of Kuwait and Iraq, stuck full of differently coloured pins, and on the floor were piles of boxes containing yet more maps. Many were the silk versions – escape and evasion maps, which wouldn't tear or fragment if wet, and which could be sewn into the lining of your combats in an effort to keep them hidden.

If things had been hectic back in Hereford, they now took on a surreal quality. We had less than two weeks before Saddam's deadline ran out, at which stage we would be at war. In that time, we somehow had to zero in our weaponry out on the ranges, get into whatever desert vehicles we could get our hands on and get out into the UAE's badlands, to try to cram up on the craft of desert driving – or Mobility Ops, as we term it in the SAS.

As I'd served a year in Mobility Troop, I was in a better position than most. Most guys from Air, Mountain and Boat Troops had little desert driving skills. And trust me, it is a finely tuned, specialist craft. It encompasses day and night navigation, freeing trapped vehicles, reading the terrain, night-driving techniques, mobile combat drills, communications, camouflage – there was one hell of a lot to cram in. Normally, it would take months to do so. We had a matter of days.

To make matters worse, Saddam was known to be fond of throwing around the odd CBRN – chemical, biological, radiological or nuclear – warhead (although no one suspected him of having any nukes right then). He'd done so against Iran, and even against his own restive populations – most notably the Marsh Arabs and the Kurds. Mustard gas. Sarin nerve gas. Chlorine bombs. He was well known for his fondness for such weaponry. Plus he had a long-range delivery system with which to target his enemies – his Scud missiles, provided courtesy of our friends, the Russians.

While the Scud wasn't exactly pinpoint accurate, it didn't have to be. The original missiles had been modified by Saddam's rocket scientists, to give them extended range. Their lack of accuracy didn't particularly matter, especially when tipped with a CBRN warhead. All you had to do was lob it in the general direction of a population centre or a military camp and watch your enemy fry, or suffocate, or choke and vomit to death.

If battle was joined, we'd have to expect Saddam to target Coalition forces with all that he could, including such banned weapons. As BCRs, we'd be slotting in to serve where the action was fiercest. We couldn't rule out Saddam lobbing the odd nerve or blister agent in our direction, especially as we'd be aiming to cause him as much of a headache as possible, and deep within his own backyard.

Any way you looked at it, getting hit with mustard gas or sarin was a terrifying prospect. Driving into the Iraqi desert in open-topped Land Rovers to face a storm of chemical agents: not the nicest way to go to war.

And not quite the way I'd described things to Emily, when saying our fond farewells.

CHAPTER FOUR

ROCKET HUNTERS

No sooner had we bagged our few precious feet of floor space than we were called for the first briefing. Our driving priority was made crystal clear. G Squadron had been out in the UAE for over two months, refreshing and refining the craft of desert mobility operations. We had just a fraction of that time to get up to speed. Acting as BCRs, we should expect to get flown in to join either of the squadrons in the midst of hostile territory. We needed to be ready to hit the ground running, taking the place of casualties suffered right in the thick of combat.

With A and D Squadrons involved in the kind of deep-desert hit-and-run missions the likes of which the SAS hadn't undertaken since World War Two, mobility was going to be key. The sand dunes of the Gulf were basically an extension of the Sahara Desert of North Africa, with just a few land borders and a stretch of sea in between. It was in the Sahara that David Stirling's originals – the founders of the SAS – had first proven the concept of special forces operations, and they had been on an incredibly steep learning curve.

In November 1941, the fledgling SAS had launched its first

ever mission, codenamed Operation Squatter, the aim of which was to raid a series of aerodromes, taking out the enemy warplanes based there. Op Squatter had entailed dropping teams of parachutists on a moonless night, to maximize the element of surprise. But as zero hour had approached, unseasonable storms and rain had swept across the desert, in the worst weather for decades. In spite of the terrible conditions, the SAS originals had insisted on the mission going ahead, so desperate were they to strike a blow against the enemy.

Battling powerful storms and near-zero visibility, the pilots had faced horrendous conditions in which to make the drop. Some of the parachutists were killed outright by the impact of landing, while others were knocked unconscious, or injured so badly they had to be left behind. Those who did survive struggled to free themselves from their parachute harnesses, a number being swept to their doom. Others were dropped so far off course they ended up being captured by the enemy, long before they could get anywhere near their targets.

Of the fifty-odd SAS originals who had taken to the skies, only twenty-one made it back alive. Though Squatter was a costly disaster, vital lessons had been learned. For their next mission the SAS linked up with the Long Range Desert Group (LRDG), the masters of intelligence gathering who used convoys of vehicles to criss-cross the desert – and thus the SAS had secured a taxi service to ferry them to and from their targets. In time they acquired their own vehicles, having learned the craft of desert navigation, survival and mobility from the longer-lived LRDG. In due course the SAS's key raiding platform would become the American-made Willys Jeep, which wasn't so far removed from the kind of Land Rovers that we would be taking into Iraq.

Those early pioneers had learned the indispensable nature of moving by vehicle, in such vast, inhospitable terrain. Taking our inspiration from the SAS originals, we got busy that first night, heading out of Camp Victor in vehicles. The base was surrounded by the kind of terrain we'd been told to expect in Iraq – soft, undulating sand-seas, interspersed with the all-too-rare water-hole and oasis. When crossing wide expanses of treacherous sand, the crucial thing to learn was how to free a bogged-in vehicle. You needed to dig away the sand from the wheels, before inserting 'sand ladders' – lengths of perforated steel sheeting, the width of your average tyre – at the front of the wheels, to enable the vehicle to drag itself free. When not in use, the sand ladders would be strapped to the side of our vehicles, slung on hooks welded there for the purpose. Foldable sand shovels were also kept handy, for the back-breaking work of digging free.

We'd move mostly at night to avoid being spotted, and night-driving in such terrain is a highly specialized skill. You proceed on 'black-light': showing no illumination whatsoever and using NVG to find your way. Navigation by stars and moon, using only the ambient light available, was another key piece of tradecraft. While we would be taking Magellan GPSs with us, the technology was still in its infancy, and in any case it was far easier for a driver simply to aim for a set point in the night sky – say, two fingers to the left of Orion – than to keep checking his GPS, the screen of which would give off a faint but tell-tale glow. The 'fingers' method referred to holding your hand at arm's length, to line up the requisite number of fingers to the left or right of your chosen guiding star. You'd marry that up with a dead-reckoning system, keeping a log of time, speed and direction travelled, and marking that off against a map, to keep track of where you were.

In addition to all this, we had to layer on the craft of formation driving and to rehearse contact drills in vehicles. That first night's practice proved intense, and it set the tone for what was to come. We'd rise early, do a stint of daylight mobility work while the temperature was still relatively cool, return to Victor for some scoff, then get busy with briefings and range packages. Out on the ranges, we also had to remind ourselves how to operate all the weaponry used by the enemy, for obvious reasons. Where we were heading, we might well run short of ammo or arms, or be forced to go on the run, and it was crucial to know how to fight using the enemy's arsenal.

Come dusk, we'd head out once more in the wagons, honing our all-important night-mobility skills. We'd return in the early hours and grab as much kip as possible, before starting all over, not forgetting to refresh our vehicle maintenance and communications skills along the way. The one big bonus was the temperature, which even during the heat of day didn't feel overly oppressive. It never got much above twenty degrees, and at night it dropped to a pleasant cool. While the schedule proved intense and exhausting, we were up for it. After all, it beat being in G Squadron's shoes – the reserve team consigned to CT duties, while every other man and his dog got to go to war.

We were a couple of days into the rehearsals when we got our briefing from the 'Green Slime' – the specialists who serve with Intelligence (Int) Corps. Their motto – translated from Latin – is *Knowledge gives strength to the arm*, but they'd earned their far more memorable nickname, 'Green Slime,' from the distinctive dark green berets they wear. One of their 'chaps' stood before us, as he proceeded to give it to us with what can only be described as both barrels.

'Do not underestimate what you are heading into, in Iraq,' he began. 'Whatever you may have chosen to believe, whatever you may have seen reported in the papers, put it all out of your heads. This is no ragtag tinpot enemy. The Iraqi military is a war-hardened, sophisticated, tech-savvy opponent, one whose DF capabilities we happen to believe are second to none. Keep your comms as short as possible, because believe me, if you give the enemy long enough to detect your signal, he'll be onto you in a flash.'

DF is direction finding: the ability of an enemy to track your radio or other signals, and to nail the location of your patrol as a result. An adversary with a shit-hot DF capability – that was the bane of behind-the-lines operators such as us.

'The unit you really want to avoid is the Iraqi Republican Guard,' he continued, handing around a file of photos. 'Unlike the regular Iraqi forces, these guys report to Saddam Hussein himself. They're better armed, better motivated, more highly trained and more disciplined.' I glanced at one of the grainy images. It showed a group of fit-looking men in smart green combats, sporting black or red berets – the latter of which reminded me of the headgear worn by the Paras, of course. Each had a thick, Saddam-lookalike moustache, which I guessed was all the rage right then, plus they sported a distinctive unit insignia – a red triangle set against a black background.

'If there is an elite in the Iraqi military, these guys are it,' the briefer continued. 'They're not conscripts, like most of Saddam's forces. They're fiercely loyal and immensely battle-hardened, after almost a decade at war with their neighbour to the east, Iran. Every man serving in the Republican Guard is a volunteer, and in return they're given better pay, good cars and the best housing. They're up for the fight, and they're the best the nation has to offer.'

'Sounds a lot like us,' a voice from the audience quipped, 'minus the bonus pay, the slick wheels and the luxury accommodation.'

There was a ripple of laughter, but it soon petered out.

'Underestimate them at your peril,' the briefer reiterated, without cracking the barest hint of a smile. 'They are fanatically loyal to Saddam, and in the area where you will very likely be asked to operate, there is an added layer of allegiances you need to be aware of. You'll most likely be heading into Anbar Province, where the local population is fiercely loyal to Saddam. If you are spotted by any locals, you should not expect to receive help. They will more than likely hand you over to the Iraqi military, and being taken captive is something you really do not want to countenance.'

'One final point on the Republican Guard: during the war with Iran they attained hero status in Iraq, after their 1988 retaking of the Fao Peninsula, one of the most fiercely contested stretches of terrain. They did so with a savagery that, well . . . demands a certain respect. Before going in, they laid down a thick barrage of nerve and cyanide agents, which wiped out everything in its path. That was an action that proved instrumental in forcing Iran to the negotiating table and in bringing that war to a close. The

Fao Peninsula was not the first use of such banned weapons by Saddam Hussein.'

The briefer paused for an instant, eyeing the room.

'As many of you know, and it's been all over the news, Saddam has a habit of using NBC weapons against his enemies, even against his own people. Don't pretend he'd baulk at doing so with Coalition forces, especially with elite units operating in his very backyard. In short, you need to go in prepared for the worst in terms of those kind of weapons being used against you, at least in the areas where you will operate.'

The briefing broke up with each of us being reminded pointedly to get all the recommended NBC (nuclear, biological and chemical) shots and antidotes. We'd each been handed a course of NAPS tablets – 'Nerve Agent Pre-Treatment Sets A1L1', to give them their full name – upon arrival at Camp Victor. Most of us had pretended to take them, then flushed them down the shitters, for the side effects of the NAPS course were rumoured to be horrendous, including reports that they made you impotent. With my recent promise to Emily about trying for a baby, that was a risk I wasn't willing to take.

But the anthrax jab couldn't be avoided: no jab meant no deploying. Within hours of having it, scores of the lads came down with fever and nausea. It felt like having a monster dose of flu, and some began coughing up great gouts of phlegm. With a few, the injection site itself turned septic, which meant it needed opening up, cleaning out and sterilizing.

As for myself, I had something else to worry about right then. Even as I'd sat through that utterly sobering briefing from the Green Slime, I'd felt the first stirrings of trouble: a rumbling in my guts, plus a familiar stabbing pain towards the top of my abdomen. *Oh shit*. This feeling was horribly familiar, and for all the worst reasons. It took me right back to the hell of Selection – first and second time around.

As discreetly as I could, I made a beeline for the Camp Victor ablutions block, dreading what was coming. Sure enough, I ended up emptying my guts from both ends –crapping and vomiting all at the same time. I don't know if you've ever experienced diarrhoea and vomiting (D & V), but the only way to deal with it in any modicum of 'comfort' is to get it all out in the showers. That way, you can sluice the entire mess down the drain, and clean yourself up at the same time. But that does not make it one iota less draining. Almost nothing takes it out of you like an attack of D & V.

Being an experienced medic, I knew the only way to deal with such an affliction was to try to get the fluids back into my body, using doses of rehydration salts, while necking Imodium to block up the other end. Without that, I'd be incapable of undertaking any more training, for obvious reasons, and once word got around, I was bound to get binned. No one was about to permit a guy with such an affliction to deploy, just as they would not have allowed me to complete Selection, had they actually found out.

As I languished in the showers, trying to deal with the shock of it all and the mess, my mind drifted to the Jungle Phase of Selection, 1985, first time around. We'd been practising close quarter combat drills amidst the thick and suffocating bush. It was all carried out with live ammunition in an entirely realistic fashion, utilizing maximum speed and aggression. Little light filters through the thick jungle canopy. We were moving as a patrol, alert for any threat, eyes out on stalks as we tried to penetrate the semi-darkness. When the first rounds erupted, I had to check that the guy covering me knew I was about to move, as I tried to get out of the enemy's line of fire – otherwise, with the low-visibility, your buddy might shoot you by mistake. But one day I went to punch through a screen of thick foliage, and as I moved I felt something snag into and then rip apart my left wrist. I knew right away that I'd hurt myself: the pain was clawing through the adrenaline. When the drill was over, I checked what had happened, and I could see where a series of thick wooden spikes had stabbed into me, piercing skin and flesh. A number had broken off in the process, leaving a dozen of the world's biggest splinters embedded in my arm. Apparently there was a tree thereabouts whose trunk was lined with these vicious wooden spines. I must have blundered into one of those.

With a sinking feeling, I was airlifted out of the jungle and whisked away to the nearest medical centre. After undergoing an operation to remove all the splinters, I had a visit from one of the SAS Training Wing staff, who gave me the bad news: I wasn't going to be allowed to return to the jungle, for fear the wounds would turn septic.

'Sorry, Des, you've not done enough of the Jungle Phase for us to allow you through,' he added. 'We'd like to invite you back to try again, but you'll have to start Selection from scratch.'

I tried to argue that I was more than willing to push on, but I was told that the risk of infection was simply too great. It was a massive blow. I wondered if I could find the willpower and the strength of character to go for it a second time around. Could I really face reliving all the trials and tribulations that I had just experienced? I was two and a half months into Selection, my body was wiped out, and it had taken pretty much everything out of me. Was I hungry enough to risk trying again?

I was flown back to Hereford, where I was called before the Training Squadron OC, Major Dominic Pitman, who just happened to have been my Company Commander in the Parachute Regiment.

'Just one of those things, Des,' he announced. 'Just unfortunate you got injured. But we'd like you to come back again. Take a year off, get yourself fully recovered, then come back and try again.'

'Thanks, boss, but can I not do that?' I asked him, in typical blunt Steel City fashion. 'Can I come back right away? Can I get on winter Selection?'

'Don't you think that's a bit too soon?'

'Boss, if I don't come back then, that's likely me done. I'll ask Para Reg if they'll give me time off right away, to train for winter Selection.'

With the OC's reluctant blessing, I did just that. A few months later I arrived back at Hereford to attempt it all over again. Not surprisingly, second time around it proved even harder, just as Major Pitman had warned it would. I had not allowed enough time for my body to recover. I felt this deep, bone-wrenching fatigue. I found it harder to focus. But worst of all, I started to be plagued by this horrible sickness – by the urge to vomit. And when I did throw up, it was this revolting acid mixture that I brought up.

The stomach contents are strongly acid, and I realized I was suffering from acid reflux. The only way I found to deal with it was to take pints of milk on the tabs – speed marches – to douse the acid (milk can have a temporary alkaline influence on the stomach contents). Undertaking two back-to-back Selections, I'd been training solidly for eighteen months, and I'd pushed myself way too hard. That was painfully obvious, as I found myself necking more and more milk, in an effort to neutralize the acid and keep going on the hills.

The DS – directing staff; the SAS veterans who run Selection – dictate what you carry in your Bergen during Hills Phase. That includes cold-weather gear, emergency rations, Gore-Tex water-proofs, a bivvy (survival) bag, a green maggot (sleeping bag), plus navigation kit, after which the rest of the weight is made up by whatever you choose. Increasingly, mine consisted of pints of milk. Before and after attempting a tab, the DS weigh your pack, to ensure the weight is adequate and that no one is cheating. Often they inspect the contents. All it would take was for one of the DS to clock that I was carrying so much milk, and they might get wise to my condition, in which case I'd get binned.

I managed to cope with it during the day, but at night, while I was lying down trying to sleep, it would flare up. I found myself vomiting as much in the block as I was on the hills, plus I started to suffer from diarrhoea as well. The DS have the right to voluntary withdraw (VW) you – to force you to pull off Selection – on medical grounds. I had to hide my condition from everyone – from the DS, but also from the other bruised and battered recruits.

The weeks took on a darkly familiar routine: on Monday I'd be pretty much okay, but by Wednesday I'd be suffering badly. Thursday I'd be on my chinstrap and come Friday I'd just about manage to crawl through. Every weekend I opted to stay on camp, and I'd sleep and eat for England, trying my best to recuperate. Then I hit my lowest ebb, right before the grand finale, Endurance, the 64 km death march.

We were on what they call the Pipeline, a massive forced march in the midst of the godforsaken wilderness of the Brecon Beacons. It was a freezing cold and hell-pit-dark January and I came across a fast-flowing stream, which you have to cross as part of the Pipeline. You're taught to take off your Bergen and sling it across one shoulder when fording such an obstacle. That way, if you fall, you can slip yourself out of it, so the weight doesn't pull you under. You might lose your pack, but in the process you'd save your life.

But I was worried that I was behind time. Breaking the cardinal rule, I decided to keep my pack strapped on tight, and use the butt of my weapon to feel my way across, like a DIY walking stick. I launched into the stream, and within seconds I was up to my waist in the freezing, powerful flow. Suddenly, around halfway across I lost my footing and went down. The current was so strong my legs were swept out from under me.

Moments later, the weight of the pack dragged me under. I turned turtle completely and had icy water streaming over my face, threatening to suffocate me. I tried to lift my head to grab a breath, but the weight of the pack wouldn't let me. I lay there thinking I was about to drown. There was a saying that we used to bandy about: *Death is nature's way of telling you – you failed Selection.* It came back to haunt me then, as the water cascaded over my face and the weight of my pack pulled me further and further under, and I felt gripped by this paralysing fear.

As I fought against the urge to black out, I tried to wriggle one shoulder out of the straps. If I didn't, I was dead. Somehow, by a herculean effort I managed to extract one arm, after which I rolled onto my front, executed a kind of press-up in the water and succeeded in dragging myself free. Gasping for breath, I felt around for my rifle, grasped it and hurled it onto the far bank. I then managed to grab hold of my Bergen and drag that free, and with my last reserves of strength I hauled it to the far side.

Frozen to the marrow and utterly spent, I collapsed onto my pack. I glanced around, scanning the horizon, to check if anyone had seen what had happened. As far as I could tell, there was not another soul within sight. I figured I was three and a half hours into the Pipeline, with a similar amount to go. It struck me then how easy it would be to die out here – unnoticed and unremarked by any other human soul.

The very thought seemed to ignite something inside me – a spurt of burning fury. I jabbed a finger at the sky and roared, screaming and yelling expletives, my teeth gritted in a paroxysm of rage.

'Don't you dare do this to me! Don't you fucking dare! I will not fail Selection again! Don't you fucking dare!'

Coming back to myself, I glanced around, only to spy three sheep staring at me, as if to say: *Yeah – that guy's totally lost it.* That was the moment that grounded me, bringing me back to planet earth.

During my first Selection I'd been advised that if you had 'a moment of madness' – and I was definitely experiencing one now – you should take a few seconds squatting on your Bergen, to settle your breath and gather your thoughts. To reset. I did that now, before grabbing my map and working out exactly where I was and how far I had to go.

The more I thought things over, the more I realized that I had no option but to crack on. I was soaked to the skin and shivering uncontrollably. I didn't have a set of dry clothes, for my pack was absolutely soaked through and through. The only way I had of getting warm was to get moving and to keep moving. If I stayed where I was, no one was riding to my rescue any time soon. I could easily die.

So I pushed on.

In due course I completed the Pipeline and I even managed to nurse my way through the last stages of Hills Phase. Those few of us left – maybe thirty guys, from an original lot of two hundred – then had three weeks' instruction in the classrooms at H, before heading for the jungle. This was precious time in which to allow bruised, battered and blistered limbs to heal. But my sickness just wasn't going away. I suspected by now that I had a stomach ulcer, and if the DS got wind of it, that was me done for. One day there was a smoke break, but I just hurried outside and vomited, even before I managed to make the toilet block.

One of the DS saw me. He came over and asked: 'Des, you okay?'

'Yeah, just feeling nauseous. Think I've caught a bug.'

He eyed me for a long second. 'Yeah, but Des, I've heard you've been sick before, haven't you?'

Someone must have said something. 'Yeah, but it's just a bug. A stomach upset.'

'Look, Des, go see the medic and get yourself checked over. You need this sorted, before we head to the jungle.'

I knew now that I'd come to their attention and that the focus was on me. But I told myself that if I could get through Selection nursing an ulcer, I could do just about anything. I vowed that if I did, I would come clean and get my condition diagnosed and properly seen to. I'd pretty much completed the jungle phase first time around, so I knew what lay ahead of me. I figured I could do this.

In due course we flew out to Brunei. It all went swimmingly – I was mentally prepared, having been there before – until we were three weeks in and we had a jungle resupply. At the time they were using these ancient-looking Hueys – Vietnam-vintage helos – to make the drops. In the midst of the thick jungle the pilot often can't find a place to land, so they have to lower a line to winch down supplies, and to haul up anyone who might need extracting – anyone who's sick or injured. The party on the ground signals its location by sending up a marker balloon, so the pilot has something to home in on.

The resupply went without a hitch, after which the DS turned to me and said: 'Des, can you clear up all the rubbish – the balloon, the packing and all that crap?'

The marker balloon came with a chemical crystal component, to which you had to add water, giving off a gas lighter than air, which inflated the balloon and lifted it up through the trees until it emerged above the canopy. I set about clearing up all the detritus, the spent balloon included, and added it to the heap of trash that we would remove when we were done. But as I did so, I felt this slight burning sensation on my thighs.

I glanced down, but couldn't see anything that might be causing it, so I cracked on. Over the next few minutes the sensation intensified, until it felt as if my legs were on fire. I went and reported it to the DS. He told me to drop my trousers, and as soon as I did we could see that the skin of my thighs had turned red raw and was starting to blister.

'Have you been bitten by something?' the DS asked.

'Not that I know of.'

There was a medic on the camp and he got me to drop my trousers for a second time. He bent to examine my thighs, remarking that I had suffered some kind of burns. Then he checked out the fabric of my combats, figuring out that the chemical from the marker balloon had leaked onto them, which in turn had burned my legs. The DS decided he had no option but to call the Huey back again, to get me airlifted to a hospital. I had an awful sinking feeling that this was going to be a re-run of the tree-splinters incident.

I hurried down to my basha – my DIY jungle sleeping shelter – still with no trousers on, slung my pack over my shoulder and dashed over to the Huey, where the pilots had the blades turning and burning. I went down on one knee and glanced to the cockpit, got a thumbs-up from the pilot and leapt aboard. Moments later, with turbines screaming, we hauled ourselves out of the jungle, and I just knew in my heart that I wasn't coming back again. We were only days away from completing the Jungle Phase, and the way my skin was blistering, no way was I getting flown back in.

I seemed blighted by the jungle. Cursed by it.

Sure enough, after several days' treatment for the chemical burns, I was returned with the rest of the blokes to Hereford. Then came that moment that every man on Selection dreads – the early-morning call to the Training Wing classroom, to learn who has passed and who has failed. I had little doubt what category I was in, and my mood could not have been darker.

A handful of names were read out, mine included, and we were told to head to one of the nearby rooms. Oddly, as I stood up to leave I figured amongst our number were the blokes who'd performed to the max during the Jungle Phase, and who should have passed. Binning those guys didn't make the slightest bit of sense.

Once we were gathered in the side-room, one of the DS came in, glanced at us and then smiled. 'Congrats, guys, you've passed the Jungle Phase. You need to be back here same time tomorrow, to start Escape and Evasion.'

So, just like that we were the chosen few.

It turned out that I'd done enough in the jungle to prove myself, especially as I'd all but completed it two times over. But by pushing it as hard as I had, and ignoring how sick I was, I'd stored up a shitstorm of problems.

In due course I was badged into the SAS and sent on a medical placement – working in the accident and emergency wing of a real-life hospital. The best way to learn how to deal with sickness, injury and trauma is to deal with it live on the job. While there, I mentioned to one of the doctors my worries about having an ulcer. He arranged for me to see a top specialist, who sent a tiny camera down my throat to have a look. Sure enough, I had a duodenal ulcer – an open sore on the lining of my small intestine – which would need surgery. Even after that, I'd still need medication to keep it in check. It would flare up at times of intense physical or psychological stress – just as it had now, at Camp Victor.

*

I finished scrubbing myself down in the Camp Victor showers, dried and dressed, and made my way to my lair in the hangar, the best place to lick my wounds. I lay on my cot, my mind a whirl of thoughts: *Fuck, I'm going to get left behind. If they realize I'm sick, they'll pull me off BCR. But if I deploy and I'm sick as a dog, I'll be useless – I'll be a total liability. I'll be a dead weight around the blokes' necks.*

No one can fight or function properly when plagued by diarrhoea and vomiting. I decided I needed to get a grip on this within the next forty-eight hours. Otherwise I'd have to pull myself off the mission. And that could be read in either of two ways. Unlike a highly visible injury, there was little outward sign that I was in bad shape. People could choose to believe what I said – that I was sick. Or they could reach the easier, darker conclusion – that I had bottled it. That I'd pulled myself off ops because I was afraid.

That could lead to a collapse in morale amongst the squadron. And no matter how unjustified or unwarranted it might be, no one could ever recover from that kind of rumour doing the rounds. *Did you hear about Des? Fuck me, he's bottled it. Pulled a sickie, so he doesn't have to cross the border. Who'd have thought it of Des?*

I resolved to dose myself up to the nines. As one of B Squadron's designated medics, I had made absolutely certain I had deployed with a full medical kit. My medic's bag would ride in a specific place on the wagon, so I knew exactly where to grab it, should the shit go down and someone get hit. It was a standard Army Bergen, but one that I'd divided into two. One side was stamped 'T', in big black marker pen – T standing for trauma. That compartment included all the kind of kit I'd need if someone took a gunshot injury – field dressings, bags of fluids and cannulas for drips, tourniquets to stop bleeding, shots of morphine and the like.

The other compartment was marked 'M' – M for medical – and it was that which I set about raiding now. I grabbed a handful of paracetamol, just to take the edge off the pain and to lower my temperature, and amoxicillin, a broad-spectrum antibiotic, in case I had a gut infection. Plus I necked the Imodium, stuffing extra doses into various pockets, to make sure I always had some to hand.

Despite such precautions, I found myself waking in the early hours and racing to the showers, only to vomit and have the shits just as soon as I got there. One time I came out after a particularly violent session, and someone was standing there who'd clearly heard all that had been happening.

'Fucking hell, Des, you okay?' It was Dinger, no doubt up early doors to get his first kick of nicotine.

'Yeah. Just a bit under the weather. Must be something I've eaten.'

I turned and hurried away, before he could fire any more questions at me. I just had to hope to hell I could weather the storm. I figured I'd be okay, as long as the head shed didn't clock how ill I was. Then a thought struck me that was truly dark. If I didn't get through this, if I did need to bail out, rather than Iraq being the golden opportunity to prove myself, it might end up being the time that I was 'proved' to be a coward.

As things tend to when you're feeling truly dog-rough, the next few days blended into one – a whirlwind of training, range work and briefings, all interspersed with long sessions in the showers, voiding myself from both ends. With the burn rate from all the preparations, plus the added stress of the illness and not eating properly, I was close to finished, and we hadn't so much as put a toe across the Iraqi border.

It felt like being on the Combat After Capture exercise, which is the grand finale of SAS Selection – the culmination of the Escape and Evasion phase, where they keep you awake and under hostile interrogation for days on end. At a purpose-built facility, they put you into stress positions, hooded and with 'white noise' – tuneless, formless radio interference – blasting into your earholes. The only 'respite' comes when you get dragged into the interrogation rooms, and your hood gets ripped away, only to be faced by grey guys in woolly jumpers offering you sweet tea and biscuits, or peroxide blondes with Russian accents taking the piss out of your manhood, or big bruisers threatening dire violence – anything to mess with your head, and convince you that your capture is very much for real.

I survived the hell of Combat After Capture, one of the few to do so. But I sure as hell wasn't convinced I was going to survive Camp Victor.

As bad luck would have it, another problem was about to raise its ugly head. US General H. 'Stormin' Norman Schwarzkopf, the overall commander-in-chief of Coalition forces in the Gulf, made it clear that he didn't want to use special forces. A veteran of the Vietnam War, Schwarzkopf argued that US elite forces had failed to cover themselves in glory during that conflict. As a result, he was determined to fight this war his way: he'd use Coalition airpower to degrade Saddam's forces, before rolling his troops and armour across the border. He didn't see the need for special operators like us at all.

In Stormin' Norman's view, there was nothing that we SF types could achieve that an F16, with its unrivalled precision optics, sensors and 'smart weapons' – laser-guided bombs and the like – couldn't achieve from the air. Desert Shield, the Coalition war effort, was going to be first and foremost an air war, backed by massed ranks of infantry and armour. On the viewpoint of one man, who just happened to be the commander-in-chief, it looked unlikely that any of us – A, D or B Squadrons included – would get used.

The 15 January deadline for Iraq to withdraw came and went, and clearly Saddam's legions were going nowhere. He had 300,000 troops in Kuwait, and as far as he was concerned they were staying put. Hours later, just as Stormin' Norman intended, the air war began in earnest. During the night of 16–17 January, a total of 671 sorties were launched, including airstrikes by state-of-the-art F-117 Nighthawk stealth fighters and volleys of cruise missiles.

But Saddam was nothing if not cunning and wily. In a belt-and-braces approach, the Iraqi leader had vowed to rain down hellfire on Israel, should the Coalition try to drive him out of Kuwait. In the early hours of 18 January he proved true to his word, launching a salvo of eight Scud missiles against Tel Aviv, Israel's technological and financial centre, and Haifa, a key population hub, plus a few more against the Saudi airbases from where the Coalition was launching air missions, for good measure.

At over 40 feet in length and with a range of over 600 km, the Al Hussein – Iraq's much-improved Scud – was a tactical ballistic missile with a cruise speed of Mach 5, or over 6,000 km per hour. That meant that it took a matter of minutes to travel from Iraq's Western Desert across Jordan to hit targets in Israel – which left precious little time for any hardware that Desert Shield might boast to intercept the missiles and take them down. The Americans had stationed Patriot anti-missile batteries around the key airbases, but they could do precious little to stop Saddam's Scuds from hitting Israel.

The Scud campaign was Saddam's seeming masterstroke. The impact craters of those first Scuds were tested for CBRN residues, for the fear was that Saddam would lob a Sarin or VX warhead into one of Israel's major cities. No signs were found: it appeared as if that first salvo of Scuds was carrying conventional high explosives only, rather like the V-2s that Nazi Germany had rained down on London and other European cities in World War Two. Even so, there was no guarantee that Saddam, in desperation, wouldn't resort to using such banned weapons as the war ground on.

Israel responded by threatening to send her forces into Iraq, to hunt down the Scud-launchers, many of which were mobile. Overnight, almost, the war was in danger of spiralling out of control. The Israelis were preparing to dispatch paratroopers to go Scud-hunting, and if that happened the Arab nations would have no option but to side with Saddam, fatally dividing the Coalition. All it would take was for one chemical warhead to fall on Tel Aviv and all hell would let loose.

Just as Saddam had intended, this was Third World War kind of stuff.

Many of the Scuds were fired from giant Transport Erector Launchers, eight-wheeled behemoths known as TELs in the trade. The TELs were mobile and easy enough to hide, which made them a nightmare to track and hit via airpower. Saddam was reckoned to have as many as forty of them, with many more Scud missiles on hand.

This meant that suddenly there was a clear and obvious role for special forces: Scud-hunting. With former SAS director General Sir Peter de la Billière serving as General Schwarzkopf's right-hand man, the US commander was all of a sudden ripe for the convincing. In short order the men of the Regiment did seem to have a role to fulfil, and it was a vital one. They would be the Scud-hunters, and upon their efforts might hinge the fortunes of the entire war.

Very quickly, the only thing preventing Israeli leader Yitzhak Shamir from sending in his battalions of paratroopers to Iraq, along with air support, was the promise that Special Air Service patrols would be there to do the job for him. Otherwise, Israeli troops would be rushed into the 'Scud Box', as we now termed it, a vast expanse of desert that stretched from the far side of the Saudi border several hundred kilometres to Baghdad.

That was one hell of a lot of territory in which Saddam could hide his missiles. Likewise, it was one hell of a lot of desert in which we would have to go looking for them. With the air war in full swing, the Coalition had already stirred up a hornet's nest on the ground. Any SAS patrols would be operating amongst Iraqi ground forces already stung by airstrikes, and a civilian population that might well have suffered 'collateral damage'.

As luck would have it, A and D Squadrons had already been dispatched – first into Saudi Arabia by C-130 Hercules transport aircraft, and from there driving their convoys of heavily armed desert-adapted vehicles overland towards the border with Iraq, in preparation for the ground offensive. What De la Billière – and Schwarzkopf – needed right now was a force that could be flown deep into Iraq, to reach the Scud-firing fields, several hundred kilometres inside the country, so as to put a stop to the launches. And that, of course, left only us – the Disco Squadron boys.

From being Battle Casualty Replacements, the least-prepared Squadron had suddenly become the very tip of the spear.

CHAPTER FIVE

THE BRAVO PATROLS

As I was feeling so sick, the past few days seemed to have merged into a blurry mush, but one thing did stick in my memory, largely because it was just so way-out weird. Around the same time we learned that B Squadron were to serve as the Scud-hunters, Brigadier Andrew Massey, the deputy director of UK special forces, put in an appearance at what passed for the Camp Victor cookhouse.

With the drugs finally seeming to take effect, my innards appeared to be stabilizing, with the result that I was ravenously hungry. All I wanted to do was to eat and eat and eat – making up for lost time, or lost stomach contents, more like. Along with the other Disco Squadron lads I was wolfing down a plate heaped high with scoff, when the distinctive figure of the brigadier strode in. Without further ado he clambered onto a table, with a junior officer flanking him on either side, and cleared his throat.

'Gentlemen,' he began to speak, 'when the Coalition war machine starts whirring, you will be the lead cog. You will be heading directly where the action is at its fiercest.' The brigadier thrust his hands down the front of his trouser belt, taking up a stance that officers – 'ruperts', as we like to call them – tend to have a habit of affecting. 'Make no mistake, you're the most intensively trained, best-organized and best-equipped SF outfit there is, and the area of Iraq assigned to you is there for the taking. Seek out, locate and destroy your targets as you find them and create havoc and confusion for the enemy. I must congratulate you now in preparation for what is to come. We are going to war and the Regiment's actions – your actions – will go down in history.'

With that, he jumped down from the table and marched right out again.

I glanced around at the others. Their expressions said it all: *What the fuck was that all about?* For sure, it was all very dramatic and stirring, but it was just a little bit too gung-ho and rupert-like for our liking. We knew what the brigadier was trying to convey: *This is your moment; the Regiment is going for it big time, and you guys are the tip of the spear.* It was just the over-the-top style and the delivery that left something to be desired.

If he'd taken just a little longer, delivered just a little more practical information, and paused to take just a few questions from the floor – hell, involved the blokes serving at the tip of the spear in his cogitations – that would have made all the difference, especially in a unit where, historically at least, merit was supposed to trump rank.

During World War Two, David Stirling had stressed that respect in the SAS had to be earned; it was not conveyed by rank alone. When operating in small-scale teams far behind the lines, any man, no matter his rank, had to be ready to continue with the mission, alone if necessary, if all others on his team had been put out of action. From the outset, Stirling had also sought to forge a unit where class had no place, and where any man should feel free to voice his opinions.

I had a rake of questions that I'd have liked to ask of Brigadier Massey, as I felt sure the others did too, if only we'd got the opportunity.

First off: *Okay, boss, so what's the timeframe here? Are we talking tomorrow? Next week? Or when?*

Next: *Are you referring to us lot only, or are A and D also going Scud-hunting?*

Then: *As A and D are already committed to their overland infil, that must make us the furthest forward troops?*

Plus: *Other than Scud-hunting, are there any other tasks likely to come our way?*

But with the brigadier having made his dramatic exit, all any of us could do was turn back to our scoff and wonder.

Pretty swiftly the first eight-man patrol was stood up to go Scud-hunting. With little further ado, the names of the chosen were posted to the Camp Victor noticeboard. First up was the patrol commander, seasoned SAS Sergeant Andy McNab, as he would come to be known. McNab was an obvious choice: fit, disciplined and well respected, he'd already won a Military Medal (MM) when serving with the Green Jackets in Northern Ireland, before he even came to the SAS.

As McNab and I were both from Air Troop, we knew each other well. He was a Londoner with a Cockney wide-boy twang, and I used to rip the piss out of his accent. He'd retort by tearing mercilessly into my broad Sheffield burr. Around the same height as me, McNab was noticeably stockier and more thick-set – he had a physique built for tabbing. Blessed with that East End gift of the gab, plus a cocky attitude and a ready smile, whenever there was fun to be had McNab would be right in the thick of it. But likewise, if it came to getting serious he was at the forefront of that too.

Dinger was also on the list, as was Bob Consiglio – my Blow Monkeys buddy on the block back at H. Chris Ryan was also on it, another bloke with whom I shared a special bond, for he and I had both completed Selection two times over, pretty much. Chris had first joined the TA SAS, for which you are put through the same Selection process as for 22 SAS, the regular outfit. But to come across from the TA unit, you then had to undergo Selection all over again. Chris Ryan had my ultimate respect for having done just that.

Then there was Tim Orr, known to all as 'Kiwi'. I'd first run into Tim in New Zealand, when he was serving in that nation's SAS. We'd been on a training package off the coast, which culminated in a parachute jump at night, diving off the ramp of a C-130 Hercules and plummeting into the dark sea. We made the leap wearing black 'dry-bags' – ultra-warm diving suits – and bedecked in full combat and survival gear. Just as soon as we hit the water, I could feel the powerful current dragging me out to sea. We'd jumped at last light, so the waiting RIBs – rigid inflatable boats – were just visible, as they zipped about plucking blokes from the water.

From the RIBs we transferred to a trawler, where we changed into our assault gear, before being dropped on a midnight-dark shoreline. A 70-foot cliff-climb followed, after which we formed up for a forced march across wild and windswept bush, to attack an 'enemy camp'. On this exercise it was a remote farmstead, and we had the Kiwi SAS – Tim Orr included – playing the role of the bad guys. Come first light we went in all guns blazing, and having faced some ferocious resistance we 'killed' some of the hostiles and cuffed the others, after which it was mission accomplished.

During the six weeks we'd spent in New Zealand, I'd been hugely impressed by the Kiwi operators. Natural born bush trackers, they were unbeatable at jungle warfare – so much so that those of us in the Brit SAS who chose to specialize in tracking were sent on a three-month embed with the Kiwis – known as 'Long Look' – to learn from the masters. It was during our New Zealand training package that Andy McNab and I had chatted to Tim Orr about joining the British SAS. In short order he'd done just that, meaning he was another guy who'd completed Selection two times over.

Tim was short in stature – no taller than me – with dark hair, and he was a very likeable bloke, always chatty and approachable. We'd often get together for a brew and a chinwag. I was forever slagging him for being a Kiwi, but in truth he was tops: fit as a butcher's dog. I rarely if ever saw Tim complain, and he remained resolutely upbeat, regardless of what life threw at him.

The big surprise, for me at least, was that I was also included on that list of eight names to make up the patrol. Whatever else that might signify, it had to mean that my hale-and-hearty act over the past few days – my attempts to conceal how tortured and messed up were my innards – must have passed muster. The other two lads on the patrol I knew less well, but with McNab, Bob Consiglio, Dinger, Chris Ryan and Tim Orr on my shoulder, I felt I'd be in the very best of company.

Ours was a classic SAS tasking – a mission set deep behind enemy lines, where we were to gather crucial intelligence on enemy targets. It was not a full-on combat role: we were to remain hidden and undetected, while radioing back Scud locations, so they could be hit by Coalition airstrikes. Even so, every other B Squadron guy was green with envy that the eight of us had got this gig.

The Scud threat rapidly escalated. The Coalition proved incapable of shooting down all the missiles bound for Israel, no matter how they might rush Patriot batteries into position in an effort to do so. Hour by hour the pressure mounted. All US President George Bush and Prime Minister John Major could do was repeat to the Israelis the same promise – that the SAS were being sent in, and that we would deal with the Scuds. It was only that which was keeping the Israeli troops from going in.

No pressure, then: just the need to prevent World War Three resting on our shoulders. But within a matter of hours everything was set to change.

We were called to an urgent briefing. The OC of B Squadron, Major Phil Carpenter, was about to address the men. Major Carpenter was a tall, lean bloke, with dark hair and the typical pointy-sharp features of a rupert. He spoke with a distinctly cut-glass accent, or so it sounded to my Steel City ears, but I didn't hold that against him. Though I'd not had a great deal to do with him during my time in B Squadron, our few interactions had been fine. In fact, I'd found the major a surprisingly approachable bloke.

We 'other ranks' tended to slag the ruperts, and that's just the way it was. But I'd once had a senior officer take me to one side for a quiet talk, presenting to me the other side of the coin.

'I realize the staff sergeants up here don't think very highly of the officers,' he'd ventured. 'And that tends to filter down to the rest of the ranks.'

'Err, yeah. It's the Rupert mentality they object to. All those brains and degrees and letters after their names, but not an ounce of common sense between them.'

'I get that,' he conceded. 'But when you pause to think about it, Des, for a major to make it back to the SAS to run a Sabre Squadron, he's got to have something about him, hasn't he?'

Any officer who made it into the SAS had to complete not only the same Selection as the rest of us, but what they call 'Officer Week' – an extra trial, in which they would get utterly roasted. That alone demanded respect. If they made it through, they'd first command a troop, but after two or three years they'd have to leave, to go to staff college and continue their career path. The chances of making it back again, as a major, to command a squadron, were remote, and it was rumoured not to be a particularly smart career move. Any man of that rank who aspired to the SAS was seen as prioritizing hands-on action over senior command, which tended to be frowned upon.

As I settled down to hear what Major Carpenter had to say, I tried putting myself in his shoes. Overnight almost, he'd gone from commanding what was basically the reserve squadron, to being in charge of the much-vaunted Scud-hunters, upon which world leaders had pledged their reputations. The stakes could not have been higher. As a major, he'd have around two years in the SAS during which to make his mark. So this was either Major

Carpenter's golden opportunity, or it was going to prove an utter disaster.

Growing up in the Steel City, everyone in our neighbourhood was either a Sheffield Wednesday or a Sheffield United fan – me mostly the latter. In fact, the rivalry between the two sets of supporters had become so intense that it had spilled over into violence on the terraces. Some of the foremost hooligans were seen as celebrities, or at least they were where I grew up. Using a football analogy, I figured Major Carpenter had his team on the pitch in the Premier League, with everything to play for.

He stood before us in distinctive desert camouflage uniform, with a sandy-coloured smock thrown over the top, for it was chilly in the air-conditioned hangar. I'd never seen either the desert cam or the smocks before deploying to the UAE, as this was my first time in the desert theatre. The smock struck me as looking uncomfortably tight on the major's tall, rangy frame. I'd learn later that these were ancient bits of kit, dating back to World War Two, and back then blokes tended to be smaller in stature, hence the cut.

'Okay, chaps, this should come as no surprise,' the major began, 'but every hour Israel is talking more and more volubly about coming into the war, all due to the Scud threat. Saddam is targeting Israel deliberately and everyone knows it. Promises have been made at a very high level that he will be stopped, and so we have decided that one patrol is not enough. It makes little sense having SF elements sat in the rear, when this is what we're up against. So, the one patrol will now become three, and each will go forward to get eyes-on the means by which Saddam is sending his Scuds to their launch sites.'

'We've already decided the make-up of the three patrols. Names will be posted on the noticeboard.' The major paused for a second. 'Suffice to say – and this should be self-evident – with three patrols now deploying, that means every man will get used. This will be chiefly an OP tasking, so your priority is to remain covert and to keep reporting in the Scud coordinates. Go check your patrols, break down into those units and start your detailed planning, because you should expect to deploy very shortly.'

By the time Major Carpenter had finished speaking, there was almost a scrum to get to the noticeboard. I didn't feel so much of a need myself, for I presumed I was still on McNab's patrol. Instead, I did a quick bit of mental arithmetic. The major was right. With a bunch of our guys busy training Sheikh Zayed bin Sultan Al Nahyan's elite guard, every man attending that briefing – barring the senior figures in the head shed – was going to deploy.

I reached the noticeboard to find that Geordie Straker – B Squadron's SSM – was giving the guys an impromptu pep talk, in his typical calm, considered way.

'Right lads, you've seen your teams, and all patrols share the same tasking: to go forward and establish OPs on the key MSRs which run east–west to the Jordanian border.' MSR: main supply route; the key roads that the Iraqi military was using right now. 'We believe Saddam is hiding his Scuds in transit along those MSRs, possibly under road bridges and flyovers, using his mobile launchers to lob them into Israel come nightfall. You'll spread your patrols along the MSRs, ID the Scuds as they pass and radio back coordinates, after which we'll take care of the airstrikes.

That's your key mission. Any questions, feel free to ask. And trust me, you guys are going to do great out there.'

I glanced over the lists of names, only to discover that I was wrong about the make-up of my patrol. I'd been allocated to another team completely, and not one man from the original lot was on it. Of course, I was disappointed. McNab's patrol was a top bunch of operators. But it was the head shed that had reconfigured the patrols, and they'd have done so in an effort to spread key disciplines – chiefly mobility – across each. I had neither McNab nor any of his guys with me, and that was just the way the cookie crumbled.

My new patrol commander was Sergeant Jim Dickson, like me a former 1 Para guy. Though in the future Jim and I would come to blows, I liked and respected him. Jim's time in 1 Para had overlapped with my own, but he'd come up to Hereford earlier, and being a former Para, he shared that go-getting attitude that typified the unit. Hailing from the east of England, he was pale-skinned, with blond hair and blue eyes, and a little shorter than me, but stocky with it. I knew him to be a tough, strong, determined individual.

I was pleased to have a Para in command of the new patrol, as I knew my own kind. It also seemed that I had enjoyed something of a promotion. As a corporal, I'd been assigned as the patrol's second-in-command, whereas in McNab's unit I'd just been one of the blokes. Under Jim Dickson and myself, we had six other guys, none of whom I knew overly well, even though we were all in the same squadron.

Of them, Lance Corporal Phillip Jeans was the guy I was closest to. Another former Para Regiment guy, Phil was dark-haired, squat and powerful, with a gruff, gravelly voice – the product of too much smoking. Of course, I was forever slagging him about it, just as I did with Dinger. But Phil's really distinctive feature was his right hand: it was missing all of one and half of another finger. Inevitably, it was the first thing you'd notice about Phil, when you went to shake hands.

It was while serving in the Paras that Phil had lost his fingers. They'd been on exercises in the Belize jungle when a fellow soldier had run amok with a machete. Typically, Phil had stepped forward to disarm the bloke, but had lost a good chunk of his hand in the process. That defined the man: he was up for a fight, always. Despite his missing fingers, Phil had made it through Selection, proving he was as capable as the rest of us. We'd nicknamed him 'Drill', as in Phil the Drill, cause he could always be relied upon to drill a target, but it had evolved from there to 'Driller' these days.

Next on the list was Lance Corporal Trevor Moriarty, a small, fiery redhead with a rapid-fire Geordie accent, one that was so thick I could barely understand a word he said. I wasn't the only one who would have problems. The catchphrase in our patrol would become: 'What the fuck did Trev say?' Trev's red-haired gnome look was made all the more convincing in that sticking out from under his ginger thatch was the most enormous nose, plus these wide blue-green eyes like saucers.

With skin that was hyper-sensitive to the sun, Geordie Trev wasn't exactly ideal desert material. He was married, and he was a fitness fanatic to a degree that well eclipsed the likes of me. Trev was a serious triathlete, and he was also said to embody proof that perpetual motion does in truth exist. He never stopped moving or talking or working out, and his catchphrase was: 'Yeah, really good fucking training.'

Next was Lance Corporal Will 'Chewie' McBride. If Geordie Trev was the patrol's Hobbit, then Chewie McBride was its cave troll, or its Chewbacca – hence the nickname. Chewie was a six-foot-four man-mountain of a bloke, with craggy features and scruffy, sandy hair worn long. Hailing from the West Country, he had a Somerset cider-drinking accent, plus the mellow, sunny disposition that tends to go with it. Despite his imposing physique, he had honest, no-nonsense features and was forever in good spirits. With me he'd rip the piss mercilessly out of my diminutive stature – and for sure, you could fit two of Des into one of Chewie.

I had extra respect for Chewie, over and above his striking physical presence. As with Chris Ryan, Chewie had come into 22 SAS from one of the TA SAS units – meaning the both of us had been put through the mill twice. Chewie was our signals and communications specialist, so no doubt he'd have his work cut out in Iraq. It would be his responsibility to ensure that the all-important target coordinates for Scud-launchers were transmitted back to headquarters, so they could be taken out.

Next there was Trooper Alex Switcher, truly the grey man on the patrol. (Trooper is the SAS equivalent rank to private.) Alex was fresh into B Squadron and a complete unknown. Small in stature and unremarkable looking, he hailed from the Hereford area, and had that typical slow-talking rural way about him. Alex had come out of the shadows to bolster our Iraq contingent, having spent several years serving in a reserve element that supports the SAS, being made up of former members and some civilian territorials. Alex was a man of few words. He was the least experienced on our patrol and was a shadowy individual that none of us knew well.

Then there was Scouse, a Liverpudlian – real name Jeff Fisher, and another trooper. A little taller than me at around six foot, Scouse had a pockmarked face, rugged features and a strong, muscled physique. He hailed from Boat Troop, had an easy-going manner and was forever inviting me to visit his folks in Liverpool. I sensed that Scouse was a hard man who knew how to use his fists and he wasn't the type to take a backwards step.

After Scouse, the last man was Trooper Joe Ambler, like me a married guy. Joe hailed from the RAF Regiment, which is not to be confused with the RAF. The RAF Regiment guys are basically paratroopers whose mission is to safeguard RAF operations wherever they might find themselves at war. But of course to us the very letters 'RAF' were the perfect excuse for some spirited slagging.

'When you RAF guys go to war, you do so in carpet slippers, don't you, mate?' we'd rib Joe.

'Yeah,' he'd retort, 'plus there's better food on our base and sometimes even pretty ladies.'

Slightly taller than me, with dark hair and eyes, Joe was a runner – a 'racing snake' – as opposed to being a gym queen. Suffice to say he was incredibly laidback, and nothing any of us could say ever seemed to faze him. As with the rest of us, I sensed that Joe was well up for a fight. All eight of us brought something distinct to the party. But what united us was our tendency to think differently, as events were shortly to prove.

It was left to each patrol to decide exactly how they intended to execute the mission. Some things were a given. We were slated to be spirited across the border deep into Iraq, riding on twin-rotor heavy-lift Chinook helicopters, flown by the RAF's Special Forces flights. But from there onwards the means of deployment for each patrol was pretty much its own affair.

A and D Squadrons had headed off each with fourteen Pinkies, the long-wheel-base desert-adapted Land Rovers fitted out with every piece of kit imaginable, and bristling with weaponry: 7.62 mm general purpose machineguns (GPMGs), .50-calibre heavy machine guns, Mk 19 grenade launchers, and MILAN anti-armour missiles. Several even had US-made Stinger surface-to-air missiles strapped to the roll-bars, plus MIRA thermal-imaging sights, which could detect the heat given off by vehicles, buildings or even human bodies, constituting a superb tool for battlefield reconnaissance.

A and D Squadrons were also equipped with Mercedes Unimogs, an all-terrain truck perfect for carrying extra ammo, rations, water and spare parts. In short, they were a force to be reckoned with, one that could take on anything up to heavy armour, via the MILAN missiles, and even marauding Iraqi warplanes, via the Stingers. Likewise, we were looking forward to getting our hands on some equally serious pieces of kit with which to go to war.

As Jim headed off to join the other patrol commanders for a planning session, I took the lads to check out the vehicles. But when we got sight of what was on offer at Camp Victor, we could barely believe our eyes. From somewhere, the powers that be had rustled up a handful of 90 Land Rovers, the short-wheel-base versions, plus one lone 110, the long wheel-base model. We stopped short and eyed them, incredulously.

I don't think I'd ever seen a short-wheel-base Land Rover on an SAS base, not unless one of the blokes happened to own one to shuttle to and from work. For very good reasons the Regiment never uses the 90: it is less stable over rough terrain, has far less room to accommodate four blokes plus all their gear, and doesn't have the space to house the vehicle-mounted heavy weaponry, our chief firepower.

To make matters worse, none of the wagons sported any of the specialist kit we'd expect: no sump-guards, winches or sand ladders, nor any extra fuel and water tanks. SAS Pinkies have stubby grenade launchers welded to the front bumper at a forty-five-degree angle – perfect for laying down a smokescreen when on the move and withdrawing from a contact. They have double roll bars running across the cab and pick-up-style rear, to protect the vehicle's occupants should the wagon flip, and offering the perfect place to strap bulky kit, like camouflage netting. They have lugs for sand ladders, so they can be slung along the sides above the rear wheels, plus brackets for holding LAW 80 anti-tank rockets.

These vehicles had none of that.

But the very worst was the lack of any weaponry. There was not one single 7.62 mm GPMG mounted on any of the vehicles, nor any of the heavier weaponry that we would expect: no .50-calibre heavy machineguns (HMGs), no grenade launchers, no MILANs and certainly no Stingers. In short, they had no mounted fire-power of any nature at all. Not to put too fine a point on it, but these wagons – painted a dull brown colour – were little short of what you'd find your average British farmer driving around in, on a dirt track in rural Herefordshire.

The Regiment's 110s are far removed from your standard Land Rover, even before we start bolting on the weaponry. The spare wheel is mounted flat on top of the bonnet, all the glass is removed, there are no doors and no roof, and the entire vehicle is painted end to end a pinky beige shade of desert camo – hence the 'Pinkie' nickname. All lights are removed, painted out or disabled, so not a glimmer would show at night, and all shiny surfaces are dulled or painted over. Each has a powerful winch bolted to the front, for pulling the wagon out of serious trouble. With the cut-down nature of the Pinkie, that 3 tonne battle-wagon is capable of carrying four blokes, at a pinch.

The Camp Victor wagons were a far cry from all that. We had an MT (motor transport) specialist attached to the squadron, who was responsible for all matters vehicle-related. I dragged him over to where the wagons were parked and gave voice to the obvious question.

'Mate: what – the fuck – are these?'

Sheepishly, MT Toby tried to explain. There had of course been rakes of tip-top SAS battle-wagons shipped out from Hereford, but unfortunately A and D Squadrons had bagged the lot. As we'd been slated to be BCRs, no one had thought to question it, for when we got flown in to replace any casualties, we'd be joining either A or D Squadron in their vehicles, so what was the harm?

But with the sudden, unforeseen developments over the Scud-hunting, the Regiment had had to make do and mend. The wagons on offer were apparently RAF vehicles, ones that the head shed had somehow managed to pilfer from RAF Akrotiri, the British airbase on Cyprus. It was all they could manage to get their hands on in the time.

I gritted my teeth. 'Let me get this fucking straight. We've gone from BCRs to Scud-hunting, and you're sending us into Iraq . . . in those? I'm just checking if I'm hearing you right.'

'Erm, yep. Well, *I'm* not, of course. The head shed is.' MT Toby glanced at the sorry excuse for SAS chariots and shrugged. 'Look, Des, they might not look like much, but they're road-worthy and functional and they won't let you down.'

'Listen, mate, we're not making a run down to fucking Tesco.' I kicked up a boot-load of dust frustratedly, before deciding to let it go. 'Fuck it. It is what it is.'

MT Toby talked us around the wagons a bit, but frankly there was bugger all to show or tell. These were just standard run-arounds – nothing less and nothing more. Nothing to see here at all.

I told MT Toby we'd bag the lone 110, plus what we figured was the best of the 90s. Apart from being the comms specialist, the Big Friendly Giant, Chewie, was also our resident wizard on vehicle mechanics and maintenance, and I let him be the judge of which was the least worst of the short-wheel-base Land Rovers. That decided, we checked over their vital statistics: fuel, oil, water, tyres.

We stood back to survey our steeds. 'A crap Pinkie and an even crapper Dinky,' I remarked, in disgust. That was it. For the 90, that nickname – 'Dinky' – just stuck.

'Right, if we break down just outside of Baghdad, we've got you to blame for it, eh?' I jabbed our MT guy in the ribs, just to let him know there were no hard feelings.

For sure, it wasn't his responsibility that the wagons were in such rag order. In fact, you had to wonder exactly whose fault it was. The head shed had doubtless done their best – this was all they could rustle up in the time available. If anything, you had to point a finger at the lack of kit and budget that generally plagues the British military. It wasn't the first time we'd been saddled with the worst gear imaginable. It wouldn't be the last.

As always, there was no option but to crack on.

CHAPTER SIX

A PINKIE AND A DINKY

When Jim rejoined us, I gave him a tour of our sorry excuse for some wheels. But if anything, the news from his end was even more of a shocker. Seeing the state of the wagons, the other two patrol commanders – Andy McNab and Patrick Johnson, an equally experienced and respected soldier – had decided they weren't about to go anywhere in those. As far as they were concerned, taking those vehicles into Iraq would be asking for trouble. You couldn't fight from them, as they had no vehicle-mounted weaponry, they'd stick out like the pro-verbial dog's nads, and all they'd end up serving as was bullet magnets. As a result, they'd decided that once the Chinook dropped them in the midst of the Iraqi desert, they would proceed from there on foot.

To say we were surprised at learning this is the understatement of the century. Despite the shite state of the wagons, this was an OP tasking, so for argument's sake we were unlikely to need to go speeding about brassing up targets. This Scud-hunting lark was far more likely to involve sneaky-beaky softly softly stuff than it was shoot-n-scoot, hit-n-run pyrotechnics – in which case the shit Pinkie and the even shitter Dinky might just do the job in Iraq, or so we tried convincing ourselves.

Going in on foot, the other two patrols would have a stupendous amount to carry – Bergens, belt kit, personal weapons, jerrycans of water, extra ammo and the OP kit they would be dragging along with them. Even so, Andy McNab's and Patrick Johnson's patrols were determined to stick to their legs. They argued that riding into the Iraqi desert in a fleet of Dinkies – there was only the one 110, and we'd bagged it – would very likely get them all captured or killed, and as we appreciated, there was one hell of a lot of experience amongst the sixteen guys on their patrols. There is an unwritten rule in the SAS that the man on the ground is always right, regardless of rank.

Either way, for us this was decision time.

We headed to a bit of open ground where we could grab a group chat – what they term a 'Chinese Parliament' in the Regiment, in which every man is free to speak his mind. Although it was something of a regimental tradition, Jim wasn't known to be the greatest fan of the Chinese Parliament system. 'Fuck all this democracy shit,' he was known to remark; 'I'm in command and what I say goes.' It had won him both friends and enemies. But right now, with a decision as monumental as this one, every man deserved to have his say.

We squatted in a circle where we couldn't be overheard, as Jim eyed us, his face set like stone. 'Right, guys, it's fucking decision time. You heard the gen: the other patrols are going in on foot. They're walking in. I say fuck that for a game of soldiers: we take the vehicles, complete pieces of shite though they might be. But it's up to all of us how we do it, and I'm putting it to the vote. So, what's it going to be?'

I liked the tone that Jim had set here: *I'm for going in with wagons, no matter what the others say.* It was the stance of a strong-headed commander who knew how to back himself. But there was no telling how the other blokes might take it. Either way, as 2iC – second-in-command – of the patrol I figured I should be the next to throw my hat in the ring.

'Vehicles – got to be,' I piped up. 'I mean, what happens if we get bumped? On foot, we're going nowhere. At least with the wagons we can turn tail and run.'

I pointed out that the most weight you ever carried on SAS Selection was 55 pounds in your Bergen, plus weapon. That was a lesson learned over countless years – what a man can effectively load on his back and remain operational. The other two patrols would be heading in with *several times* that amount. How on earth they expected to move – heaven forbid fight – when laden down like that beggared belief. They would be staggering about like drunkards. In short, the vehicles might well be utterly crap, but they were better than nothing.

I finished speaking, and Driller gave a smoker's growl of assent: 'We take the wagons. Got to be.'

That was the three former Para Reg guys in agreement – good to see the 'Concrete Reg', as we Paras were known, holding firm.

Chewie gave a nod. 'They're crap, but the mechanics seem sound enough. Lovingly looked after by a bunch of RAF slipper queens, no doubt.'

All eyes turned to Joe, our very own slipper queen. He grinned. 'You know me – I'm all for an easy life. We take the wagons. After all, they're RAF, so what's not to like?'

Next, our very own Hobbit Trevor Moriarty rattled off a slew of words in machine-gun-fire Geordie, liberally peppered with expletives, but I was damned if I could make sense of it.

'I take it that's a yes?' Jim queried. Clearly, I wasn't the only one having problems.

Trev confirmed that it was, after which Scouse – Jeff Fisher – made clear his thoughts in equally colourful language: not taking vehicles was borderline insane. That was seven of us in agreement, which left only the cloak-and-dagger grey man, Alex Switcher.

'Alex? Jim queried. 'You in?'

'That I am,' he confirmed, simply.

You had to really listen to hear Alex, for he spoke in that soft Hereford lilt and seemed to want to swallow his own words almost before he'd got them out. I coined a nickname for our grey man there and then: from now on, to me at least, he would be 'Quiet Alex'.

Anyhow, that was it: all eight of us – unanimous. Despite the cruddy state of the wagons, we were going in with wheels.

We now needed to work out our configurations – who would ride in which vehicle. One thing was for sure: Jim would bagsy the 110, which left me with the Dinky. With Jim having the bigger wagon, he would obviously get Chewie, which was a bit of a bummer, because I really rated our Big Friendly Giant. But as a consolation for not having the BFG, I managed to grab Driller as my driver, which was no small bonus. Not only were we Para Reg brotherhood, but Driller had bags of mobility experience. If anyone could nurse a Dinky through the Iraqi desert, I reckoned he could.

I volunteered to take Quiet Alex in my wagon, along with Geordie Trev, mainly because no one else seemed keen to have our grey man for company, or the guy who spoke in Hobbit language. I gave Quiet Alex the role of Minimi gunner, as I'm a fan of the old saying: *Big dogs don't bark*. I had an inkling that he was the kind of guy to wield the superlative Minimi Squad Automatic Weapon (SAW) – our light machine gun, and our single greatest piece of firepower. That left Jim and Chewie taking Scouse plus Joe on the 110, and I felt sure the RAF slipper queen would appreciate the extra space and comfort.

Next we needed to bodge up the Pinkie and Dinky for where we were heading. Using gaffer tape, we'd need to black out all possible sources of illumination. We'd nicknamed the stuff 'maskers', for that very reason – we used it for masking out all light. We'd use strips of hessian to enshroud all our heavier equipment, in an effort to prevent it clanking and banging as we got on the move. We'd use yet more gaffer tape to cover over anything that might give off a tell-tale glint in the sun – mirrors being a prime example.

But even when all that was done, I still didn't like the look of either wagon. The 90 I felt sure would let us down. Yet to me the alternative – legging it – was unthinkable.

Jim gave orders for us to gather together food rations, communications gear, navigation equipment, vehicle maintenance kit, jerrycans of water and fuel, camouflage nets, sand ladders, shovels, medical gear, NBC suits and masks, plus the all-important weaponry and ammo, to see how we could somehow cram it all onto our wondrous steeds. We were to budget for a two-week deployment, at the end of which we'd aim for a resupply by helo, if we were to remain in the field.

As we were slated to be out for fourteen days without resupply, we broke the ration packs down to what were the bare essentials. We set aside the main meals – corned beef hash, baked beans, chicken and ham pasta and the like – plus the all-important coffee, tea and sugar sachets, and the chocolate bars, while throwing the remainder on a heap to be discarded. Anything to free up a little room.

With the vehicles we had to hand, space was at an absolute premium and every item had to be stowed with infinite care. Riding in the Dinky, we'd have two guys up front – Driller driving, with me beside him – and Quiet Alex plus the Hobbit behind. Luckily, they were both relatively small guys, especially as the cramped rear compartment of the 90 was where we had to cram enough kit for two weeks on operations.

Normally, you reserve your Bergen for personal kit and weaponry, with your twenty-four-hour emergency kit slung on your webbing. But with space being so limited, the four LAW 66s that we were taking with us – portable anti-armour rockets – would have to be strapped across the tops of our Bergens, adding 8 pounds of weight to each. The LAW fires a HEAT – high-explosive anti-tank – warhead, capable of penetrating up to 400 mm of armour, which meant it could take out just about any battle tank that the Iraqis had in service, if hit in the right spot. With no vehicle-mounted heavy weaponry, those LAW 66s were our single most potent piece of firepower.

We also had to find room for our ammo, including L2 grenades – nicknamed the 'lemon' due to its distinctive profile. The L2 had a worrying habit of the pin working itself free, especially when jolted around in a vehicle. With only a 4.4 second fuse, that left precious little time to dive to cover. Consequently, we bastardized them, by crimping the pin tight to the grenade's body and using tape to doubly secure it. We also loaded up smoke grenades – for providing cover if we had to bug out under contact – plus the wild card of such weapons, the white phosphorus (WP) grenade.

An incendiary weapon, the WP grenade was known to be something of a double-edged sword. Packed with white phosphorus, which ignites violently on contact with air, it was perfect for setting alight an enemy vehicle or bunker, or for laying down a smokescreen. But it had to be used with care. If the grenade wasn't thrown far enough, or the wind was in the wrong direction, globs of burning white phosphorus might blow back onto your own side, with horrendous consequences. We certainly couldn't afford to have one of those detonating by accident in a shaken-about Dinky's rear.

As we dashed about grabbing kit and piling it on wherever there was room, I just kept reminding myself what it would be like to have to carry all this on our backs. With vehicles, surely we were better off than the other patrols? Surely to God we were?

Even so, I found myself experiencing these nagging doubts. Maybe Andy McNab and Patrick Johnson were right? Maybe the vehicles simply weren't up to the job? Maybe we'd got it all wrong? Maybe we too should be heading in on foot? Maybe, by sticking with the Pinkie and Dinky, we were riding into a whole world of trouble?

I was pulled away from such thoughts by the arrival of Geordie Straker. He handed around eights sets of maps. From their lightweight, silky feel I could tell that these were something special.

'Yeah, guys, you'll like these,' Geordie reassured us. 'They're for E & E, so guard them with your lives and keep them close.' E & E – escape and evasion: maps to guide us, in case we had to go on the run.

I opened mine and took a good long look at where we were headed. I figured the map would be fine for basic navigation in the vehicles while on the move. Rolled tightly, it collapsed to around the size of your average handkerchief, which made it perfect for slipping into the pull-cord lining of our desert combats. That way it would always be handy, and would remain on your person in case you had to leg it on foot.

Geordie told us we were also getting issued with ten gold sovereigns apiece, plus a sheet of paper printed in Arabic. The note explained that the sovereigns were a reward for any Iraqi who might shelter any SAS personnel and guide them to safety. If he or she did so, the British Embassy promised to pay the Good Samaritan £50,000, on top of the sovereigns.

After taking possession of the sovereigns, there was the small matter of what to do with them. The safest thing turned out to be to fasten each one onto a strip of tape, and then to sew that into the waistband of your combats. That way, the gold was nicely concealed and would be with you as long as you didn't lose your trousers, in which case you'd very likely be in a whole world of trouble anyway.

Next on the to-do list was signing wills. It didn't matter if you'd already written one – with what lay ahead of us, the Regiment wanted to be sure that every man's last will and testament was bang up to date. Mine was simplicity itself. I left the new house and my Ford XR3i to Emily. I had little else worthy of note and no one else to bequeath it to. My father had died when I was nine years old, my mother a few years after that.

As I filled in that last-minute paperwork, all of a sudden it started to hit home. I thought of Emily, trying to get settled into our new home, but with reports of the Gulf War playing 24/7 on the news. How was she bearing up? There was no way of knowing. Just as soon as we'd left Hereford we were in isolation – no further communication with the outside world. Of course, there were good reasons for that: if one careless word somehow leaked to the enemy, it could have disastrous consequences.

But I wondered how us lot would really fare in Iraq. We were going in as one lightly armed patrol of eight men, as opposed to a kick-arse squadron-strength force. Inserting far in-country, we faced the most likely chance of getting compromised and captured or killed. It was a sombre moment. Suddenly, it all felt very, very real.

We'd picked up the vibes at Camp Victor: we knew there was disquiet amongst the head shed regarding the other patrols' intentions to go in on foot. Both the B Squadron OC, Major Carpenter, and Peter Radcliffe, the blunt-spoken regimental sergeant major (RSM), had had words with the patrol commanders. They'd done so in an effort to convince them that it was asking for a whole heap of trouble, at least in the head shed's view.

None of us in our patrol particularly disagreed. But in terms of suicide missions, driving into the heart of enemy territory in a painfully overloaded Pinkie and a Dinky sure came a close second. A lot of the blokes were throwing around that phrase pretty liberally by now – 'suicide mission'. They might have been doing so tongue in cheek, but never a truer word was said in jest.

I couldn't understand why the OC hadn't ordered the other patrols to take vehicles. True, we did have a system of leadership that was based upon merit above rank. Often you'd have a sergeant or a staff sergeant commanding a patrol, with an officer under him. But in this case, Major Carpenter and Peter Radcliffe would have had rank *and* merit on their side, and neither McNab nor Johnson could have refused.

Knowing the guys on McNab's patrol well, I felt sure they must have thought through their decision. Apart from Bob Consiglio, the other guy I counted as a good mate was Chris Ryan, a real thinking man's soldier. He'd just completed the eighteen-month mountain leader's course, which takes real guts to get through, and in the process he'd become more or less fluent in German. Some achievement. I went to find Chris, because I was burning up with curiosity about why they'd made the call they had.

'I hear you guys are going in on foot,' I ventured, once we'd got the small talk out of the way. 'You happy with that?'

We'd got a brew on, so there was a good bit of tea-stirring before Chris replied. 'How are you lot going in?' Typically, he'd answered my question with one of his own.

'We voted for vehicles,' I replied. 'As far as we're concerned, if we get bumped and we're on foot we're in the shit. At least with vehicles we can turn tail and run.' That was typical Steel City – no beating about the bush and straight to the point.

'Yeah, but it's a trade-off, isn't it, Des?' Chris remarked, pensively. 'It's bloody hard to camouflage vehicles and to hide them. On foot you can go into an OP and be utterly hidden; covert.'

'Maybe, but you're waltzing about in the enemy's backyard, and someone's bound to notice you sooner or later.'

Chris shrugged. 'Maybe, maybe not. Anyhow, that's what we voted for.'

I asked him what kind of weight they were going to be carrying. Momentarily, his face darkened. They had around 140 pounds in their Bergens, 30–40 pounds of belt kit, personal weapon weighing in at around 12 pounds, plus extra water, food, OP kit and more. When all was said and done, he reckoned they had some 250 pounds of weight per man.

'Err, Chris, that is one hell of a lot of weight to try to move anywhere.' It was stating the obvious, but sometimes that's exactly what needs saying.

'It is,' he confirmed, 'but we figure it can be done.' They had good reasons for reaching the decision they had, he explained, and it hadn't been made lightly. 'We put in an OP, Des, in the desert around here. We put sand into sandbags, built ourselves a hide and got all the ammo, water, rations and everything stashed inside. It's doable. Fourteen days' worth, no problem.'

He paused, taking a sip of his brew. None of the guys on his patrol intended lugging 250 pounds of kit anywhere in one go, he explained. As this was an OP mission, they'd lie low wherever they could find a vantage point offering views across the MSR – the Scud-transport arteries. They'd ferry their excess kit from the drop zone (DZ) – the Chinook drop-off point – to the OP nice and easy, in a number of relays.

'When our time's up, Des, we'll call in a resupply helo, or if we're being extracted we'll get lifted out of there. Done and dusted. Like I said, it's all doable.'

'Yeah, but it's still one hell of a lot of kit, Chris, even with vehicles, never mind walking in,' I repeated. Typical me – like a dog with a bone.

'It is. But once we're in position, we're covert and unseen. Static. Like I said, it's all doable.'

'It's a tall order, but I guess it can be done,' I conceded. But I still couldn't hide the doubt and the scepticism in my tone.

Chris eyed me for a long second, as if weighing his next words carefully. 'Des, have you seen the state of the vehicles?' He paused. 'This mission doesn't call for movement, Des – it's all about concealment. That's the whole reason we're going in on foot – to keep a low profile. You won't manage that for very long, not with those sorry excuses for wagons.'

'Maybe, but what happens if you do get bumped, Chris? Two hundred klicks inside enemy territory – you're going nowhere fast. You're deep in the shit.'

Chris figured the reverse was true. If they took the vehicles, they'd be far more visible and vulnerable. It was now that he delivered the real sucker punch. Having first stripped them of all unnecessary weight, they'd tried using the Dinkies in the desert around Camp Victor. Pretty quickly they'd reached the conclusion that the wagons simply were not fit for purpose. You could fit sixteen jerrycans of spare fuel onto a specially adapted SAS Pinkie, plus four blokes and enough kit for two weeks of operations. By contrast, the Dinkies were a liability as far as they were concerned.

Part of me agreed with Chris. Part of me felt deeply unsettled by what he had revealed: they'd tested the wagons and found them *not fit for purpose*. Erudite and thoughtful, Chris had shed real doubt on our patrol's decision, as far as I was concerned. I left him feeling shaken, and thinking: *Jesus, going in on foot – that's some ballsy move. But maybe it's the right one too.*

I returned to my patrol and we talked over what Chris had said. Any which way we looked at it, taking the wagons still seemed the common-sense option. Inserting deep behind enemy lines, the wagons were our exit strategy. If we were seen, we'd be hunted, and on foot you'd have no rapid means to extract – to make a break for friendly lines. If we opted to dig in a static OP, like Chris had suggested, we'd split the patrol in two. We'd have the wagons set back a good distance, sheeted over in camouflage netting. We'd rotate teams between the two positions, to relieve the tension of keeping watch 24/7.

No matter how we looked at it, or tried to argue the other side's viewpoint, we were sticking with our wagons.

Inevitably, 'mission creep' began to set in now. On the verge of departure we were given a secondary tasking, over and above Scud-hunting. We were to seek out and disable Saddam's fibre-optic cables, via which command messages were sent to and from the Scud launchers. Those cables were strung along the MSRs in deeply buried tunnels, the vulnerable points being the inspection shafts placed at regular intervals.

McNab and Johnson's patrols had to add cutting equipment to their already stupendous loads, to take out those cables. But that wasn't all. According to the Green Slime, the Iraqis were keeping a close watch on the fibre-optic network, checking for any breaks via a system of electronic monitors. All three patrols – ours included – were ordered to load up a case of C3A1 'Elsie' anti-personnel mines, for placing around any areas we might have sabotaged. That would deter the Iraqis from making any rapid repairs.

Somehow, we found space on the wagons for a case of the mines. But we decided to adopt a more prosaic approach to the cable destruction itself. We lashed a heavy chain to the Pinkie, the only wagon with any space left to accommodate it. We'd hook that around the guts of the fibre-optic cable, and using the grunt of the wagon we'd rip the thing to pieces. It was rough and ready, but sometimes the simplest approaches are the best.

With kit and transport sorted as best we could, there was one last matter to attend to, as far as I was concerned. With all the talk of 'suicide missions', I figured it was high time to give the guys on my patrol their medical briefing. This was going to be down and dirty, but where we were headed I figured it was entirely necessary.

I gathered the guys. 'Right then – show me your morphine syrettes.' I checked that all the blokes had two of the pain-killing devices – much like a mini toothpaste tube with a hooded needle attached to one end – slung around their necks. That way, if anyone did get injured, whoever was treating him would know where to grab some morphine, so they could punch it into the wounded man's veins.

'Right, next I'm going to show you how to cannulate someone and how to set up giving sets, which you'll need to do if they're losing a lot of blood.' I gave a quick demo of how to insert the cannula into a vein in the forearm, so that a drip could be attached. 'Now, pair off and practise on each other. That's the only way you'll get any good at it.'

Chewie was the medic on Jim's wagon, but he wasn't as experienced as I was. Likewise, I knew sod all about vehicle maintenance. It was the sign of a patrol that was functioning well when we each recognized the others' key disciplines, and let that guy take the lead, as Chewie did now with me. Once they'd cannulated each other a few times, I moved the guys on.

'Remember your four Bs: Breathing. Bleeding. Breaks. Burns. Or some people prefer Bones to Breaks. Either way, that's your hierarchy of priorities. As bleeding looks dramatic, it's only natural to try to stop that first. No point, if the guy's already swallowed his tongue. Remember, you can survive having lost over half your blood, but you can suffocate in the time it takes to get a cannula in, so always check the airway first. If it's clear, you can stop the bleeding. If it's needed, get a drip going. Then check for broken bones and burns. Got it?'

'Got it,' the lads confirmed.

'Oh, and remember: if you do give a guy a jab of morphine, do not leave him unattended. If you do, someone else comes along, sees him in rag order and gives him another shot. Bish-bash, he overdoses and the cure becomes the killer. If you *do* have to leave him, write a big bold "M" on his forehead.'

'With what?' Driller demanded. Of all of us, he was the most squeamish when it came to the sight of blood, with our slipper queen, Joe, coming a close second.

'There are marker pens in the med-kits, which Chewie and I have packed onto the wagons. But if you can't get to one of them, use anything that comes to hand. You can even write it in the guy's blood. An "M"'s still an "M", regardless.'

'Bit of a morbid bugger, isn't he?' Joe quipped.

I smiled. 'You could say that. But where we're headed, this could just save your life or one of us lot's lives, so no apologies.'

'Yeah, we all know the sketch,' Driller interjected. 'You're a dour northern git and you'll say what you like and like what you bloody well say.'

Trev added something in machine-gun-fire Hobbit language. It sounded a bit like: *Yeah, he needs an expletive-riddled needle rammed up his ass.* But I couldn't quite be sure. Still, you had to laugh. Practising medical drills was always an excuse for a good bit of slagging, so what else did I expect. But beneath the bravado, it was a sobering moment for us all.

I didn't know if the patrol medics on the other teams had done such a hands-on run-through, and I didn't particularly care. Unsettling it might be, but there was little point shying away from the hard truth. We were small teams inserting deep behind enemy lines in sub-standard wagons, or on foot, and wherever we ended up we would be outnumbered and outgunned. Disco Squadron were going to take casualties, and I didn't doubt our medical knowhow would be much in need. So, morbid though it might be, we needed to go in with eyes wide open and ready for the worst.

It may sound like a cliché, but death is a way of life in the Regiment – or at least, it had been ever since I had joined. In fact, we'd lost the first guy before I'd even completed Selection. I wasn't even done with the Hills Phase before two guys peeled off a high-altitude climb, and one lost his life as a result of the injuries suffered in the fall.

Then, on my second attempt at Selection, we were in the

cookhouse at H just a few days before deploying to the jungle, when all of a sudden a brooding and dark atmosphere settled across the entire camp. I knew something bad had happened, I just didn't know what. It was as we filed out that one of the blokes pulled me to one side.

'You heard what happened in the Killing House? One of the guys on the CT team's been shot. Going through the CT drills, he caught a stray round.'

'Shit. How is he?' I asked.

'How is he? Not good, as it happens. He's fucking dead.'

In an instant my mind flashed back to the first time I had ever seen one of the mysterious winged-dagger warriors. It was at the Para Reg camp in Aldershot when I'd first noticed this guy. What drew my attention was his longer hair, his relaxed kind of dress and the sheer presence and confidence he seemed to carry with him.

'Who's that?' I'd asked one of my Para mates.

'That guy? Yeah, they're the ones who deal in the Death Business.' I'd asked my mate what he meant. 'Those guys deal in stuff you don't need to know about,' he answered. 'Like I said – they're experts in the Death Business, and a damn sight more than we'll ever be.'

I was seven weeks into my second attempt at Selection when I heard about the guy getting shot in the Killing House. I learned he was well respected and that he had been serving for many years. It was then that the penny dropped. *Fuck, this SAS stuff really is a dangerous kind of business.* I'd barely made it into the Regiment and was doing my initial parachute training when a bloke piled in on a night jump and ended up very, very dead.

That was three guys who'd lost their lives and I'd only just got in.

Shortly, another guy would die in a vehicle accident, in Northern Ireland. So, like I said, no matter who you were or where you were or what exactly you were doing, death tended to come with the territory. The Grim Reaper was always there, looking over your shoulder, scythe poised at the ready. And in truth, once we did hit the Iraqi desert I would get to use my medical kit big time – but not at all in the way I had expected.

Yet all of that lay a while in the future.

Shortly before mounting up the C-130 Hercules to fly out to Saudi Arabia, Jim was called to a meeting with the head shed. He returned with the news that the OC, Major Carpenter, had handed out the callsigns for the three patrols.

'Right, we're keeping it simple stupid – so Bravo One, Bravo Two and Bravo Three Zero.' That made good sense: we were B Squadron, hence the 'B' – Bravo – callsign. 'Johnson's lot are Bravo One, McNab's lot are Bravo Two, and we're Bravo Three Zero.'

No one took particular note of the callsigns at the time. It was only later that one in particular would come to have the high profile – the notoriety – that it does today.

We headed for our final orders briefing, plus a cross-brief with the Chinook pilots, to get the lowdown on how they intended to insert us into Iraq. The one bit of good news in the orders brief was that after our two weeks' Scud-hunting, we would have the option to link up with either A or D Squadron, to carry on the war. They would be driving in from the Saudi border, so it was good to know we had them racing up from behind. If nothing else it meant we'd have less distance to cover if we did have to turn tail and run.

But as the senior Chinook pilot got up to speak, outlining exactly what the aircrews intended, I detected a certain shiftiness – almost an us-and-them attitude – about some of the things that he was saying. Or rather, the things he seemed unwilling to say. Apparently, for some reason he was not able to share the aircrew's escape and evasion plans with us.

'If we do get into an E & E situation,' he announced, 'we've got an E & E procedure which is something we've practised and rehearsed separately, and it's our own personal package.'

Should we get shot down or crash land, at that point RAF aircrew and SF types would be going their separate ways, he explained. I happened to be standing next to Andy McNab for the briefing, and we exchanged these perplexed glances.

'So what's the score with that?' I whispered. 'They don't want nothing to do with us, is that it?'

'Leave it. We'll chat about it later.'

After the briefing was done, I asked McNab again: what was the sketch with the Chinook crews not wanting to have anything to do with us, if we were forced to go on the run?

'Simple. They don't want to be associated with SF troops,' he explained. 'If we get caught behind enemy lines and the Iraqis realize we're SF, we'll get topped. That's what everyone's saying. But if they separate themselves from us, they'll be classed as cabbies – aircrew – so they'll get treated as POWs. At least, that's what they're hoping.'

'But if they stay with us, they'd have more numbers and fire-power. Doesn't that make better sense?'

'Look, Des, they're RAF, we're SAS. If they can argue they're only ferry crew, they figure they can get away with their lives. Us lot – we'll face execution.'

'Fair enough. Still doesn't feel very nice though, does it?'

'No. But you can hardly blame 'em, either.'

For sure, we'd been briefed on how the Iraqi military had treated captured Iranian troops, during the long years of that war. Suffice to say they'd given no quarter. Likewise, it stood to reason we'd face a dark fate if captured. Realizing this, the Chinook crews were distancing themselves from us lot. While it might make me feel uncomfortable, McNab was right: no point any more lives getting wasted than was necessary.

'Look, Des, if we do have to E & E, the only way to go is west towards Syria,' McNab added, 'so make sure you've got your Levis stuffed in the bottom of your Bergen. Dump your military kit at the border, slip on your Levis and make like a civvie.'

I couldn't tell if McNab was joking or not. With us lot driving vehicles, we'd figured the shortest distance to run was south, back towards the Saudi border. That had the added advantage that A and D Squadrons would be racing north, holding out a promised offer of linking up with them. I suggested as much to McNab.

He shook his head. 'Des, I'm telling you – if we get bumped, if the shit hits the fan, only one way to go. That's west, on foot, towards Syria.'

I decided to let it go. McNab was a senior rank to me, he'd been in far longer and was far more experienced. Syria was sympathetic to the Coalition and it was one of the closest countries to where we would be operating.

Briefing done, we mounted up a C-130 Hercules and flew out to Saudi Arabia, heading for our forward-mounting base, at a place called Al-Jouf. Despite the lack of planning, preparation and even the most basic of kit, we were raring to go. That is a defining feature of the Regiment – the utter positivity and can-do attitude.

I carry a notebook with me whenever I deploy. In it I've written the odd phrase or saying. Fragments of poetry. Memories. For me at least, they sum up the collective ethos of the unit with which I was going to war. I found those lines running through my head now. One was from 'Invictus', the classic warrior poem, the first and last stanzas of which seemed to epitomize the spirit of the men riding on that C-130:

'Out of the darkness that covers me,
Black as the pit from pole to pole,
I thank whatever gods may be,
For my unconquerable soul . . .
It matters not how strait the gate,
How charged with punishment the scroll,
I am the master of my fate,
I am the captain of my soul.'

Another was a George Orwell quote that runs something like this: *People sleep peaceably in their beds at night only because rough men stand ready to do violence on their behalf.* That struck me as being so very true of the moment, not to mention my upbringing; what had made me who I was today. At many times in my life I'd come across bullies: at school, on the streets of the

Steel City, on the football terraces. I'd learned you had to stand up to them.

The first bullies I'd come across were twins, like characters out of a Tarantino film: bleached-blond skinhead haircuts, pale skin and piercing blue eyes. Just looking at them used to put the fear of God into me. But I can thank the twins for toughening me up. Going to my junior school was like entering a war zone. Eventually, we had a set-to. I gave a good account of myself and we became pals after that. They went on to be alright kids – not bullies at all.

When I left school at fifteen there were two jobs you could take: working in the steel industry or coal mining. Both were hard, hard professions. The blokes who worked in them were tough, and in any case the Steel City has always been a fighting city – it's produced dozens of world-class boxers. There was never a shortage of guys who wanted to forge a reputation for themselves. A lot of that involved picking on weaker types.

I guess a lot of my life had been about reputation; proving myself. Taking a job in the steel industry, then going for the Paras and ultimately the SAS – each was a bigger, tougher challenge. But what I liked about the Regiment was their attitude: if you think you're good enough, tough enough and ugly enough, come and give it a whirl. But you don't need to sing and shout about it. No bravado needed here.

Fittingly, in the Regiment we used to say: *You travel the world, you fight terrorism and tyranny, and guess what – you get rid of the bullies.* I'd noted down these words, too, in my notebook. They summarize David Stirling's founding principles when creating the SAS: humility, a classless society, humour, discipline and the relentless pursuit of excellence. It was in that spirit that we were speeding north, heading into the unknown; into a war from which some at least might not return.

Then I thought of something one of the Old and Bold had once said to me, about those who serve in the Regiment: 'We're doing one of two things, Des: we're either chasing angels or running from demons.'

I wondered which we would end up doing most of in the deserts of Iraq.

CHAPTER SEVEN

BEG, BORROW AND STEAL

No one could wait to get that C-130 flight done and dusted and to get whisked onwards, across the Iraqi border. In a sense, we were in a race against A and D Squadrons, and quite unexpectedly we'd got the upper hand. By the time we reached Al-Jouf, 1,900 km northwest of Camp Victor, the squadrons were long gone, heading overland towards the border with Iraq. But they had a 200 km drive ahead of them, just to reach their start point. They'd then have to fight their way across 300 km of enemy terrain to get to the Scud-launching grounds.

Even before that, there was one other major barrier that stood in their way. All along the border Saddam had constructed this massive berm – an artificial ridge made from bulldozed sand. Its purpose was simple: it was there to prevent the passage of armoured and tracked vehicles. It was Iraq's border rampart, and of course it posed a serious impediment to the passage of wheeled vehicles – SAS Pinkies and the heavier Unimog supply trucks included. No one knew quite how they would surmount the berm: they would have to get eyes-on and hope to come up with a plan. Meanwhile, we were about to leapfrog their columns, heading into the heart of the fire.

By the time we reached Al-Jouf, I figured my diarrhoea and vomiting was a thing of the past. Barely forty-eight hours earlier I'd been on the verge of going to have words with Geordie Straker, B Squadron's SSM, to tell him I couldn't deploy. Plagued by D & V, I wouldn't have been able to physically do the job, and I would have endangered the rest of my patrol. But somehow I'd managed to medicate my way out of it.

That was the good news. But at Al-Jouf, we were to be made painfully aware of our shortcomings. It was a brand-new civilian airport, which had yet to be brought into service. Instead, various Coalition forces had made it their forward HQ. While the head shed set about commandeering a corner in the terminal for B Squadron business, using a luggage conveyor belt as DIY desks, we set up camp as best we could on the far side of the runway.

But frankly, with our green Army maggots – standard sleeping bags – laid out on the sand, we looked like some sad-ass desert hobos, especially compared to the US Navy SEALs, who were also in residence. As the American military tends to, the SEALs had deployed with *everything*. We had no tents or shelters of any sort. We had to eat where we squatted and to crap in an open pit dug in the dirt – and with zero privacy, for this was one busy kind of an airport. Our campsite lay on one side of the oval perimeter road, while on the central runway were lined up rank after rank of US warplanes. With the air war in full swing, those guys didn't seem to rest.

Flights of squat, ugly A10s Thunderbolts – more commonly known as the 'Warthog' – kept heaving themselves noisily into the skies. Ungainly, heavily armoured and relatively slow-flying, with a cruise speed of 340 mph, the Warthog would prove itself a fearsome ground-attack aircraft in Iraq. Poking out of its stubby nose was a seven-barrel 30 mm 'Gatling gun', plus it could carry Maverick air-to-surface missiles and laser-guided bombs. But it was the F-16 pilots who really put on the show at Al-Jouf. As soon as they lifted off, they'd point their spear-like noses at the sky, perform a barrel roll and thunder into the heavens. If anything, the aerobatics executed by the returning top guns were even more impressive: they executed these loop-the-loops, plus screaming circuits of the oval perimeter road, showing off how this was their time.

At dusk we found ourselves huddled around a campfire trying to keep warm, as flight after flight of warplanes thundered into the skies, executing night missions. We'd set up camp gathered loosely in our patrols. All of a sudden, some kind of alarm started to blare out from the far side of the runway, emitting an ear-splitting wail. We glanced at each other: *What the hell is that?* In the distance we could just make out figures dashing about, and seemingly trying to find some shelter.

'I think that may be a Scud warning,' someone ventured, trying to make their voice heard above the deafening noise. 'I think we're supposed to take cover.'

'Too fucking late now,' a voice retorted.

No one had mentioned a thing to us about being on the lookout for Scuds, as a result of which we sat through that first, very noisy warning sipping our brews and wondering what was up. A little later word came over from the terminal confirming that it had been a Scud alert, and that from now on we were supposed to grab our NBC kit and take cover in one of the concrete shelters ranged around the runway whenever we heard the alarm.

It was at times like these – facing a shedload of crap, chaos and uncertainty – that I'd often wondered how I'd even found my way into the military. For sure, it was a long way from the tough streets of inner-city Sheffield to Al-Jouf. Most likely, the answer lay in my family – especially my grandad, who'd won the Military Medal in World War Two.

My grandad had lived just a few doors down from us. Every evening mum would grab my hand and say: 'Right, we're popping down the street to say goodnight to grandad.' He had been gassed in the war and his lungs were bad, so he was forever spitting on the fire. From an early age, I did the same. We'd go into his house, and he'd ruffle my hair. 'How have you been today, little 'un?' he'd ask. There was so much potential for getting into trouble where I lived, but my grandad, my dad and my mum kept 'little Dereck', as they knew me, firmly on the straight and narrow.

I didn't realize then, but that was the military discipline side of my upbringing shining through: respect, family unity, close-knit camaraderie. Too young to fight in World War Two, my dad had done his national service, before taking up work with a local Co-op as a delivery driver. Some years later he was chatting with some mates when a driver lost control of a truck and crushed him against a wall. There was a knock at the door giving us the bad news. Right then I was nine. I had a big sister, Lorraine, who was thirteen, and a baby brother, Mark, who was just two years old.

Mum rushed to the hospital, only to find dad laid up and not looking well.

'You've got to keep a close eye on the family,' he told her. 'Especially the big one, as you may get a few problems with her. Plus little Dereck and Mark.'

'Don't you worry about the kids,' she reassured him. 'I've got it covered. Just you get well.'

'I don't feel right,' dad continued. 'I don't feel right in me body. I can't seem to feel me legs.'

'Don't you worry. After the operation you'll be as good as new.'

Mum was thirty-two years old and she was in denial. Dad was trying to shield her from the truth, while simultaneously preparing her for the worst. He doubted if he would make it, and even if he did pull through, he would very likely be in a wheelchair. I've often thought back over what he did then, when I've been in dire situations myself.

Mum and dad had just agreed to purchase a new house in Brinsworth, a village midway between Rotherham and Sheffield. That signified getting out of the inner city and making good. We'd got there due to dad's hard work and graft. He told mum that she had to go ahead and purchase the house, no matter what. It was a new-build, and we used to drive there every weekend to see how the construction was getting on.

Mum had left the hospital ward, knowing that dad would be operated on later that day. She'd glanced back and dad had his eyes upon her, watching her walk out of the door. I'd often wondered how he found the courage to dig deep and to put a brave face on it; to give mum the strength and the guidance to carry on when he was gone. She went to see the surgeon later, to hear what she was convinced would be the good news.

Yours truly, Des Powell, in 1980, while serving with the Parachute Regiment in Hong Kong, where we'd have a go at starting WWIII, picking a fight with the Chinese People's Liberation Army (PLA) … but for all the right reasons. I was a fitness and martial arts fanatic, needless to say.

Author Des Powell, left of photo, with Andy McNab, after a parachute jump into the Tasman Sea off New Zealand. This is two years prior to the 1991 Gulf War, in which Andy would command patrol Bravo Two Zero and I'd serve as second-in-command on Bravo Three Zero.

Yours truly, Des Powell, left of photo, 1984, lugging a hulking great GMPG on the Parachute Regiment's Exercise in the Brecon Beacons. Three years later I'd pass selection to make it into the SAS, where I became the unarmed combat and fitness instructor for B Squadron.

Pictured during the nightmarish escape and evasion phase of SAS selection, yours truly, Des Powell, second from left. Injured by a viciously-spiked tree on the jungle phase, I would have to attempt selection twice, before finally making it into the Regiment.

Air Troop, B Squadron with yours truly, Des Powell, sixth from left, back row. Behind is the famous SAS clock tower, upon which are inscribed the immortal words: 'We are the pilgrims, master, we shall go, always a little further it may be ...'

Training with Norway's special forces yours truly, Des Powell, centre, *above*, and right of photo, *below*. We learned how to survive with sub-zero temperatures and extremely hostile conditions, with the right kit and equipment and knowhow. But few of us ever expected Iraq in 1991 to suffer heavy snowfall and freezing, life-sapping conditions, especially as we'd been briefed that it would be 'like Britain in springtime.' Consequently, the three *Bravo* patrols headed into the Iraqi desert woefully ill-prepared for the freezing hell they would encounter.

Yours truly, Des Powell, during counter-terrorism (CT) training, wearing all the specialist 'black kit'. On CT operations, the pistol often proved the better weapon for close-quarter combat. When B Squadron were scrambled for Iraq operations in late 1991, we'd spent months on CT duties, and we were neither prepared or acclimatised for the deserts of Iraq.

A mixed group of B Squadron's Air and Mountain Troops, in black CT gear, showing some of the guys from the Bravo patrols: left to right, back row: No. 3, author Des Powell; No. 7, Andy McNab; No. 10, Chris Ryan; No. 15, Bob Consiglio. Front row: No. 9, Joe Ambler; No. 10, Trev Moriarty.

B Squadron deployed from the UK to the United Arab Emirates (UAE), for high-intensity desert training, which included deploying in cumbersome NBC (nuclear, biological and chemical) protective gear, known as 'noddy suits'. The hulking figure on the left of the photo is none other than Will 'Chewie' McBride, Bravo Three Zero's signaller, with yours truly, Des Powell, second from right.

Above – hanging from a Westland Lynx, SAS blades prepare to leap into the void. Yours truly, Des Powell, is sat in the doorway, in the white suit, poised to go. *Below*, I'm with a Puma helicopter crew, about to test a .50 Calibre HMG. These special forces aircrew and pilots are the very best in the business, as our low-level-hell insertion by Chinook into the Iraqi desert would prove.

Ready to raise merry hell – yours truly, Des Powell, centre of photo in hat. Nothing remotely like the Gulf War deployment had been tried by the SAS since WWII, and the days of SAS founders Colonels David Stirling and Blair 'Paddy' Mayne. Deploying in fleets of specially-adapted, heavily-armed Land Rovers – 'Pinkies' to those in the know – with quads and motorbikes in support, we could take on just about anything, including Iraqi armour and warplanes. Fast, mobile, agile, we would pack a real punch, especially as three entire SAS squadrons – A, B and D – would be heading into the Iraqi desert. Or at least, that was the theory. In truth, we would be plagued by kit and equipment shortages and, most painfully, in the provision of proper vehicles.

'I've tried everything I possibly can, but it just wasn't possible,' the surgeon said, trying to break it to her gently.

'I know things are bad, but we can wait,' she replied. 'We can take him home when he's better, there's no rush.'

'No, you don't understand. He's passed away.'

Grandad had died shortly before my dad, so I had lost the two main influences in my life one after the other. But they'd done their job. In those first nine years of my life they'd made sure I was forged in fire. As I went into my teenage years with only mum to keep the family together, I kept resolutely to the right path, barring one incident. I was in my mid-teens when I smashed some street lamps and was charged by the police. My mum was so disgusted she reassured them she would deal with it, and of course she demanded of me what my dad would have thought.

That was it. I never strayed from the path again.

That night, curled up in our doss bags trying to keep warm at Al-Jouf, there was a series of further Scud alerts. At first we tried doing what we'd been told: grabbing our NBC kit – respirators, gloves, heavy suits and over-boots – simultaneously hopping about trying to pull it all on while dashing for the bunkers. Needless to say, it wasn't a pretty sight.

No one doubted that Saddam was targeting Coalition forces – particularly the airbases. Likewise, we all figured that sooner or later he'd be lobbing over some kind of chemical warheads. But after the first alert we reasoned that if there had been no Scud impact on the airbase – no *kaboom* – then we'd not been targeted, so best not make a big song and dance.

'D'you know something, the sooner we get out on the ground the better, as at least then we're in control of our own fate,' Jim remarked.

I nodded. 'Too right. For sure this airfield's going to keep getting zapped. We're vulnerable here. It's an obvious target.'

'Tell you another thing,' Jim added. 'If we're supposed to be the Scud-hunters, we're better off out there stopping this kind of shit.'

'Yep. Better that than running around here in our noddy suits like headless bloody chickens.'

'Noddy suits' was slang for NBC kit. But in fact, where we were heading we were going to be needing our NBC kit as a matter of life and death – only not in the way its designers had ever intended, not in their wildest dreams.

After several more alerts had come to nothing, the next time someone shook me awake, I just mumbled: 'Guys, leave me where I am to sleep, okay.'

After a night plagued by such noisy interruptions, sun-up proved equally lively. Never a dull moment at Al-Jouf. The SEALs fired up their fleet of gleaming dune buggies and took them out for a spin across the desert. To say they were absolutely awesome bits of kit was the understatement of the century: like everything US special operations tended to possess in terms of kit, they were top-notch. Each had a gleaming M60 7.62 mm machine gun mounted on the roll bar, and several had Stinger anti-aircraft missiles strapped to their sides.

Compare those to our Dinky, I told myself, ruefully. *What a fucking joke.*

The nearest equivalent we had in the SAS was something called the Ricardo Cobra Light Strike Vehicle, or LSV for short.

Rushed into service in the run-up to the present conflict, they'd been tested by the G Squadron boys in the UAE desert, but had been found seriously wanting. The LSV was designed to carry two blokes, seated side by side, but it simply wasn't robust enough for this kind of terrain, nor substantial enough to carry sufficient kit for extended operations.

No one was planning on taking an LSV anywhere near the war in Iraq. But we did have one at Al-Jouf, just as a run-around. As the SEALs were busy showing off their peachy dune buggies, I figured we'd do the same with our sorry excuse for one. It might help further the mission I had in mind – which, being a typical blagging northerner, was all about going on the scrounge.

I called for a volunteer. Being a fellow beg, borrow and steal up-north type, Trev the Hobbit stepped forward. We mounted up the LSV and set off along the perimeter road, making for the SEAL camp. So low-slung is the LSV you feel you're sitting in it almost lying down. Unfortunately, on the way there we managed to clip one of the 50 gallon steel drums that served to demarcate the road, and as the LSV rebounded, one of the wheels came free, catapulted right over the top of us and carried on going.

I did have something of a reputation in the Regiment when it came to road traffic accidents, but I wasn't actually driving the LSV – Trev was. Either way, its sorry fate pretty much typified the quality of our kit at the time. We stopped. Trev ran after the missing wheel and, being the Duracell Bunny made flesh, he caught up with it, after which he managed to dump it on the rear luggage rack contraption of the LSV (yeah, trust me, it did have one).

The LSV was renowned for having dodgy suspension, but we hadn't realized it was *that* dodgy: the wheel had simply sheered off. But as the thing was just about drivable on three wheels, with the odd axle-graunch thrown in from time to time, we decided to continue on our way. So, scraping and grounding a good deal, that was how three-wheeled flat-cap Des and his pal the Hobbit arrived at the American SF end of camp.

I could see the SEAL guys eyeing us, thinking: *Who the fuck are you guys, and what the fuck is that?*

Why had we come? Well, we were on the cusp of deploying and one of the hardest things to remain upbeat about was our sheer lack of firepower. It wasn't simply about not having any vehicle-mounted weaponry. It came down to the very basics. Somehow, all of our 9 mm Browning Hi-Power pistols had got 'lost in transit'. This was akin to British Airways losing your luggage, only this was life-or-death kind of stuff. No pistols meant no secondary weapon, if you had a problem with, or ran out of ammo for, your assault rifle.

It's not a game-changer being deprived of a sidearm, but it sure is an embuggerance. If you had a stoppage on your M16 – your 'long' – you'd let it drop on its sling and draw your 'short' – your pistol. That way, you could stay in the firefight and deal with the blockage on your main weapon whenever there was a lull in battle. It was a similar drill if your long ran short of rounds. Plus the pistol was arguably better for close-quarter battle – like fighting in urban and built-up areas – as it was shorter, lighter and more handy.

Far worse than the missing pistols was that each squadron's claymores had also been lost in transit. No one had a clue where they were. This was something close to a disaster. It's standard operating procedure if you're being pursued to stick down a claymore and detonate it, sending out a scything wall of steel ball-bearings into the face of the enemy. That would seriously slow them down, as they dealt with their injured and checked for any more such devices. They're also great for securing hidden positions, like OPs. As we all appreciated, not having any claymores left us at a serious disadvantage.

When we'd raised this back at Camp Victor, one wise owl in the head shed had suggested we go visit the cookhouse, grab some empty ice-cream containers, fill them with plastic explosives, detonators and a good dose of 'shipyard confetti' – gravel, scrap iron, nuts and bolts and the like – and hey presto, a DIY claymore was served up. Only, no one was buying it. Where we were heading, no one fancied having a make-and-mend 'ice-cream claymore' go off prematurely in a wagon, and kill or maim all aboard.

But worst of all was that we had no 'golden eggs', slang for the 40 mm rounds that our M203 grenade launchers use, the ones that were mounted beneath our M16 assault rifles – the combination being known as the M16/M203. The grenade launcher is a superb weapon, one of my all-time favourites. On the battlefield it is a real game changer, capable of destroying soft-skinned vehicles at around 500 feet. As an area-suppression weapon against ground troops it's effective at around twice that range. We had the launchers, just no ammo.

But being a straight-talking northerner, I aimed to find a way around all that. Trev and I had hardly made the most auspicious of arrivals, but the SEALs had already clocked the sad state of the British contingent at Al-Jouf, so they weren't entirely surprised. A big, rangy guy wandered over to where we'd pulled up in the LSV.

He eyed the missing wheel. 'Hey, guys, what the fuck happened there?'

I shrugged. 'The wheel just came off. These things are shit.'

He laughed. 'You're telling me they are.'

They made us typically welcome, with lashings of coffee, chocolate and biscuits, before asking why we were 'all over the place' – camped up like a bunch of vagrants and bedded down in the open *with nothing*. I made some excuse about being rushed and supplies being delayed, but frankly it was embarrassing. Here we were, the mighty SAS, and we'd come to beg, borrow and steal.

I swallowed my pride and launched into serious scrounge mode. I told the guys we were about to deploy, but we lacked just about everything. Did they have any Meals Ready to Eat (MREs) – US ration packs? I just loved their meatballs in sauce, plus the MREs came complete with heat packs, so were self-heating. With the British Army rations you had no option but to spark up the tiny foldable stove that came with them. Where we were heading, self-heating jobbies would prove far more convenient and covert.

Did they have any spare medical kits, by any chance, plus Gore-Tex gloves or hats, and tents? Plus did they have any proper, detailed, up-to-date, accurate satellite imagery or mapping? But most of all, did they possibly have any golden eggs they could spare, and maybe some spare boxes of 5.56 mm ammo while they were at it? All those things had been either non-existent or in very short supply at Camp Victor.

The main man, a SEAL petty officer, the equivalent of a sergeant in the army, stared at me in disbelief. 'What is it with you guys? You turned up with fuck all?'

I pretty much admitted that we had. He told us to give him and his guys ten minutes. We did, and they came back dragging several heavy ammo crates, boxes of MREs, sacks bulging with assorted goodies, and best of all, two tin cases crammed full of the gleaming, bulbous forms of 40 mm M203 rounds. It was like all our Christmases had come at once.

They handed it over, with a lot of hale and hearty 'Hey, man, yeah – take this and take that and take that.'

All of it was very much appreciated, and I guess our expressions spoke volumes. The SEAL sergeant waved away our words of thanks. 'Hey, guys, anything for the British SAS.'

'Really?' I perked up. 'There is one more thing . . .'

Did he happen to have a spacing bar for a Browning .50-calibre heavy machine gun, I ventured. I knew we didn't have any .50-cals with us, but I was the squadron's expert on the weapon and it had a nasty habit of suffering stoppages, and the spacing bar was the only way to get around it. If we were lucky, we might get some proper vehicles and weapons flown in on a resupply, hence my request. It took the guy a while longer, but eventually he even found me one of those.

We'd also scrounged whatever cold-weather kit the SEALs had to spare, for there was a decided nip in the air at Al-Jouf. I'd noticed those guys had thick duvet jackets, plus Gore-Tex everything, even down to their gleaming Danner boots. In our intel briefings, we'd been told that the weather in Iraq would be like 'England in spring'. But like so much else, that would turn out to be a crock of shit.

For some, that would prove a screw-up with catastrophic consequences. People would die because no one had thought to call up the BBC forecasters, or to ring one of the hundreds of Shell people who'd been working for decades in the Iraqi oilfields, to ask them what the weather was like in January in the Western Desert of Iraq. The excuse: OPSEC. Short for 'operational security'.

Believe it or not, the weather picture was called so wrong because no one wanted to let the cat out of the bag that we were deploying to Iraq. *Guys, it's in the newspapers. It's on the TV.* That was the obvious retort. It was for the same reason that I had to try to scrounge some usable mapping and satellite imagery off the SEALs. The Americans had it. They had it all. I'd actually been on one mission where they'd offered to move a satellite over our objective, to get real-time imagery.

But no one in our intel cell would ask them for any, due to OPSEC – because it might risk revealing to them where we were going. *Guys, they're on our side.* We used to joke about it in the Regiment. We used to say the SAS was so secret, it didn't even know it existed, let alone what it was doing. If you didn't find ways to laugh about it, you'd go stir crazy. But once we crossed the Iraq border it wouldn't seem so funny any more.

Chris Ryan must have had some kind of premonition at Al-Jouf – a sense that bad things were afoot. He went to have words with the head shed, pointing out in no uncertain terms that the three Bravo patrols were a disaster waiting to happen.

In the process, he made it clear that he figured we were on a 'one-way ticket'; that a lot of us – himself included – weren't coming back, or at least not unless it was carried in a coffin.

The deployment had been too rushed. The kit was too make-do-and-bodge-it. That had led to patrols breaking some of the golden rules of such deployments, to try to make amends. The intelligence picture was way off accurate, although a lot of that was still to be proven, one way or the other. This was mostly just Chris Ryan's gut feeling at the time, and he made certain that some at least were aware of it.

Bravo Two Zero was slated to be the first patrol to deploy. Just after dusk on 19 January they headed out on a Chinook, but not long after they were back again. Apparently, the air cover was so thick over Iraq, and the airstrikes so unrelenting, that US air controllers had ordered the lone British helo to turn right around, for fear it might get shot down.

Friendly fire – we'd been worried for a while now that it was going to dog our every step. This just confirmed it. If Coalition pilots couldn't identify a massive twin-bladed Chinook as being friendly – and the Iraqi military certainly didn't have any of those highly distinctive airframes – what hope did we have when deployed deep behind enemy lines? But it was a case of once more unto the breach . . . What other options were there?

Second time around, all three Bravo patrols were ordered to squeeze onto the two Chinooks – Bravo One and Bravo Two Zero with all their kit stuffed into their bulging Bergens, plus us and our sad excuse for wheels, cram-full to bursting with their cargos. Before mounting up, we made a final check that we were 'sanitized' as a patrol: no aerial photos, no markings on any of the maps we carried, no grid references scribbled in any notebooks.

Back at Camp Victor we'd been warned that if anyone was caught taking photos once we crossed into Iraq, that was an RTU-able offence. Likewise, we were supposed to carry not a single personal photo – no family snaps – on our person. It was fair enough. From the escape and evasion phase of Selection, we all appreciated how an enemy only needs the slightest thing, and they can exploit it as a chink in your armour.

It was a weird, wired, sombre, yet strangely buzzing atmosphere as we walked out towards the waiting Chinooks, the rotors turning and burning, the familiar smell of hot avgas pricking our nostrils. I turned to Reggie, a close mate of mine, and one of the few who was slated to remain behind. We put our backs to the helos, so we could have a few final words.

'This is going to sound over dramatic, mate,' I began, 'but if anything happens – anything at all – you tell Emily from me, not to worry. She's got the new house, half my pension and my savings in the bank. Once she's done mourning, tell her to move on with her life. Tell her I enjoyed every minute we spent together, the *Sun*'s fittest couple competition included, and that she's a good lass.'

'No problem,' Reggie replied, laughing. Everyone knew about our saga with the *Sun*. 'Tell you what, do I get the XR3i? You won't need it where you're going. I could even take Emily out for a spin.'

I smiled. I'd often clocked him eyeing up my missus. 'Wanker.'

'Tosser,' he retorted.

We shook hands and I climbed up the ramp to join the others.

We gathered as a patrol, clustered around the two wagons. As we were slated to be dropped first, we were positioned the nearest to the ramp. Further back amidst the dim red light that lit the Chinook's cave-like interior were some of the other Bravo patrol guys, together with their massive, bulging backpacks.

Rather them than us, I told myself, grimly. I was amazed that there hadn't been a last-minute change of heart. *Yeah, maybe we should take vehicles.* But if there's one thing that defines your average SAS guy, it's that we have a tendency to be as stubborn as the proverbial mule.

The RSM, Peter Radcliffe – the one who'd tried talking McNab and Johnson into taking vehicles – was known to be fond of saying: 'Opinions are like arseholes. Everybody has one.' It was his way of telling everyone to shut the hell up and listen. But self-reliant blokes with the ability to think outside the box and to give voice to their thoughts were exactly the types the Regiment claimed they were after. I knew from having attempted Selection – twice – that what got you through was not so much the physical side, but mental toughness.

We were a strong-minded and strong-willed bunch. Opinions – they came with the territory.

The first leg of the coming infil would be a thirty-minute flight north to a place called Arar, a town in the far north of Saudi Arabia. On the outskirts, Coalition forces had established a refuelling base, and it was there that we would get the final thumbs-up or thumbs-down as to whether we were cleared to cross the border into Iraq.

With the distinctive *thwoop-thwoop-thwooping* of the twin

rotors cutting the air above us, the helo shook herself free from the concrete runway and took to the skies. The noise was deafening and there was bugger all chance to talk. I spent the flight repeating a mantra in my head: *I hope it doesn't get called off. Please God, not this time.* I wasn't sure which deity I was praying to. Anyone that would listen, I guess.

After all the build-up and the tension, plus the rollercoaster ride of all the changes of plan – not to mention all the let-downs with the kit and intel – I just wanted to get in there and get busy. I was also acutely aware of how I'd been burning the candle at both ends. We all had. In truth, we were shattered. We were sucking on hope, nervous energy and adrenaline.

The CH47 came down to land at Arar, the ground crew rushing to refuel her, as one of the pilots went to check if we had got the green light. They kept the blades whirling, in the expectation of an onward journey and the ride of our lives.

Despite our differences over the us-and-them E & E plans, the Chinook aircrew were the very best. They were top grade military pilots who'd volunteered to fly such extremely hazardous and challenging missions, for no extra pay or comfort and for a damn sight more danger than you'd ever get piloting any other airframe that the RAF has to offer. And for sure, these kind of flights were risky in the extreme.

As just one example – and it was one that preyed heavily on my mind – the single biggest loss of life suffered by the Regiment since World War Two was all due to a helicopter going down. Nine years back, on 19 May 1982, at the height of the Falklands War, a Sea King transport helo packed full of SAS troops had gone down in the freezing swell of the Atlantic. Having lost power following a freak collision with an albatross, one of the world's largest seabirds, the helo hit the surface and turned turtle, the heavy turbine and rotors on the roof dragging it over, as the windows imploded and dark water flooded in.

Survivors fought each other to reach a tiny pocket of air, and then to exit via an escape hatch. There were thirty-one men aboard that Sea King: only seven would survive. Some of them would be traumatized for life by what they had experienced during those terrible moments trapped in the sinking helo, and afterwards, fighting to stay afloat and to remain conscious in the sub-zero waters.

As with all such flights, whatever had happened to those men riding in that Sea King had been completely out of their hands – just as it was with us, right now, on this Chinook. I'd got to know two of the survivors of the Sea King accident well. One, a D Squadron guy called Mark Bradley, never once spoke to me about it. He kept it all locked up inside. The other, Sam Pinter, proved the opposite. He told me about it chapter and verse.

'Des,' he'd said, 'remember this: no matter how special or well trained you are, the air-taxis are just a means to get you from A to B. They can crash, get hit or just fall out of the sky, and there's sod all you can do about it. You are totally at the aircrew's mercy and your fate is determined by the vagaries of that machine.'

Sobering words, especially now, when waiting for the Chinook pilot to get the go-go-go. He was back after a few minutes, his face beaming, as he flashed around a thumbs-up. *We were on.*

The Chinook clawed skywards once more, turbines howling. As it did, I locked eyes with Jim, our patrol commander: I sensed that he was well up for the fight. In fact, as I gazed around the

Chinook's shadowed hold, I figured to a man we all were. Despite the crap equipment, the rushed deployment, the useless intel and the frankly laughable state of the vehicles, we were itching to get busy. In spite of the other patrols' misgivings, we'd embraced the Pinkie and the Dinky. *Our beloved wheels.*

We all knew that life-and-death decisions lay ahead of us. One moment's lack of vigilance, one wrong call now, and it could spell death or capture. Our fortunes might turn on a sixpence. At the same time, we understood exactly why we were here. We appreciated the desperate urgency to get eyes-on the Scuds, and to get intel winging its way back to headquarters, so the fast jets could thunder in and take them out. We knew how crucial our role was to the fortunes of the entire war.

No pressure, then.

I settled back in the helo's fold-down canvas seat and grabbed a set of headphones. Via those, I could listen in on the aircrew chat, as the pilot and co-pilot conversed with each other and the navigator. I could hear the talk going back and forth, and I sensed the calm and the confidence radiating out from the cockpit, but with just a hint of underlying tension. We were still in Saudi airspace, just minutes from the border.

Soon now.

I tried to relax in the dark, the avgas fumes swirling all around. Each of us was in his own space now, zoning into the coming mission. Thoughts – questions – crowded into my head. What was going to happen in the days and weeks ahead? Had we prepared enough? Planned enough? Did we have enough ammo for extended operations deep behind the lines? How long could we go without food or water, if the resupply failed? Did we have enough firepower to batter through an Iraqi position? There were only eight of us in two thin-skinned vehicles, yet we were heading into the heart of the storm.

My mind was dragged back to the present by a voice on the headset: 'Crossing into Iraqi airspace.'

I felt the Chinook lurch lower, as the pilot endeavoured to hug the contours of the night-dark landscape. We were going in at around 50 feet above ground level, in an effort to avoid enemy fire. The pilot would be following the terrain, to hide our signature from any watching eyes – flying 'nap-of-the-earth', they call it. In the briefing at Camp Victor the aircrew had made clear they'd be flitting over and around any obstacles: electrical pylons, signal masts, trees, Iraqi military outposts. So be prepared for sudden movements, and likewise if they needed to evade enemy ground fire, or lock-ons from heat-seeking missiles.

Unerringly, I felt the Chinook drop lower, as it thundered across the dark terrain at approaching 300 kph. Not a great deal of room for any error, at that kind of altitude and speed. No doubt about it, we were in for a bumpy ride.

'Power cables coming up front,' a voice intoned, from the cockpit.

'Roger that.'

I felt the helo blip up a few metres, then flip back down again, as it hurdled that first set of obstacles. The calm chat from the cockpit had the tendency to lull you into a false sense of security. But not for long. Not on this ride.

With zero warning, I felt the aircraft bank a hard right, keeling over alarmingly on its axis, before flipping back just as violently the other way. No matter that they had warned us this might happen, I felt my adrenaline spike, my pulse thumping like a machine gun. *What the hell was that?* If I hadn't been strapped in, I'd have been thrown across the hold.

I stole a glance at the vehicles. They were lashed tight to steel lugs bolted to the floor. Thank God the ties seemed to be holding fast. Over the intercom I could hear voices from the cockpit, but they sounded garbled and erratic, distinctly alarmed. Moments later a cloud of spear-like bolts of fire went flaming past the Chinook's porthole-like windows. A series of rhythmic flashes pulsed down the hold, illuminating the figures crouched there like spectres, faces white and strained in the light.

Was that ground fire? Was someone shooting at us?

The loadmaster – the member of the aircrew who commands all that happens in a helicopter's hold – managed to communicate by hand signals that this was chaff. The Chinook was firing off clouds of blinding flares. They were being released on all sides, in an effort to confuse any heat-seeking missiles that may have been launched. Basically, the flares produced scores of false heat sources, shielding the helo from any incoming warheads.

It wasn't exactly a comforting thought, for what kind of Iraqi force was deployed into the far Western Desert equipped with heat-seeking SAMs? There was clearly someone trying to knock us out of the skies, and a good chance we mightn't even make the DZ. A quarter of an SAS squadron killed or injured, and before we'd even set foot on enemy soil.

Not a great outcome.

Then another thought struck me. If the pilot was evading such fire 50 feet above ground level, that had to leave zero room for any error. It was just as my Sea King crash survivor buddy had warned me: my life was entirely in someone else's hands, and I wasn't finding it a particularly enjoyable experience.

But maybe this wasn't the Iraqis at all? Maybe this was some American top gun, cruising high above us in his F-16 through the dark night skies. Due to all the priority placed upon OPSEC, did the Yanks even know we were here? They did have a tendency to be decidedly gung-ho, as we all appreciated. Here we were leading the way in an effort to prevent World War Three, and it would be sod's law to get blown out of the sky by our own side.

I'd barely had time to consider that thought when the same thing happened all over again. The Chinook flipped violently left and right, then righted itself, before the bursts of ghostly light seared through the dark night to either side of us. I gazed into the far recesses of the hold. In the pulsing flashes of illumination I figured I could see the features of the other Bravo guys. Was that fear written in their eyes? Could they read the same in mine?

Fuck knows.

I managed to catch the eye of the loadie. We leaned closer, to have an exchange of words. Sure enough, on a previous flight they'd had the pilot of an F-16 challenging them very aggressively to identify themselves. The Chinook pilot had done as requested, after which he'd still opted to execute evasive manoeuvres and to fire off the chaff, just in case the guy cruising high above them had decided to unleash a Sidewinder missile.

Better safe than sorry.

The loadie had no idea if it was the same tonight, or if we were being 'painted' by a SAM operator on the ground. By one of the enemy. No option but to sit back and say our prayers.

By the third time the Chinook executed the same manoeuvre,

I'd decided to let it go. There was sod all – zilch – that any of us could do about it. If we were brought down by ground fire or a fast jet flying high above us, we'd just have to hope we would survive the crash landing. Even if we did, we'd probably be in little state to fight, or to go on the run, and we'd never even have got close to the targets.

And that was just the way it was.

CHAPTER EIGHT

GOING IN

Not a moment too soon, the loadie gave us the ten-minutes-to-target signal – ten fingers, flashed before our eyes. He got busy now, loosening the wagons from the chain-and-ratchet system that held them locked to the floor. His movements became ever more frantic as we neared the DZ. We'd backed the wagons in, so we could drive them directly off the ramp into whatever might await us on the ground.

At the two-minutes-to-target mark we clambered aboard. Driller turned the ignition key, and the Dinky's engine coughed into life. In no time, the hold began to fill with thick diesel fumes. All of a sudden I could sense the Chinook flaring out to land, its rear end dropping, as we descended towards the dark desert floor. The vibration caused by the sudden deceleration was immense, and quite suddenly there was a sharp bump and a deafening crack, the rear end hitting the deck much harder than I had anticipated.

Moments later a high-pitched whine filled the hold, as the ramp cracked open and began to descend. Thick, choking dust billowed in. I grabbed my shemagh – my Arab-style headscarf – plus my freefall goggles, pulling them tighter around my features, in preparation for landing in what we call a 'brown-out', a swirling storm of dirt, sand and rocks thrown up by the rotor blades.

But the next thing that struck me felt like a sledgehammer blow to the head, it was so totally unexpected: lancing in through the Chinook's lowering ramp there was a blinding white light, as if someone had a searchlight trained upon the helo even as it came in to land.

What the fuck is that? Do we have a reception party? It sure as hell looks that way.

I grabbed my M16, ratcheting in a golden egg to the grenade launcher, while giving silent thanks to the SEALs at Al-Jouf. I turned to Quiet Alex in the rear, motioning for him to ready the Minimi. This far into Iraq, it could only be the enemy, which meant we must have been tracked by Iraqi radar. We'd chosen the present DZ with real care, for it was positioned away from human habitation or military facilities, at least as far as we could tell from the maps.

But if this was a searchlight, that had to mean vehicles, and this far into the Western Desert of Iraq that could only mean some kind of highly mobile frontline troops. As our wagon was perched rearmost on the helo, we were slated to be first off, which meant we would be heading out to meet our fate riding in a Dinky. What chance did we stand?

Involuntarily, my hand went to my chest, to grab my dog tags. 'Let's get the job done, Des,' I intoned. 'Let's get the job done and fuck off home.'

But somehow, this time, those words just felt so totally inadequate for whatever might be out there. I glanced at the loadie, who was gesturing frantically for us to move off the ramp. *Fuck it.* Whatever might be awaiting us, we were rolling out to meet it head on. I signalled to Driller to get us underway.

As we nosed forward into the blinding dust storm, one that was backlit by that weird, ghostly light, the ramp was so steep if felt as if the Dinky was about to tumble onto its nose. Moments later I felt the front wheels hit and the rear bump down. I scanned my arcs, searching for the source of the light: *the enemy.* But it seemed to be all around us, almost as if we were at the very heart of a burning vortex. It seemed to illuminate the entire swirling brown-out, transforming it into some giant howling fiery beast of the desert.

What the hell was going on?

You can't drive far from a Chinook when it drops you like this. The reasons why are simple: if you try to move any distance at all, at the angle the helo is perched and with the diameter of the rotors, you risk colliding with the rear blades, which would prove very terminal for a Dinky and those riding in it, and not too healthy for the Chinook, either. We halted just aft of the ramp, and waited in that weird, eerie, unnerving light for whatever might be coming, our eyes down our gun barrels.

If this was the enemy, why hadn't they shown themselves, or opened fire? If they did, they could very likely bag the Dinky, plus maybe even get a shot at taking out the Chinook. The lack of any hostile action – it didn't make the slightest bit of sense. We'd just been dropped by the biggest taxi this patch of desert had doubtless ever seen, and the noise and the downdraft were stupefying. Here we were trying to be stealthy and covert, and instead we'd got searchlights pinning us in their glare.

We had to have been compromised.

I chanced a look behind, into the helo's gaping hold. Shadowy figures were dashing about in the dim red light. I caught the loadie's eye, and he flashed me a thumbs-up. As far as they were concerned, we were good to go. *But what about this fucking light?* I felt like yelling. Not that anyone would be able to hear.

Moments later the ramp juddered to a close. The Chinook's turbines started to scream, as it began to claw its way skywards. The weirdest thing was this: as the Chinook lifted off, the brown-out became thicker and more intense, but so too did the light. Maybe that was why the enemy hadn't hit us: the cloud of choking dust kicked up by the rotors was just too thick to see through. The Iraqi military did have helicopters, and maybe they couldn't open fire for fear that this was one of their own.

Then, as the helo pulled further away and the dust began to thin a little, the penny finally dropped. *The Chinook itself was the source of the blinding illumination.* There is a phenomenon called the 'halo effect', one that I'd heard about but never actually seen. Basically, the spinning rotors suck up clouds of dust, and the blades striking the silicon in the sand create heat and light. You end up with the rotors generating a truly ghostly effect, which looks exactly as if the blades are two giant circles of fire.

As the Chinook pulled away still further and the dust thinned, I'd finally got to see it for what it was . . . Still, my adrenaline was spiking like crazy, my pulse pounding in my ears. Gradually, the deafening noise of the Chinook's turbines began to fade. The quicksilver effect was also gone now. The contrast could not have been more absolute. The desert was dark and seemingly utterly deserted. So much for a convoy of enemy vehicles with searchlights.

I watched as the helo pulled further away, flying low and

fast across the open terrain, the faint glow of its twin exhausts flickering on and off, as it drifted in and out of vision. The noise stayed with us long after the helo was completely lost to sight. The rhythmic juddering beat that has given the Chinook the nickname 'the wocka-wocka' echoed across the desert, as the rotors cut a path through the night skies. If that hadn't woken the dead, nothing would.

I began to notice the temperature and the terrain now: it felt noticeably chilly and the landscape was not what we'd been led to expect. Not at all. As far as I could tell, it was billiard-table-flat on all sides.

With the Chinook gone, Jim pulled his Pinkie in front of ours, into pole position: this would be our line of march whenever we were on the move. I saw him dismount: time for a chinwag. We gathered by the bonnet of the Dinky, heads close. Of course, after all the deafening noise and the spectacular light show, if any hostiles were anywhere hereabouts they'd know all about our arrival. Even so, the vast, brooding emptiness of the desert seemed to demand a respectful hush.

'We'll make three to four klicks heading east,' whispered Jim, 'then stop for a listening watch, see if we've been followed.'

'Roger that.' No more needed to be said.

But as Jim went to mount up the 110, I noticed there was a small sliver of light visible to the rear of his vehicle. In terrain this pitch dark it shone out like a beacon. We'd thought we'd taped up everything at Camp Victor, but in all the rush we must have missed something.

'Hang on a minute,' I hissed, 'there's a light at the back of your wagon.'

I dashed forward. Of all things, we'd forgotten the bloody numberplate light. I raised my M16, and with a blow from the butt smashed it in. Jim and his lot were good to go now. We'd move off like this, driving on 'black light', using the ambient illumination from stars and moon to navigate.

We got going, the Pinkie first and us following, keeping a good few vehicle lengths apart. That way, we would be able to put down covering fire for each other, but didn't present one easy target. I noticed Driller was sticking to the lead wagon's tracks, to try to minimize our signature. It also meant that if the front vehicle hit trouble – a ravine; an enemy minefield; an ambush; shed a tyre even – we would get maximum warning, and should be able take evasive action. Good drills.

We could keep tabs on the Pinkie easily enough via the ambient light. We'd brought two sets of night-vision goggles per vehicle – the very same kind that Emily and I had used when stalking around our Peterborough garden. But wherever possible it was preferable to navigate by the naked eyeball. Over long periods of use, the weird frog-green glow of the NVGs tended to strain your eyes and to burn out your natural night vision. Not good, if you bumped into the bad guys and triggered a full-on firefight.

As our two-vehicle convoy crawled across the pitch-dark desert, several things became clear. First, the terrain here was nothing like the UAE, or Saudi Arabia for that matter. This was no undulating sea of sand. The way the heavily laden Dinky was bucking and groaning, we had to have rocky terrain underfoot. In the light thrown off by moon and stars I could see the desert far and wide. In every direction it was dotted with these hard, angular, blocky silhouettes. Far from being a sand-sea, it looked as if we were driving through a field of rocks, the largest of which were around the size of a man's head.

In the still quiet of the open landscape, the racket made by the wagons – the ceaseless creaking, banging and rattling – sounded deafening. No matter how we might have tried to muffle and mummify the heaviest kit, by wrapping it all in hessian, there was little hope of keeping silent when moving across such ground. Smooth sandy terrain like we'd found at Camp Victor makes for quiet driving. This was the complete opposite.

I figured we were making ten klicks a hour, if that, but the Dinky for sure couldn't go a lot faster. Lying low on her suspension, the short-wheel-base wagon was like a dog-eared mattress that had seen far better days: any sharp knocks, any serious impacts, and the springs were likely to give way. Even proceeding at this kind of pace, anything not bolted down – or firmly sat upon by Trev and Quiet Alex – was at risk of getting bounced out of the wagon, and there would be no soft landings anywhere hereabouts.

With the Dinky – and her load – clanging and rattling like a thing possessed, there was almost no way of communicating, bar hand signals. No one spoke much. Plus it felt damn cold now. Not the cold like we'd experienced at Al-Jouf; this was something altogether more chilly. In fact, it was almost cold enough for me to want to grab the Gore-Tex gloves and hats that I'd scrounged off the SEALs, to hand out to the lads.

I glanced around our vehicle. Driller was hunched over the wheel, concentrating on the task at hand. Quiet Alex had the Minimi cradled in his arms, as he scanned his arcs to one side of the Dinky's open rear. Geordie Trev was doing the same with his M16 on the opposite flank. No one was saying a word. I could sense the tension. We felt as exposed at the proverbial dog's bollocks, and equally vulnerable. This was not what we had been led to expect at all.

After thirty minutes crawling across such terrain, Jim called a halt. It was 0200 hours, and we remained in our vehicles, silently scanning our arcs and straining eyes and ears for the slightest sign of the enemy. This was what we call a 'listening watch', but it was also a chance to get a feel for the environment and the terrain. We'd pulled up in the midst of a dark and empty field of rocks, which stretched from horizon to horizon with seemingly not the slightest variation.

The horrendous racket made by the vehicles' progress had been replaced by a deep stillness, such as I'd never experienced before. Plus I was struck by the wild, empty, dust-dry scent of the desert night. It was so utterly deserted and silent out there that my own breathing sounded loud in my ears. As we sat and studied our surroundings, it seemed so completely devoid of life. Not a thing moved. Not a vehicle backfired, not a headlight cut the night, nor a dog barked.

It felt like you could see practically forever amidst such terrain, even at night. As my eyes adjusted to the gloom, off in the far distance I could just make out some kind of illumination. A faint halo pricked the horizon. I couldn't work out what exactly it was, but I figured it had to be some kind of human habitation. It was our first sign of the Iraqis. Of the enemy. One thing was also pretty obvious to us by now: there was no sign whatsoever that we had been compromised. Noisy and spectacular it may have been, but the infiltration by Chinook seemed to have gone unnoticed.

We'd pulled the vehicles to a stop in tight formation, so we could talk without dismounting. After ten minutes' listening watch, and not seeing the slightest sign of any movement, Jim and I leaned across to exchange words.

'Hard going, mate,' I whispered. 'Potholes, boulders, the works. Not what we were expecting. Plus it's quiet enough out there to hear a sparrow fart.'

Jim nodded. 'It's as flat as a bloody pancake, Des, which means fuck-all cover. If the other patrols have put down on ground anything like this . . .'

He left the rest unsaid, but it was exactly what I had been thinking.

If Bravo One and Bravo Two Zero had stepped off the Chinook into similar territory – this barren, featureless moonscape – there was no way they were digging any kind of a hide any time soon. Not in this kind of terrain. We'd brought in empty hessian sacks, supposedly to fill with sand to shore up any position. That wasn't happening anywhere around here. More to the point, this kind of billiard-flat surface left absolutely nowhere to run. Being out here on foot and laden down with 250 pounds of kit apiece, as the other patrols were – it simply didn't bear thinking about.

'Not at all what the intel briefs led us to expect,' I hissed to Jim, through gritted teeth.

He shrugged. 'Fucking intel.' Then, after a short pause: 'You know what, Des, I don't see us putting in an OP anywhere around here, and as to hiding the fucking vehicles . . .'

'Yeah. Come sun-up we'll stand out like the dog's nads.'

I knew instinctively what Jim was thinking. He had every right to put a radio call through to Al-Jouf, to bring the Chinook back again, aborting the mission on the grounds that the terrain made it untenable. To make that kind of decision would be a massive call, especially when we knew what was at stake here: preventing World War Three. It was the kind of decision only all of us could make, for we'd have to live with it for the rest of our lives, and with the – all-but-inevitable – accusations that we'd bottled it.

Jim shrugged again, then glanced at me. 'Fuck it, Des, we're here now. We're here and we're staying. Let's do what we can.'

'Agreed,' I told him. 'We're here, so let's fucking do the job we were sent out for.'

Jim was a hard, tough commander, and I wasn't surprised that he'd made the call that he had. I was more than happy to argue my case and tell him exactly what I thought, and we'd already had a few cross words back in UAE. They'd generally ended with Jim telling me: 'I'm the fucking senior rank here and we'll do as I say.' But at the end of the day I liked his attitude and I was 100 per cent behind him.

With three former Concrete Reg guys on the patrol, that mentality was bound to shape our decisions. We were hardly known for taking a backwards step. In fact, we were far more likely to get accused of being too gung-ho. There was always the chance that we'd made the wrong call. Maybe come sun-up we were going to get seen, chased and comprehensively wiped out. Maybe we'd just signed our own death warrants. But either way, we were staying, and we were going to do our utmost to get busy. That just left the thorny question of where on earth we were going to set up our hide.

*

As we sat there, pondering our predicament, my mind flipped back to when I had been pulled off Selection with the splintered arm. What had happened then epitomized the Para Reg mentality, and it had caused me no end of trouble. There was a Guards Regiment bloke called Lance Smith who'd also made it through to Jungle Phase. With my arm lacerated with tree spines I was out of the running, while Lance was one step closer to being awarded the prize – his beige beret.

We'd had words in the block back at H and it had ended in a full-on showdown. He was five foot ten and far more bulky than me. No matter.

'I don't fucking like you,' I told him. 'Fucking come here and get some.'

'Des, what's your fucking beef?' he retorted. 'You didn't get through. You're out. Deal with it.'

'Don't you talk to me like that.'

'I'll say what I want.'

'Okay, come and say it in the drying room.'

We had a saying in the Paras – 'If you need to sort it, go sort it in the drying room.' Most military bases have one – a closed room, no windows, full of pipes and radiators, for drying sodden-wet kit. Invariably the drying room stinks of sweat, piss, rancid socks and unwashed gear. It was a place where no one would hear you scream. Some of the guys had seen the two of us flash. They tried to talk us down, but it was too late for that.

Lance and I headed for the drying room. Once we got there I went to shut the door, only for him to square up to me. 'You're just pissed 'cause you failed. It's sour grapes. Grow up and get over it.'

Red rag to a bull.

I turned away from the door and in one fluid movement I brought my left fist up in an arc, executing a classic upper cut to the point of his jaw. I followed it instantly with a haymaker from the right, and Lance went down on one knee, dazed, and without getting in a single blow. I stood over him as he swayed on his knees, making it absolutely clear that if he talked to me like that again, he'd get more of the same.

When the senior commanders found out what had happened, I was in no end of trouble. 'You don't do that up here,' I was told. 'You leave that Para Reg mentality at the gates, if you want to have any chance of making it into Hereford.' After that set-to in the drying room, I was very lucky to get invited back for a second attempt at Selection.

Eight months later I'd made it into the Regiment. I'd earned my beige beret the hard way. I walked into the canteen at H one lunchtime, only to spy a familiar figure near the front of the queue. I walked up to Lance and extended my hand. Like I've said, I'm a plain-spoken bloke and I say it like it is.

'Look, mate, we had words, but as far as I'm concerned it's over. I'm up here now and I just want to get on with what we're here for. So, how about you?'

'Fair one, Des. Far as I'm concerned it's finished.'

We shook hands.

After that we didn't exactly become blood brothers, but the hatchet was well and truly buried. Lance's older brother was also in the Regiment and he was at a more senior rank. He could have caused me no end of trouble. Quite the reverse was true: he helped me out in no end of ways. As far as I was concerned, that was the mark of a man. No back-stabbing. No slagging. You sort it out, after which it is all forgotten. In the same way, Lance would go on to prove himself a fine soldier. He had my respect.

Likewise, there would come a time when Jim and I would come to blows. Strong-headed, we could rub each other up the wrong way. But when the chips were down, as they were right now, he had my absolute 100 per cent support.

Jim glanced around the spot where we'd pulled up. 'You know what, sod it – this is as good a place as any to set camp. You okay with that, Des?'

'We could try over there, or there, or there, or there – but what's the fucking point? It's all much of a muchness, Jim.'

'Yeah. Fucking intel.'

We figured there was a slight depression nearby, so we'd manoeuvre the wagons into that. Decision made, Jim turned to speak to those riding in the rear of the vehicles.

'Right, lads, listen up. This is as good a place as any, so we're stopping here. Let's get into our night routine. We'll dig trenches, at the front and back of the wagons, so at least we'll have a bit of cover. Then cam nets over everything and get into stagging on. Plus Chewie, break out the comms so we can get a report into base.'

We shunted the wagons back and forth a bit, after which we got busy with the shovels, as we went about setting up our first lying-up place (LUP) – hide – of the mission. Trouble was, the ground proved as hard as cement. It turned out that beneath the boulders lay only compacted rock and gravel, baked solid by the relentless sun. The most we could manage was a few very basic shell-scrapes – like shallow graves that a man can crawl into, and which provide the barest modicum of cover.

The aim of the LUP was to keep us hidden during the hours of daylight. All had to be readied under cover of darkness. But over and above being a simple hide, a good LUP should also offer decent defensive positions. Normally, you'd take careful note of any obvious avenues of attack, especially any 'dead ground' – terrain via which the enemy could approach unseen. It was in those areas that you'd normally set your claymores. You'd work out your 'arcs of fire', interlocking your killing fields, so that each wagon's heavy weapons covered your key vulnerabilities. Finally, you'd decide upon your 'bug-out' plan – your escape route – set a sentry watch, and then try to get some shut-eye.

You generally only get the one chance to establish a LUP. Come daylight, you don't want to risk breaking cover and searching for a better spot. Of course, with no vehicle-mounted weapons, we were limited in what we could achieve defensively, plus we were lacking in any claymores. Amidst such terrain, we could get spotted from just about any point of the compass, leaving all avenues open for an attack. There was sod all that we could do about that, other than ready those weapons we did have and maintain maximum vigilance.

Once we'd got the Pinkie and Dinky sheeted over, and the cam nets suspended on their collapsible poles, we figured their outlines were at least semi-obscured. That sorted, we took it in turns to stand sentry or to glug down a cold sachet of food. We were on 'hard routine', so there would be no heating meals or firing up stoves to make a brew. While on exercises or operations, a favourite meal was an 'all-in' – baked beans, pasta, hotpot, sausages, oatmeal biscuits and more stirred into a formless mush, often with some spices chucked in for flavour. There would be none of that here in Iraq.

On hard routine we'd also be defecating in plastic bags and carrying it all with us, so as to hide our presence from the enemy. Of course, amidst such terrain that meant taking a crap in full sight of the others, for there were certainly no rocks or vegetation large enough to offer even a modicum of privacy. As they say, shit happens.

I tried catching a few minutes' kip, but the ground proved horrendous. I kept turning this way and that, yet I still seemed to have sharp, angular rocks digging into my ribs. Eventually, I decided to give up and go help the Big Friendly Giant call home. Chewie had broken out our Clansman HF radio set and begun the complex procedure of preparing to transmit. It was a thankless task, hence my crawling over to lend a hand.

Normally we'd have two means of making contact from the field – via the HF set, or via a satcom, an early version of a satellite phone. The big advantage of the satcom is that it's a quick, dial-up system. All you have to do is wait for enough satellites to be passing overhead – which usually takes a matter of minutes – and you can call through. By contrast, the Clansman takes an age to set up. Normally, we'd use a satcom for transmitting low-grade information, as it was too vulnerable to intercepts. But right now we wouldn't be doing even that, because there had been no satcoms left at Camp Victor by the time we got there.

Consequently, our only means of reaching Al-Jouf was via the radio. What we needed to do, now we were firmly in our LUP, was to send a 'sitrep' – a situation report – summarizing our position, status and intentions. Keyed into a ruggedized laptop, the message would be sent in a quick, coded 'burst' of HF radio waves. In fact, the burst was flashed into the ether, only to hang there until the signallers at base plucked it out for decoding. Headquarters would use the same means to send messages back to us, so at the end of a long night's move we might have several bursts waiting to be downloaded.

Sending daily sitreps is crucial for the prosecution of an SF campaign, for the simple reason that it enables the head shed to keep track of each individual patrol. That in turn should prevent any two SAS teams from bumping into each other, mistaking each other for the enemy, and proceeding to brass each other up – what's termed a 'blue-on-blue'. As we sent the daily sitreps, HQ was supposed to send back 'advisories', alerting us to where the other patrols were, plus any key intel.

That was the theory. In practice, it was a complex and challenging procedure to get the Clansman operational, as Chewie was about to experience. His sitrep was short and to the point: 'Bravo Three Zero, establishing comms. Location grid: 123456. LUP.' Right now, that was all that needed to be said.

After stringing up an antenna and punching various buttons, Chewie figured he'd sent the message, but he received no acknowledgement. Now, that might mean HQ hadn't downloaded it yet, or it might mean the message hadn't been transmitted at all. I did my best to help, as the Big Friendly Giant tried messing about with various configurations of the antenna – laying it out across the ground, erecting it on poles, and trying different lengths and orientations, but still he couldn't get the sniff of a response.

Eventually, he turned to me and shrugged. 'Fucking ionosphere.'

I cracked a smile. The Clansman's HF signals are supposed to be bounced off the ionosphere, one of the outermost layers of the earth's atmosphere. But the procedure was famously unreliable, and that had become something of a catchphrase amongst the comms guys: *Fucking ionosphere.*

'You know how it is, Des,' Chewie added, 'comms always works until you really need it to. Not too worried. I'll keep trying. Sometime or other, it's sure to get through.'

It was around 0500 by now – an hour or so from sun-up – and I figured Jim and me needed to have a word. I crabbed across to where he was laid out beside the 110, wriggling under the camo netting. From the looks of things, he'd had little better luck trying to get any kip than I had.

'Mate, this is nothing like the UAE,' I remarked, joining him with my back propped against the flank of the 110. 'Nothing like we trained for. No soft sand. Nowhere to dig in an OP. Nowhere much to hide the vehicles.'

'Don't I know it,' he grunted.

'Plus Chewie says he can't be sure the sitrep's got through. He's got no response.'

'Fucking ionosphere.'

'Yeah, but that's serious though, mate. If we've got no comms, we've got no way to execute the mission. We can hardly radio in Scud locations, with no comms.'

'Good point. We can't.' Jim paused, seeming deep in thought. Finally, he shrugged. 'Any which way you look at it, Des, there's nothing we can do about it. Either the comms comes good or it doesn't. Just got to crack on.'

'Yeah. Agreed.' I glanced at him, searchingly. 'Any thoughts about the others? I mean, the other two Bravo patrols.'

He turned his face towards me, his expression set like stone. 'I'll tell you something, Des. If we're having problems with vehicles, then they're utterly, totally screwed. Let's just hope they aborted. If not . . . Well, they're as good as dead.'

Shit. Those were dark sentiments alright, but truth be told I'd been thinking pretty much the same thing. If Andy McNab and Patrick Johnson had stepped down the Chinook's open ramp and seen what we'd seen, they'd have had every right to walk right up again and tell the pilot to fly them all back to Al-Jouf.

If they hadn't – well, right now they were dead men walking.

I must have nodded off, for I awoke with a start to hear a short, sharp whack, followed almost instantaneously by Trevor Moriarty – our resident Hobbit – chuntering away in quick-fire Geordie-talk. He was going at it hammer and tongs and I just knew instinctively what must have happened.

Being so massively into his fitness and triathlons, Trev was big into the porridge that came in the ration packs, which put him in a minority of just about one. We'd got used to it back in the UAE – Trev, wolfing down an early-morning sachet, followed by the pronouncement: 'Love it. I've got all this energy, 'cause I just ate me fucking porridge.'

The lads had taken to launching dawn porridge attacks, the best of which was a direct hit with a full sachet on the back of the neck. Trev tended to take it a little too personally to my way of thinking, for it was all in a good cause – boosting morale. As I glanced around right now, I could see the other lads' shoulders going up and down, as they tried their best to stifle their mirth and to keep their eyes firmly down their weapons' sights. It was first light, the most common time to get bumped by the enemy.

It may sound juvenile, but British Army humour tends to be centred around somewhat childish wind-ups. And the thing is, such joshing about is absolutely vital to keeping everyone's spirits up. Not another nation can rival British humour, especially amongst the ranks of their militaries. It's a long-lived tradition. When David Stirling had listed his five founding principles of the SAS, humour was right there at, or very near, the top. If you could laugh in the face of adversity, or crappy intelligence, or godawful kit and equipment, you were one big step closer to winning the war.

As tended to happen after an early-morning porridge salvo, Trev did his best to turn it back on me. No doubt I was the chief suspect, never mind that I'd been kipping, for over the past few days launching porridge sachets at the flame-haired Hobbit had become one of my favourite wind-ups.

'You're just riled, Des, 'cause there's no bread and dripping in the rat-packs.'

'Fuck-aye, I'm missing me bread and dripping,' I retorted. Like I said, always best to roll with the punches.

It was Chewie's turn to have a go now. 'Des, up in Yorkshire you live on bread and dripping. Really, though, that's dried-up chip fat. How d'you survive on that?'

'Oooh, it's fucking lovely, especially with lashings of brown and white and salt.'

Chewie raised one – giant – eyebrow. 'Brown and white and salt?'

'Yeah. Brown and white and salt. You see, up north dripping has a thick crust of white on top, which is the fat, with a layer of brown underneath, which is the congealed gravy. Put it all together with a good dose of salt – fucking lovely!'

Chewie feigned disgust. 'That cannot be good for you, Des.'

'Up north we have a saying, Chewie, which is like gospel: bread and dripping is good for you, 'cause it greases your innards.'

'It's like Cockneys with their jellied eels,' Driller cut in. 'They can't help it.'

I screwed up my face. 'No way. No way would I ever go near jellied eels.'

Driller snorted. 'Chip fat and dried gravy ain't a lot better.'

'Des, if you live on dripping, can I have your chocolate?' a voice cut in. It was Joe, our resident chocoholic, and he'd just opened himself up for a full-on broadside.

I hurled a bar of Cadbury's at him, which comes as standard in the rat-packs. 'Here you go, then. No wonder you RAF types are all fat bastards.'

'Not only does he go about in carpet slippers and is a rock ape, but he lives on chocolate.'

That last one was from Chewie. Here we were in the middle of the Iraqi desert deep behind the lines, the sun was peeking above the horizon and we were facing the utterly unknown, and it was great to see that the lads were sparking.

As the light strengthened, we were somewhat relieved at what we saw. What we'd taken for billiard-table-flat terrain turned out to have very slight undulations. Over great distances, they should help shield us from any watching eyes. With the camo netting breaking up the profiles of the wagons, we figured even if there were any watchers out there, we should blend in. In the far distance we could spy the odd flash of sunlight off glass, which had to be vehicles moving on the MSR a way to the east of us. That was where we needed to head, to get eyes-on the Scud convoys.

Best of all, we could see no sign of any human presence in any direction, apart from those distant glimmers and glints. Nothing seemed likely to come heading in the direction of our LUP any time soon. That sorted, we settled into day routine – a mix of stagging on and trying to grab some kip – with the plan of breaking camp and moving up to the MSR come nightfall.

We set a stag roster two hours on and two off, which meant we always had four sets of eyes keeping watch. I volunteered for the first stint, along with Quiet Alex, while the others went to get some kip. Out of the corner of my eye I saw Driller unroll his maggot, crawl in, curl up next to the Dinky's rear wheel where it was most sheltered, and almost instantly he was fast asleep. It never ceased to amaze me how, when and where Driller could kip. He'd barely bothered to de-rock his patch of ground. Out of the lot of us, he was the prize-winning kipper.

For sure, we were all dog-tired. The rush, rush, rush of our deployment from the UK; the intensity of Camp Victor; the ever-changing nature of our tasks and the patrol make-ups; the constant battle to get hold of half-decent kit; the pitiful scrounging; all followed by a long night's infil and setting up the LUP. It was day one in Iraq, and already we were deeply fatigued. Even so, most of the blokes just weren't able to do a Driller: climb in their doss-bag and – blam! – they were fast asleep.

As the sun clawed its way higher, those of us who weren't kipping began to realize the full, galactic extent of the screw-up made at Camp Victor. We'd been handed out a few, very basic satellite images by the Green Slime. We'd been told that the dark areas represented the higher ground, the lighter shades the more low-lying terrain. But from studying what we could see now of the lunar landscape, we realized it was *the opposite*. The dark features were actually areas thrown into shadow – they were lower-lying – and the lighter features were the sun-washed higher ground.

For the other two patrols this alone might prove fatal. They'd endeavoured to select a patch of high terrain for their DZ which offered a view of the MSR. Instead, they'd have ended up being dropped beside some wadi or gully. And there was no way that either Bravo One or Bravo Two Zero was going to be able to move from there to any higher ground, laden down with all their gear. The whole point of going in on foot was to be dropped in a spot that offered good visibility and to dig in a hide.

We talked about it amongst ourselves. We were appalled to think what kind of fate might await our fellow patrols. Surely those guys had had no option but to abort. If they had, then that would leave us as the only SAS unit this far forward in Iraq. As we were supposed to form the tip of the spear– the most advanced Coalition troops – that might mean that we eight men and our Pinkie and Dinky were it. Without establishing firm comms, there was just no way of knowing.

My first stag done, I tried bedding down, but my mind was a whirl of thoughts, and even with the cam netting over us, it didn't cut out much light. The sun's rays beat through. You can't bury your head in your doss-bag while in an LUP, because that pretty much deadens your hearing – your early warning system.

Instead, you have to try to sleep with your head fully exposed. I tried doing that, but pretty instantly I got hit by a hail of tiny grains of sand, which were drifting low across the ground on the early-morning breeze.

A carpet of sifting sand was blowing across the desert, driving scores of tiny needles into any exposed flesh. I pulled my she-magh tighter, but still they seemed to prise a way through. I curled closer around the Dinky's tyre, seeking to take advantage of the natural windbreak caused by the wheel arch. You had to resist the temptation to crawl right under the wagon. If you did get taken by surprise and had to move in a hurry, it was almost impossible to do so when ensconced in a green maggot and jammed beneath a vehicle.

Even when I did manage to nod off, I came awake to a painful throbbing where a rock was having a good dig. I tried clearing my little patch of dirt of all visible obstructions, but there just seemed to always be the one. Sod's law, it would work its way into my most vulnerable parts – kidneys, neck, shoulder blades, ribs.

After a while I gave up and broke out the maps, or the sorry excuses we had for them. We'd been provided with aviation charts, which were on a 1:250,000 scale and which were decades out of date. That was maybe okay when executing an air sortie from tens of thousands of feet and screaming along at Mach 2. But for us, they gave nowhere near enough information. I tried working out where we might find a vantage point overlooking the MSR, when we moved off come nightfall, but that kind of detail just wasn't there. Our E & E maps, at 1:1,000,000, had even less to offer.

What made it all the more galling was that I knew what the

Americans had: they'd used bang-up-to-date satellite imagery to compile large-scale, detailed mapping. They even had the ability to transmit those satellite images to analysts in Washington, who could tell if there had been any movements by vehicle or foot across any patch of terrain. Back at Al-Jouf, I'd been shown just such a set of maps by the SEALs. I'd practically salivated at the very sight of them, but as I fully appreciated, they'd needed proper clearance before handing over a bunch of them to us.

During the short time that we'd remained at Al-Jouf, permission hadn't come through, or so I assumed. Truth be told, I hadn't wanted to push it, to keep asking. It was embarrassing and, frankly, degrading. What should have happened was that the powers that be should have walked across to speak with their opposite numbers in the US military. They should have asked the Americans for help. One thing is for sure with the Yanks: if you ask and they can, they generally will. In my experience they're generous to a fault, especially where the British military is concerned. The reason why no one had asked was all down to 'OPSEC': no one was allowed to know that we were deploying into Iraq.

It would have been laughable, if it wasn't life-or-death stuff we were talking about here.

CHAPTER NINE

ROAD WATCH

Come dusk we broke camp, starting the entire LUP process in reverse: glugging down a cold meal, stowing away sleeping kit in our Bergens, and breaking out our night-vision optics. I got together with Jim to discuss the route we planned to take and our aims when we got there. Our objective was one of the main east–west MSRs, running from central Iraq to the Jordanian border. It was from there that Saddam was lobbing his missiles into Israel; this terrain had earned the nickname 'Scud Alley'.

Scud Alley stretched for several thousand square miles from Baghdad west and south to the Jordanian and Saudi borders. Right now, we were about to head northeast, every turn of the Land Rovers' wheels taking us one step closer to the Iraqi capital, less than 100 km away. In short, we were right in the heart of Saddam's backyard and cruising deeper into Scud Alley. It was some proposition.

Thirty minutes before nightfall we rolled back the cam nets and stowed them, loading them and our Bergens onto the wagons, as Chewie made one last attempt to raise some kind of response from headquarters via the radio. Needless to say, all he got was an echoing void of silence. So, with none of us any the wiser we clambered aboard the Pinkie and the Dinky and prepared for the off.

Deprived of any link to higher command, we felt horribly isolated. It was as if we had been cut loose and left to fend for ourselves. But that is what SAS Selection and training is there for. It is designed to prepare you to face the very worst kind of scenarios and to keep going; to execute the mission objective, no matter what. As Jim had rightly pointed out, we still had our task to achieve: we still had to find some Scuds and to kill them. In the absence of any orders from on high to the contrary, we were game on.

We set forth, slipping into our night configuration – Pinkie leading, Dinky taking up the rear. Although we couldn't know it, this very night Saddam would rain down eight more Scuds on Tel Aviv. All eight would be taken out by Patriot missile batteries, but even so, the debris would cascade down, killing and injuring Israeli civilians, and who knew what else might be drifting to earth, along with those blasted fragments of missile.

Sarin? Chlorine? Mustard gas? Or worse?

Saddam actually had two models of Scud in use – the Al-Hussein, with a range of some 650 km, and the Al-Abbas, with a range of around 900 km. Both were Iraqi-engineered modifications on the Soviet R-17 Elbrus ballistic missile, known as a 'Scud B' in NATO parlance. The R-17 is named after Mount Elbrus, the highest peak in Russia and all of Europe, and it was a mainstay of Soviet forces. To give an indication of how ingenious were the Iraqi modifications, the R-17 had a range of around 300 km. In order to massively increase that in the Al-Hussein and

Al-Abbas, the payload had been reduced while the rocket fuel was made to burn faster, boosting power and range.

During the Iran–Iraq war, Iraqi forces had unleashed more than 200 Scuds against Iranian targets, with the result that Saddam now boasted a dedicated cadre of experienced and battle-hardened missile-launch crews. Wily and cunning, the Iraqi leader had also developed a plethora of covert means to effect a Scud launch: in addition to the Soviet-made MAZ-543 TELs, he'd developed the Al-Waleed, a modified civilian Scania truck as a DIY launcher, plus he'd built fleets of fuel trucks and missile-supply vehicles disguised as civilian transports, and in some cases even as civilian tour buses.

All of that underlined the immense challenges of spotting Scud-launch crews from the air, and taking them out. Even if an F-16 pilot did suspect a vehicle was acting suspiciously, the risk of blowing to pieces a civilian bus packed full of Iraqi women and children by mistake was just too great – hence the need for eyes up close and boots on the ground.

The distance from Iraq's western border to Israel's main cities – Jerusalem, Tel Aviv, Haifa – is some 500 km, well within the range of an Al-Hussein or an Al-Abbas. But it was over double that if the missiles were to be launched from central Iraq, putting it out of even the Al-Abbas's reach. Hence Saddam's need to move his missiles west along Scud Alley, together with fleets of support vehicles and launch crews.

Right now he was doing that with seeming impunity, and Israel's leaders were getting more and more enraged and belligerent. Promises that the SAS would stop the Scuds had so far proven hollow, which made our mission even more vital. This was exactly the kind of information the head shed had been trying to communicate to us, via the radio, only none of their messages were getting through. All we had left to go on was gut instinct, training and sheer nerve – a determination to get the job done, even if we were the last Coalition forces in Iraq, which for all we knew we might be.

Funnily enough, as we got motoring in the Dinky, creeping east towards that far-distant MSR, all four of us in our wagon were smelling of roses. It's a myth that special forces operators can afford to get filthy dirty in the field. Over long-duration missions cleanliness is essential, which is why all of us had had a quick 'cat-lick' before breaking camp – a once-over using a wet wipe and a few dribbles from your water bottle, especially between the legs, to prevent crotch rot.

Caring for your body – 'husbandry', as we call it – may not sound particularly manly, but blokes suffering from chafing thighs, or cracked and painful hands, or feet plagued by trench rot don't make for good, capable, mobile fighting troops. In conditions like the Iraqi desert, sand gets into everything, and if you didn't do a cat-lick between your toes and powder daily, your feet would rapidly fall apart. For similar reasons we each carried a tube of baby lotion, to lather onto hands.

Having said that, there are always those in such a patrol who can't resist a bit of a dirty wind-up. Back at the LUP we'd decided upon the poo protocol for Bravo Three Zero. We'd agreed between us that while we had to remain in sight of those on watch when going for a no. 2, we were allowed to move a few paces away from camp, just to enjoy a little privacy. Preferably downwind of the LUP, of course.

The drill was simple. You'd warn your mucker: 'Okay, I'm going for a no. 2.' You'd grab a large freezer bag, and wander off to a chorus of – inevitable – muted catcalls. You'd deposit your doings direct into the plastic, then double-bag it, before stowing it in your Bergen. Or at least, you were supposed to. The temptation was always to dump it in someone else's pack – somewhere they'd only find it come endex – mission's end. Funnily enough, the biggest dirty wind-up-merchant would prove to be Joe, which for a mollycoddled RAF type had to signify something. I'd learn to watch that man like a hawk.

There's actually a very real and compelling rationale behind sticking to such hard routine, however unpleasant it might sound. A sophisticated enemy can learn a great deal even from human body waste: if several deposits are left around an LUP, that alone can betray the size of the patrol. Closer analysis of the contents can reveal the make-up of the troops. Here in the Iraqi desert, half-digested bacon, potatoes and sweetcorn would signify British and American forces; rice and beef, Arab-nation troops.

The golden rule was to leave whatever terrain you'd camped in exactly as you had found it. It's an ill-disciplined and unprofessional outfit that scatters any kind of military detritus in its wake: spent ration packs, discarded food, cartridges, cigarette butts, faeces. A group of men at arms who leave no trace – ghost-like – are a force to be reckoned with.

As we crawled towards the MSR at our signature snail's pace, the terrain became more rocky and unnavigable. Every now and again I felt a sudden impact as we collided with an unseen boulder, the thump echoing out across the desert, the impact wrenching the steering wheel from Driller's hands. Once or twice we kangarooed through a wide pothole, crashing down one side and bumping up the next. Were they bomb craters? They certainly felt as if they might be. Either way, it made for horrendous driving: noisy as hell, nerve-shredding, exhausting and horribly punishing on the vehicles.

All we needed was to damage a wheel or to suffer a puncture, and we'd be in serious trouble. In mobility ops, speed and keeping on the move is your single greatest friend. That's what Minky, B Squadron's Mobility Troop staff sergeant, had drummed into me countless times over, when I'd served my year in his troop. Unless cammed up under the nets in an LUP, you have to keep mobile. If you were forced to go static and you got spotted, it would give the enemy time to organize a hunter force and to set out in numbers. The trick was to keep on the move and to remain elusive, whenever you weren't lying low.

As we pushed onwards across the dark terrain, steering a course north and east all the time, I reminded myself of the secret to driving across such ground, something Minky had drilled into us ad nauseam. If you gripped the steering wheel tight with your thumbs on the inside, you were likely to suffer a right embuggerance. If you hit a boulder, even at the speeds we were driving at, the steering wheel could wrench so violently that the spokes would rip your thumbs out of their sockets.

'Hold the wheel lightly, mate, thumbs on the outside,' I reminded Driller, having to shout to make myself heard over the din of the wagon's progress. 'Otherwise you'll injure your hands.'

Normally, I'd expect a good deal of slagging from Driller about being such a fussing mother hen, when he was already doing it exactly as he should. Or about the fact that he was missing half of one hand anyway, so what was the big worry. But not now. Not tonight. Not where we were heading.

Eventually, we figured we had to switch to the night-vision kit, to try to steer a way through. Driller broke out his NVGs, or passive night-vision goggles (PNGs), to give them their more accurate name. PNGs work by magnifying and intensifying the natural light thrown off by moon and stars. Coalition planners had set 16 January 1991 as the start date for the war, partly because it was one of the first moonless nights after the deadline for Saddam's withdrawal. But now was several days hence and the moon hung low on the horizon, a thin sliver etched in the sky. With almost zero light pollution in the desert, even that small amount of illumination dispelled most of the shadows, especially when viewed via PNGs.

On a good night PNGs can 'see' up to about 200 metres. But the chief downside is that they are big, bulky bits of kit and very tiring to use. They slot down in front of your eyes, suspended on something that looks like a head-torch's cradle. But after just a few hours with around a kilogram of kit strapped to the front of your face, your neck muscles start to burn and spasm with the strain. Over long periods of use, the optics make your eyes and your brain throb, because your senses are having to process a massive information overload, as they try to make sense out of the artificially boosted imagery.

Worst of all is the blinding effect. If a driver using PNG is suddenly faced with an intense light source – vehicle headlamps or the flash of a muzzle firing – the PNG is 'whited out', becoming awash with intense light, leaving the operator with no natural night vision to speak of. It takes several minutes for the eyes to readjust, during which time he's blinded – fumbling around like a drunkard – leaving him at the mercy of the enemy.

Using PNGs also gives you little ability to judge distance. Driller might see a boulder up ahead very clearly, but misinterpret how close it actually was. In no time he could run the wagon onto it, with catastrophic consequences. The answer was for me to make intermittent use of my pocket night-vision-scope, resembling a smallish pair of binoculars, which I kept slung around my neck, along with the dog tags and the morphine syrettes. I could take a quick butcher's with the scope, scanning the way ahead, then let it drop onto its straps, leaving me free to talk Driller around whatever was coming.

'Okay, mate, you've seen that large boulder up ahead, 11 o'clock? About the size of a 50 cal ammo tin.'

'Got it.'

'Right. It's 70 yards away and closing. I'll talk you around it.'

'Got it.'

Like this we nosed ahead, trying to keep the two wagons spaced around 100 metres apart. If the ambient light lessened, we'd close up the gap, doing the reverse if it grew brighter. The strict discipline of night navigation had to be maintained no matter what, and the toll and strain of such constant watchfulness was immense. The psychological stress was magnified by the fact that such mind-numbing monotony might be punctuated at any moment by savage eruptions of combat. We had to remain alert to our location on the ground, and in relation to the other wagon, while mastering the complex art of dead reckoning, and also keeping a lookout for the enemy, at the same time as fighting the urge for rest and sleep.

In this way, moving at a little above walking pace and with the tension rising with every turn of the wheels, we crept ever closer towards the MSR. We were doing everything we could to try to minimize the sound we made and the dust thrown up by the tyres. This close to the main artery of Scud Alley, the slightest thing could draw the enemy. But no matter how carefully we tried to drive, the wagons were creaking and groaning like a couple of bedframes suffering a severe case of demonic possession.

I was painfully aware that we were closing in on the enemy, yet we were so glaringly overt – bang, crash, wallop, bang – and it sent the adrenaline spiking. Surely Saddam's Scud routes had to be closely guarded, and here we were about to execute a very noisy arrival. Nothing like making an entrance.

After two hours crawling across the night-dark desert, Jim's truck finally ground to a halt. We pulled up alongside it and killed our engine. He lent across for a word. By his reckoning, Jim figured the MSR was no more than half a kilometre away. We double-checked and our calculations pretty much matched his.

Close now.

We dismounted to get a look at the ground, only to discover that the terrain here was even worse than where we had spent the previous night. It had a consistency not far removed from con-crete. No one was about to dig in an OP anywhere hereabouts, meaning the very idea of hunkering down in sight of the MSR was out of the question. It was impossible for us with the wagons, but even eight guys moving on foot wouldn't be able to dig any kind of usable hide.

Up ahead we could see the odd flash of light, so we figured this had to be the MSR. We reasoned we had no option but to keep watch from our present position, while remaining in the wagons. Should anyone glance in our direction, what would they see? Two distant vehicles parked up in the open. We knew the Iraqi Army had GAZ-69 jeeps, a Russian-made 4x4 manufactured by Gorkovsky Avtomobilniy Zavod. At a glance the short-wheel-base, two-door GAZ, with its canvas back and pick-up-style rear, didn't look a great deal different from our own vehicles, the Dinky especially.

Ironically, bringing the Dinky might actually prove a bonus here in Iraq. At a distance at least, it could double as a GAZ. We decided this would be our modus operandi – hiding in plain sight – for tonight. Indeed, there was no other option.

Via our KITE sights, a long-distance night-viewing scope, we should be able to keep a close eye on anything moving up and down the MSR. With 4x magnification and a 500 metre reach under clear starlight – and more than six times that in moon-light – we should be able to take note of any vehicles of interest and their coordinates. Designed to bolt onto an array of weaponry, the KITE sight's reticule displays a three-armed cross-hair for targeting, plus a scale for calculating range.

Sadly, some bright spark had forgotten to pack the mounting rails, via which the KITE sight would attach to our assault rifles, and I'd been unable to scrounge any. But as a handheld night-spying device, it was perfect for what we now had in mind. Via the KITE sights and our Magellan GPSs, we could nail the location of any target and radio coordinates through to headquarters. That's if we could get the comms working, but right now we had to presume that Chewie could, for there was no point us being here otherwise.

Decision made, I broke out our KITE sight, removed the lens cap and nestled my left eye against the smooth rubber eyepiece. As I rotated the focus ring, all of a sudden the terrain half a kilometre ahead was pulled into sharp focus. Using one arm crooked at a right angle and propped onto the Dinky's bonnet, I managed to brace against the KITE sight's weight, cutting out the worst of the image wobble. But over time that would grow tiring as hell, so I grabbed my Bergen from the rear of the wagon, bunged it on the bonnet and nestled the KITE sight on top of that. Perfect.

With Jim doing the same in the Pinkie, now all we had to do was to wait for the first of Saddam's convoys.

All eight of us were permanently stood to, ready to move at a moment's notice. While Jim and I were focused on the MSR, Driller and Scouse – my and Jim's drivers – were poised to take notes, as we related to them anything of interest. That way, Jim and I could keep our eyes glued to the scopes. At the same time the others had their eyes out on stalks, scanning the terrain 360 degrees all around, just in case.

At first sight the MSR seemed a curious affair and not at all what I had been expecting. Via the KITE sight, I detected a wide expanse of terrain showing clear signs of use by vehicles. But here at least this was no hard-surfaced motorway. This was more a variation on the proverbial camel track, only it was much wider and more intensively used, the route having been cleared of all obstructions. With the desert being flat and rock solid anyway, maybe it made sense that no hard surface needed to be laid down. Once a route was cleared of boulders, it was a case of put pedal to the metal and let rip.

Sound travels for ever in the desert at night. We sat there

enveloped in the silence, the only noise being the gentle plinking of the engine blocks as they cooled. The first sign that anything was moving out there was the faint throb of an engine, a way to the east of us.

'Hear that?' I whispered at the others. The desert makes you speak in hushed tones, no matter how isolated you are.

There was a series of nods. Everyone could hear it.

I swivelled the KITE sight in the general direction and a halo of light appeared. Or rather there were two, moving in a slow crawl.

'Headlamps, two sets, moving west on the MSR,' I whispered. 'Stand by.'

Night after night, Stormin' Norman Schwarzkopf had had several squadrons of F-15E Strike Eagles – the long-range multi-role strike fighter – scouring these very deserts for Scud traffic. Night after night the F-15 aircrews had returned with the same frustrating reports: no targets found or destroyed. We were about to appreciate exactly why.

'Vehicles moving into view,' I related. 'Looks like some kind of Nissan-type bus, with a low-loader truck following.'

Driller repeated it back to me, so I knew he'd noted it down correctly.

As the pair of vehicles crawled closer, the low-loader pulled ahead of the bus, taking up the lead. As they passed the nearest point to where we were located, I could make out everything in close-up, grainy, green-hued detail: the grime-encrusted windows, the dirty wheel arches, the billowing dust thrown up in the low-loader's wake backlit by the bus's blazing headlamps. I could all but read the numberplates, the image was so sharp.

But what I couldn't figure out was the convoy's role or intentions. The low-loader had something big and bulky on the rear, but it was tightly sheeted over with tarpaulins. I guessed it could be a Scud, but then again it could just as easily be any kind of cargo. Plus the bus had occupants: I could tell by the shadows moving behind the windows. But as it was caked in a thick film of dust, I couldn't see exactly who or what they were. Could be a Scud crew. Could be Baghdad United FC off to play Amman FC at a game of footie.

At my side I could sense that Driller was keen for more details. Trouble was, I didn't know exactly what to say. 'One bus, one truck, civvie colours; no idea what they're carrying or the ID of the occupants.'

'So, is the bus and truck a suspect Scud crew?' Driller pressed.

'No way of knowing. Truck's a Scania, khaki yellow, six wheels on either side. Bus is a bog-standard Nissan tour bus kind of thing. White.'

'So, it's no Scud support convoy?'

'No way of calling it either way.'

Back at Camp Victor the Green Slime had briefed us about how Saddam had taken to hiding his Scuds on civilian buses, the same type of white coaches you'd see packed full of grey-rinse grannies on a sightseeing tour to Bridgend. He'd removed the seats and cut entry hatches into the rear of the vehicles, so the Scuds could be slotted aboard. So I understood what Driller was driving at. I knew how unlikely it was for a busload of grannies to be nipping across the desert for a jolly, at well after midnight and at the height of the Gulf War.

The argument was there for radioing in a target warning, one that might change the course of the war. But when all was said and done, it was impossible to be absolutely certain. We made note of the speed, bearing and position of the convoy, figuring we'd radio headquarters with a full description of what we'd seen. That way, the decision of what to do about it was out of our hands. But one thing was becoming clear as we sat there scrutinizing the MSR. It was clawing at my mind, snapping at my thoughts. *You need to get closer. You need to get closer. You need to get close enough to see the whites of their eyes.*

Of course, normally we could and we would. In the depths of the jungle, up snow-covered mountains, in remote rural terrain, in urban areas even – we could always dig, excavate, build or requisition some kind of hide. In Northern Ireland blokes would spend days on end camped out in boggy woodland or hedgerows, well dug in and soaked to the skin, remaining invisible and undetected as they kept eyes-on a suspect farmstead. But out here amidst this wide-open, rock-hard terrain devoid of cover, what were the options for getting any closer? I just couldn't seem to think of any.

I figured I'd compare notes with Jim and see what he thought; or maybe as an entire patrol – pool our ideas. But first off, we had a distant pulse of light on the eastern horizon: more vehicles inbound. I swung the scope around, as Driller hunched himself deeper into his seat to better guard against the chill, hands poised with notebook and pencil. By the looks of things, we faced a long wait until whatever it might be hove into view.

The procedure we were adopting here was tried and tested in the SAS and was known as 'road watch'. It was something that had first been developed in World War Two by the Long Range Desert Group (LRDG), the forerunner to the SAS, and it had become one of the most reviled missions. Road watch was perfected in North Africa, where the MSR ran along the thin strip of cultivable land that fringes the Mediterranean, inland of which lay only the sun-blasted wastes of the Sahara. The LRDG had figured out that a five-week drive across supposedly impassable desert would bring them to the fringes of the MSR, undetected by the enemy.

Hidden on a ridge just to the south of the MSR, they had recorded enemy vehicles passing to and fro, radioing back details to headquarters. Laid up just a few hundred metres from General Erwin Rommel's 'Panzer Alley' – the route via which his armour was rushed to the frontline – the slightest slip might spell discovery, capture or death. But much as the men of the LRDG had appreciated the value of reporting Rommel's strengths, road watch had proved a crushing monotony. In reality, none of the men could appreciate the truly war-changing nature of their work, for it was blanketed in the highest level of secrecy possible: 'Ultra'.

The 'Ultra' classification covered the top-secret work of Bletchley Park, breaking the enemy's codes. Since spring 1940 Britain had been intercepting the Third Reich's most sensitive signals. They were encoded upon the Enigma machine, an ingenious encryption device that was able to churn out an almost unlimited number of unique ciphers. Enigma's codes were so complex as to be unbreakable, or so the Germans had believed. But at Bletchley, a team of codebreaking wizards had worked feverishly to achieve the seeming impossible, prising open Enigma's secrets.

But the messages intercepted from North Africa had proved vexing. The Allies suspected that Rommel was deliberately under-reporting his strength, consistently putting forward his worst case to Berlin, in an effort to win more men, tanks and supplies. But if they were wrong, was Rommel somehow feeding the British deliberate misinformation? Was Bletchley's work being used against them? In short, had the Germans rumbled Bletchley's breakthrough and turned it against the Allies?

The answers to such questions lay in road watch, the real objective of which was to prove it either way. Hunkered down on their ridge, noting every vehicle that passed and radioing through details, the LRDG proved that Rommel was indeed under-reporting his strengths to Berlin. Such intel coups had done much to help win the war in North Africa, the first major Allied victory, one that Churchill credited with turning the tide of World War Two.

At Hereford we strived to learn from such early operations, and the tactics, techniques and procedures (TTPs) that lay behind them. Now here we were, several decades later, doing almost a carbon copy of those pioneering missions. Our personal weapons were a little more advanced, the vehicles a little more capable – though lacking the armaments the LRDG had boasted – but otherwise very little had changed. As to our chief adversary, Saddam Hussein was every bit as wily as Rommel. And the nature of the intel we were gathering had similar potential to change the outcome of the war.

With Saddam hurling Scuds into Israel, we were on the brink

of World War Three. The Israeli Knesset – that nation's parliament – had a zero-tolerance policy towards attacks launched on Israeli soil. The concept of an eye for an eye was applied towards all such aggressors. Saddam, via his Scud attacks, had wounded and killed scores of Israeli citizens, and there was a clamour for retaliatory action. If we failed in our mission, it might cause the conflict to spiral out of control.

At all costs, Israel had to be prevented from going to war with Iraq. If that happened, Arab nations would desert the Coalition, and the genie would be out of the bottle. Making the correct call about a passing convoy tonight could make all the difference between a world at peace and a world at war. As we settled down to scrutinize whatever the distant lights on the MSR might bring, my mind flipped back to the last time I'd found myself on the cusp of triggering World War Three.

It was a couple of years back and I'd been on a HALO training course in Norway. HALO stands for high-altitude low-opening – a means to insert a force of men covertly into enemy territory. Basically, you jump from extreme high altitude, plummet through a monster freefall, then pull your chute at low altitude and execute a landing. In the process of that giant rollercoaster ride, your intention is to have crossed from friendly to hostile territory, utterly unseen and undetected, even by the enemy's radar.

This time, we were jumping at night, right on the very frontier with Russia. Sensitive. Poking the bear. Not a lot of people realize it, but at Norway's far northeasterly tip the nation shares a stretch of border with Russia. It is remote, mountainous, freezing, wind-blasted and barren in the extreme. A winter jump over Norway's high northern latitudes is like plunging into the proverbial freezer: it is thirty to forty degrees below, and that's before you've leapt out of the aircraft.

Consequently, on the long flight in, our eyelids had started to ice together, it was so unbelievably cold. Whenever anyone asks me what is the scariest thing I've done in the SAS, I tell them it's the night jumps. There is just so much that can go wrong, so many ways to end up dead. And on this one, it was about as daunting as it gets, for all the obvious reasons.

We jumped in all our specialist HALO kit, looking like astronauts diving into the dark void. Sucking on oxygen, we plummeted the first 1,000 feet in a little over ten seconds. By that time we'd reached terminal velocity – 120 mph – which meant that every five seconds we were plunging through 1,000 feet of icy blue. At that speed if you collide with another parachutist, you could very easily end up badly injured or knocked unconscious. Even worse was to smash into the large and bulky cargo pack which accompanied us, and was stuffed with all the heavy and specialist kit that cannot be strapped to your person. It's pushed out of the ramp and the jumpers follow, the cargo pack's parachute being triggered to open at a point where it can be tracked to the DZ.

At 120 mph the windchill meant you were being frozen alive. Worse still, your jump devices were freezing up, including your altimeters and compasses – the means to guide you to the DZ. My goggles and my oxygen mask had crusted over with ice, which meant that I couldn't see a damn thing. I'd packed on the clothing beneath the HALO suit, layering on thermals beneath fleecy kit, until I was bloated out like the Michelin man. Even so, I could feel the air cutting into me, working its way up my body to my mask.

Much as you might try to make it otherwise, your jump kit is never symmetrical: in particular your heavy Bergen, oxygen tubes and strapped-on assault rifle prove especially unwieldy. At this kind of velocity, that can cause you to wobble and buffet violently, threatening to flip you over or to send you into a spin. So, as you plummet towards earth you're fighting against the very air itself. You have to remain stable, in preparation for the moment when you release your chute. That's when things can go badly wrong. If you deploy in a spin, you can tangle up like a bundle of damp washing. Your chute can catch on your kit, and your hands are so frozen that you can't 'cut away' – getting rid of the malfunctioning parachute, so you can trigger your reserve.

At 3,500 feet my barometric release mechanism – the automatic opening device (AOD) as it's called – triggered, and I felt the chute billow out above me. Riding under the square rig, I now had to steer myself onto the DZ, positioned on the Norwegian side of the border. Trouble was, I couldn't see a damn thing through the ice caking my goggles and cementing my eyelids, and in any case the weather guys had called it wrong. The DZ lay southwest of where we had made the jump, the Russian border due east, and sure enough the wind was blowing in the wrong direction, towards the Russian side.

No matter how I fought against it, trying to steer my chute the opposite way, I feared I was going to miss the DZ, which meant going down in unknown territory. We were eight in the jump stick, and each of us was laden down with some 200 pounds of kit and weaponry. I could feel the sheer dead weight of it hanging off my person and cutting into me, further restricting my blood supply and making my extremities turn numb.

I reached up for the steering toggles and began to try to steer my way to the DZ, but my hands were just so deadened with the cold, despite the thick gloves. If you have the breeze behind you – as we were supposed to – you turn with the assistance of the wind and it catches your chute, speeding you along in the direction you need to go. But right now I had to try to swing around into it, as my airspeed fought to conquer the headwind, to batter a way through.

It was just about first light by then, so there was enough illumination to steer a course by, if only I could see. My mind felt utterly frazzled and disorientated. Frozen to the core, light-headed with the oxygen, locked inside the iced-up world of the HALO mask, I was suffering what we term the tunnel effect – where your senses begin to close in on you and shut down. I had to scream at myself: *Focus. Focus. Fucking focus, Des!*

Not a moment too soon, I realized I was about to hit the ground. I let my Bergen drop away, falling beneath me on its length of rope, so it struck first, taking the impact of its own weight. I saw it plunge into a thick drift, disappearing completely from view. Seconds later I felt my feet plunge into the snow and I came to a halt buried up to my shoulders. I had no idea which side of the border I was on, or how I was going to extricate myself, or where the other guys in my stick might have landed.

Laden down with such immense amounts of kit, it was going to take a superhuman effort just to get out of the snow-hole. We had snowshoes strapped to our Bergens, so in theory we should be able to strap them on and move out on those, heading for friendly soil, but only if we could free ourselves. If we didn't, I didn't doubt that the Russians were coming.

Barely had my frozen senses processed all the thoughts that were jumbling through my head when I heard the rhythmic beat of an incoming helicopter cutting through the air. Either this was good news, or it was very, very bad. Either it was a Norwegian military Puma, or it was a Soviet Mi-8 Hip – their distinctive, squat, ugly-looking but bulletproof reliable troop-transport helicopter, in which case myself and some of the other lads were going in the bag.

We might try to argue it was a training exercise gone wrong, but it sure wouldn't look that way. We were fully bombed-and-armed up, and with the Soviet Union threatening to fragment, and with violent unrest sweeping many of its constituent states, it would be easy enough to see us as a covert NATO force, infiltrating Mother Russia in an effort to fuel that disquiet.

And who knew where that might lead.

As the mystery helo bore down on me, my hands were so numb that I had to keep whacking them against my sides, just to try to get some of the blood flow and the warmth back into them. The drill is that a helo can't land until you've got control over your parachute. Otherwise, the downdraft of the rotors could reinflate the chute, with disastrous consequences. Either the jumper might get dragged across the ground, or the expanse of silk might get sucked up into the rotors, bringing the helicopter crashing down.

I raced to drag in my chute, and to gather up the rest of my gear. When the helo finally hove into view, I felt a massive flood of relief. It had the distinctive silhouette of a Norwegian

Air Force Puma, complete with helo-skis fitted over its wheels. Demonstrating incredible flying skills, the pilot put it down on the snow no more than 30 metres from me, as the loadie dived off and dashed to my aid.

'Get yourself on the aircraft!' he yelled, jerking a thumb at the open side door, and grabbing a handful of my kit. 'We've got to go find the rest of your guys!'

I stumbled, crawled and dragged myself and my gear onto that Puma, and moments later we were airborne. We flew about the snowscape, gathering up the rest of the stick. Once all were aboard, we made ourselves scarce. When all was said and done, we'd got out of there with no harm done. At least, not World War Three-triggering stuff. It had been an awesome exercise, giving us a real feel for what infiltrating Russia would be like for real, never mind the kind of tasks we would have to undertake once we got there.

But here in Iraq, when executing road watch, one wrong call and who knew where it all might end.

An hour before first light we pulled back from our position overlooking the MSR. It had been one busy night. Having observed that second convoy with much the same results as the first – was it a civvie set of transports, or one of Saddam's covert Scud moves? – we'd executed a U-shaped manoeuvre, moving away from the MSR, so as to approach it again a good way eastwards, probing for a more favourable position, one that would get us closer to the enemy. But frustratingly, the ground there had proved no better than before. It remained stubbornly, resolutely board-flat and concrete-like.

Yet right now, we had far more pressing issues to deal with.

As the horizon towards the east began to brighten with the first hints of daybreak, we crawled away from the MSR, searching for a place to hide. But the terrain was about the most inhospitable and forbidding that I had ever laid eyes upon. Our flame-haired Hobbit would have had problems finding anywhere to dig a Hobbit hole, let alone locating somewhere to conceal eight blokes, one the size of the BFG, plus the two wagons.

By 0530 hours we were starting to get just a little unsettled and jumpy. *Where in the name of God were we going to go to ground?*

CHAPTER TEN

CHEMICAL WARRIORS

In Iraq's Western Desert at this time of year, the sun rises just before seven in the morning and sets just prior to six in the evening. But first light comes at least an hour earlier, and after sundown the brightness lingers in the wide-open skies for a good while. We figured we had around forty-five minutes in which to find some cover and to establish an LUP. We weren't searching for a classic hide any more – a deep ravine or wadi, offering cover from view and great all-around defence. Any dip or pinprick would do.

It reached 0600 hours, and still we'd seen the square root of sod all. Tactically speaking, this kind of billiard-table terrain made operations such as ours a near impossibility. But we were here now, and unless we found something pretty damn smartish, we were deep in the shit. As we continued to trundle across the barren moonscape, I forced myself to contemplate what we would do if things didn't rapidly – miraculously – improve.

Was that it, then? Did that spell endex? Would we turn tail and make a dash for the Saudi border? Right now we had the previous night's convoy details to radio back to headquarters: did we just abandon all that, turn tail and run? Or did we accept the fact that we'd have to park up in the open, cam net the wagons, and sit there like lemons, hoping we didn't get noticed? Hiding in plain sight, we'd have to hope the Iraqis would conclude we were some of their own, but there were no guarantees.

One thing I knew for sure – with my Para Reg mentality, I couldn't face the prospect of running for home.

More by luck than good judgement or skilful navigation, we found a place of sorts. It was little more than a slight undulation in the landscape, but if we could just nose the wagons into that and get them netted over, from a distance we might conceivably avoid notice. In any case, first light was almost upon us and we were all out of options.

Before pulling into the LUP we performed a 'short stop' – halting adjacent to our intended place of hiding, killing the engines and executing a short listening watch. As we could detect zero sign of the enemy, we snuck into our place of uncertain refuge. We did a hurried repeat of the first night's setting camp – scratching out some shell scrapes as best we could, while Chewie got on the radio.

That day – our second in Iraq – everyone was craving sleep. The sheer exhaustion of being on the go 24/7 was catching up with us all. More to the point, the constant nervous tension of driving at night and keeping hyper-alert was incredibly tiring. We set a stag roster, after which those not on sentry were free to get some kip. As for me, what I needed first was to get a heads-up with Jim and a sense of how he saw things.

We sat in the cover of the cam nets and chewed the fat. The long and short of it was this. The only way to PID – positively identify – any Scud convoys was to get closer to the MSR. Much closer. On that we were 100 per cent in agreement. But if we tried to do that, we were bound to get compromised. If that happened, neither of us rated our chances. The GAZ could reach speeds of 100 kph – around 60 mph – and it was a tried and tested performer across such terrain. The Iraqi Army also boasted some 2,000 BMPs – Soviet tracked infantry fighting vehicles – which were superlative performers off-road, plus T-72 main battle tanks. In an outright chase, any of those could outrun an overloaded Pinkie and a Dinky. But if we didn't risk moving closer to the MSR, what was the point in being here? Any which way we looked at it, there just didn't seem to be any easy answers.

It was now that Chewie put in an appearance, having been tinkering with the comms for a good while. Sadly, his news wasn't entirely encouraging. He'd transmitted all the intel gathered during road watch, or at least he *hoped* he had. But his efforts had proved massively frustrating, for there was still not a sniff of a response from headquarters. In short, Chewie had no confirmation that any of our messages were getting through.

'Alright, but what's your best guess?' Jim pressed. 'Are they hearing us or not?'

'Yeah, I think they are,' Chewie replied.

'Chewie, you're the best there is on the comms,' I told him. 'No doubt about that. So why is it you think they're hearing us, but we can't get a sniff in return?'

He shrugged. 'Truth be told, it's just a gut feeling. Instinct. I reckon our messages are being heard, it's just the responses from headquarters that are garbled.'

'What d'you mean, "garbled"?'

Chewie paused for a moment, thinking about his answer. 'Well, it's like this. I'm getting something. I'm getting some kind of a response. Just when I try to decode it, it's nonsense. It doesn't make a blind bit of sense. It's like the comms from there to here are getting scrambled.'

Jim and I exchanged worried looks. *Did that mean what we thought it did?*

'You reckon it's the enemy?' Jim ventured. 'Are the Iraqis jamming the comms somehow?'

'Remember the briefings at Victor,' I added. 'The Iraqi military's got a shit-hot EW capability.' EW – electronic warfare – is the ability of a military force to comprehensively mess with your communications.

Chewie shook his head. 'I don't think so. If they were jamming us, we'd get nothing. Diddly squat. I'm getting a response of sorts. I'm getting bursts to download. It's just they're gobbledegook; gibberish.'

None of us knew what to make of it, except that this wasn't the most heartening of news. Driller came over to join us. Turned out that he couldn't sleep, and all because he was dying for a ciggie. The sole guy on our patrol who smoked, he'd been teased remorselessly back at Camp Victor. He was only allowed to have a fag in full daylight, due to us being on hard routine, for the glow of a cigarette can be a dead giveaway. That meant he had a good few minutes still to wait.

As he sat there fidgeting away, he was like a cat on hot bricks. I figured now was as good a time as any to needle him, all in the cause of lifting the mood, of course. I made a show of patting my combat pockets all over, as if I was searching for something.

Eventually, someone took the bait. 'What's eating you? Can't you sit still, or something?'

'It's me fags,' I replied, deadpan. 'Has anyone seen me fags?'

Driller glared. 'Fuck off, Des, you northern git.'

I could see the shoulders of the other two rocking back and forth. Like with any good wind-up, you couldn't do it too often, 'cause little is best. Avoid overkill.

'Look, Driller, why don't you just pack it in?' I suggested. 'I mean, it's bad for you. This is your time.'

For a while now we'd been trying to convince Driller that this was the moment for him to quit. His chosen brand was Silk Cut, which were supposedly 'low tar', but even so no one wanted to sit in a billowing cloud of cigarette smoke, as it pooled beneath the cam netting. Hence our desire to get the guy to pack it in.

'Yeah, maybe you're right,' Driller conceded, but we all knew his heart wasn't in it.

We now had three blokes that I rated very highly – Jim, Chewie, Driller – getting our heads together over our present predicament. But any which way we looked at it, it was a total brain-teaser. It was messing with our heads. Normally, the answer would have been simple. We'd send a sitrep to headquarters, summarizing where we were at, and await guidance. Maybe the other Bravo patrols had put down in entirely different terrain, where digging in an OP was eminently possible. Maybe A and D Squadrons had surged across the desert, breaking through in force, showing us the way.

Trouble was, with no comms we had no way of knowing.

With no real decisions reached – other than seeing what the

day might bring – Driller and I wandered back to our wagon and crawled under the cam nets. I bagsied the spot beside the rear wheel, in the lea of the wind, Driller taking the front wheel arch. Trev was on watch at one side of the wagon, Quiet Alex on the other. The sun was up by now, and I figured visibility was good. Too good. We could see to about a dozen kilometres, which was a mixed blessing. We could spy them coming, but they could see us trying to hide.

There was nothing we could do about it, so I scrabbled a few rocks to one side, plumped up my Bergen to form a makeshift pillow, crawled into my green maggot and got my head down.

'Err, Driller, what's the point in smoking Silkies, anyway?' I asked, as I felt my wearied limbs begin to relax a little. 'Aren't they supposed to be "good for you"? Low tar or something? What's the point in that, when you're out here and at any moment you could get slotted?'

'Piss off, Des.' Still, he couldn't help but chuckle. 'You know how it is – Paras are supposed to smoke fags. That's what you do in the Maroon Machine.'

'Yeah, but you're not in the Paras any more, are you, mate?'

'Once a Para, always a Para,' Driller shot back at me.

'Tell you what,' I announced, 'why don't you take up smoking a pipe? Quite a few of the lads in the squadron do that. Sit in front of the fire and suck on a pipe – I've seen 'em doing it. The smoke smells kind of nice. None of us would mind that.'

Driller gave me a hard stare. No further words necessary.

As I tried to get to sleep, my mind re-ran the turmoil of the last forty-eight hours, which had brought us to this point. I wasn't kidding myself that we were anything other than substantially visible, not where we'd gone to ground. I consoled myself with this thought: the concept of 'hiding in plain sight' had a long history with the Regiment, and it was surprising how well it had worked for us on previous operations.

A few months back B Squadron had been scrambled for a highly unusual tasking. Our destination had been Somalia, the failed state in East Africa which has proven the bane of some of the world's foremost militaries, not least of which would be the SEALs, Rangers and Delta Force teams that would fight savage battles across the nation's capital, Mogadishu, as a result of a US raid that went badly wrong (immortalized in the book and the movie *Black Hawk Down*).

The griff – the lowdown – was this. Douglas Hurd, the then foreign secretary, was off to Somalia and he'd asked the Regiment to provide a close protection (CP) squad. Hurd's mission was to head for Mogadishu, to meet with General Mohamed Farrah Aidid, a leading Somali warlord, military commander, politician, diplomat and ... war criminal. With the country riven by bloody conflict, Aidid commanded one of Somalia's most powerful armed factions. Hurd wanted to convince Aidid to use his power and influence to enable humanitarian aid to reach the Somali people.

Hereford put together a team of six and I was lucky enough to make their number. Of course, we couldn't accompany the British foreign secretary into Somalia decked out in full regimental kit. Dropping an SAS team into Mogadishu would be like a red rag to a bull, especially with all the gunned-up militias that roamed the streets. The plan was to fly out and deploy dressed in civvies, and that meant we'd only be able to carry concealed weapons.

In the few days before departure we were briefed on the main issues: Mogadishu was divided into patches of territory, each of which was controlled by a rival armed faction. Trouble flared at the drop of a hat. Aid supplies were flown into the city's airport or delivered to the port, to be distributed across the country, but the militias fought amongst themselves to steal as much as possible.

Hurd figured that by getting Aidid – the most powerful of all the warlords – on side, he could quieten such troubled waters. In that spirit he was willing to fly into the heart of such a massively dangerous and volatile conflict, with only the six of us to stand guard over him, which was one hell of a ballsy move. You had to admire the courage and convictions of the man, but you also had to maybe wonder at his sanity.

Once we'd got ourselves ready, we were told to take a few days leave. I grabbed the weekend with Emily, before the call came through: we were deploying in forty-eight hours' time, so I was needed back at H. We flew out to Kenya – first stop on the journey – on a standard civilian airliner, trying to make like any normal bunch of blokes off for a stag do and a safari. Some of the guys had gone the extra mile, acquiring smart khaki safari suits and the like.

Upon arrival we booked into the Intercontinental Hotel in downtown Nairobi. Our weapons were in-country, so all we were awaiting now was the arrival of the big man. We'd be flying north to Mogadishu on an RAF C-130 Hercules, and one of our chief concerns was this: we could conceal 'shorts' – pistols – easily enough, but our 'longs' were a different matter.

We tried breaking down our M16s, to see if we could bag them up. But the more we tried to stuff our disassembled M16s in day-packs and the like, the more we realized how risky it was. All it would take was for a militia commander to demand to open our bags, and the shit would hit the proverbial fan. We figured there was far less chance of being subjected to body searches, so our pistols should pass muster. If we left our M16s on the C-130, as a back-stop, we could arm up with SIG Sauer P226s, a compact and superlative pistol for this kind of work, plus as many of the SIG's extended, twenty-round magazines as we could secrete on our person.

That decided, we headed for Nairobi airport to rendezvous with 'The Douglas', as we'd nickname him. We gathered for a heads-up: us lot, the foreign secretary, plus his two Special Branch escorts. The plan was to spend no more than forty-eight hours on the ground and for all of that time the C-130 would be on standby, in case we needed to bug out. We decided the Special Branch guys, who were also carrying shorts, should stick close to the foreign secretary, who was the high value target (HVT). Meanwhile, we six would satellite around him, with our eyes out on stalks.

All being well the itinerary would work like this: upon landing, we'd head out in convoy direct to a rendezvous with Aidid. We needed his blessing for what was to follow – a visit by Hurd to the city's main hospital, followed by a refugee camp and a shanty town, plus an overnight at the British Embassy, or what remained of it at the time – a skeleton crew was still in operation – before flying out the following day.

'I know this is Somalia, but I intend to get on with things

as normal and do what I do best,' The Douglas told us, calmly, which seemed to epitomize his general cool-as-a-cucumber, statesman-like attitude.

The next day we flew out in the C-130. It had been burning hot in Kenya, and would be just as torpid in Somalia, and it would prove far tougher than we imagined.

We flew into 'Mog', as it's known, and I will never forget the landing. The C-130 came in low over this gorgeous expanse of turquoise ocean, fringed with reefs and white sandy beaches. From a distance it looked like an archetypal tropical paradise. The reality was far different. The pilot touched down on the runway of Mogadishu International Airport, but it was pock-marked with craters and he had to dodge this way and that, to bring us to a standstill in one piece. That done, the C-130's ramp whined down and the blinding Mog sunlight flooded in. The RAF loadmaster gazed out and glanced back at us, his expression saying it all: *I really do not like the look of this place.*

Thankfully, a three-vehicle convoy pitched up, which turned out to be the deputation from the British Embassy. We loaded ourselves aboard, and headed out of the airport, whereupon we linked up with our first 'escorts' – a convoy of battered Toyota Hilux pick-ups, crammed full of teenage kids sporting string vests and shades, and packing AK-47s and rocket propelled grenades (RPGs). For good measure, each of the Hiluxes had one of the highly-distinctive Russian-made DShK 12.7 mm heavy machineguns bolted to the rear.

Fast, mobile and heavily armed, these 'Technicals' as they are known struck me as being the Somali militia's equivalent of the SAS's Land Rovers, though I doubted whether the operators were quite as intensively trained as us lot. There was a lot of yelling and bravado and brandishing of RPGs, as the convoy got underway, most of which I figured was to impress us lot. I got busy snapping a few pics, as the militia guys struck suitably fearsome poses, whilst clinging on to the sides of the Technicals. It was worth trying anything, to keep this lot happy.

Once upon a time Mogadishu had clearly been a beautiful city, with grand colonial-style whitewashed buildings and wide sun-washed plazas running down to the glittering oceanfront. One day, I told myself, I'd like to bring the wife here for a holiday. But not right now. Right now the place was in rag order. Everywhere I looked the streets were lined with blasted, windowless shells, which had once been people's homes, and piles of stinking refuse lay rotting on every corner.

As we got closer to the city centre, our 'escorts' hung back warily, for we were nearing handover time – the point at which one militia's territory became another's. Up ahead, a simi-lar-looking bunch in a similar group of Technicals were shouting and gesticulating and puffing their chests out, as they awaited our arrival. The further we ventured into downtown Mog, the more handovers seemed to take place and each 'escort' seemed to be more heavily armed and to hem us in ever more tightly.

I glanced at the others on the team: all it would take was for one militia guy to let rip with his DShK and we would be sand-wiched right in the midst of it all.

Quite suddenly the convoy vomited itself into this big, open park-like area, which actually seemed remarkably intact. I glanced around the surprisingly airy space: white-painted walls, curving pathways and ranks of palm trees galore. It all appeared comparatively clean and well-kept. But what really drew my eye was the vehicle parked right in the centre of it all. It was a gleaming white Range Rover complete with dark tinted windows, which in central Mog looked so utterly out of place it was as if aliens had landed.

We pulled to a halt alongside it. A figure stepped out, flashing a broad smile, and sporting a dapper button-down shirt, rolled-up sleeves, khaki slacks and shiny shoes.

No doubt, this was Aidid.

Douglas Hurd stepped out from our convoy, and the two greeted each other and shook hands. Meanwhile, we six fanned out, jockeying for position – for if it was going to kick off it stood to rights it would do so now. I hunkered down by a wall, trying to work out where would give our HVT best cover.

Hurd and Aidid stood there in the open chatting away, as if they had all the time in the world. I'd have preferred them to have moved into some cover, but there was sod all any of us could do about that now. If it all went noisy, we'd have to try to bundle Hurd into our vehicles and to fight our way back the way we had come, making for the airport. If we made it, we'd have to rush him aboard the C-130 and get airborne, for that was our only ticket out of there.

It was a very tall order, whichever way you looked at it.

All of a sudden Hurd and Aidid were smiling broadly, before they embraced and shook hands again. I could hear them making some kind of arrangement to meet later, presumably to cement their friendship over a good few beers. Or maybe not, as Aidid at least probably didn't drink, so maybe over a good hookah pipe or two. No sooner had they bidden each other farewell, than Aidid clambered into the Range Rover and was gone, and we mounted up our convoy and left by the other side of the square.

Noticeably, there were no Technicals in attendance any more. With Aidid's blessing it seemed we had the freedom of Mog, no escort required. First stop was the city's main hospital. With all my medical training, I could tell right away what an appalling state the place was in; it was crammed full of the starving, the sick and those with gunshot wounds. They were laid on stretchers in corridors surrounded by dirty and rusting medical kit, and with bugger all medicines. It was like something out of a Freddy Krueger movie.

From there we headed to a refugee camp, which turned out to be a bit of an anti-climax, after the hospital from hell. The place had just a few dozen people in it, whereas we had been expecting a biblical multitude. We spent the entire time during the visit circling around Hurd protectively.

'I was expecting a lot more refugees than this,' I remarked to one of the aid workers.

He shrugged. 'Only the brave make it this far. The factions kill them off or scare them away before they even make it into the city.'

He explained how the delivery day for aid supplies was generally a Tuesday, so that was the day the fighting would really spike. There was always some kind of shootout and people always got killed. Sometimes, the aid workers were caught in the crossfire. Recently, a Dutchman had been trying to ensure some of the aid actually got to those most in need, when a teenage militiaman walked right up to him and shot him in the head. No doubt about it, these aid worker types were brave souls.

From there, we made our way to the British Embassy, or what remained of it. We reached the entrance at around three o'clock, which was perfect timing for afternoon tea, as it happened. The gates swung open, we drove in, and suddenly we found ourselves amongst beautifully manicured grounds, with tables and chairs already set for what looked like a garden party. The contrast to the Freddy Krueger scenes of earlier could not have been more complete.

We took our seats, only to be served on the Embassy's finest china with English Breakfast tea, tuna and cucumber sandwiches, Rich Tea biscuits – the works. Who would have thought there was a war on? Of course it couldn't last. We hadn't been there long when word reached us that trouble had flared: somewhere in the city there had been a shooting. Tempers were running high. We advised The Douglas to curtail the rest of his trip, and to head direct for the airport, so we could get ourselves the hell out of Dodge.

To his credit, Douglas Hurd listened to us and heeded our advice, so we necked a last few sarnies and got on our way. We made haste towards Mogadishu International Airport, which thankfully lay not so far from the Embassy. As we drew closer I could see the solid, reassuring form of the C-130 awaiting us out on the runway. *Thank Christ for that,* I told myself. *At least the whirlybird looks unmolested and good to go.*

Barely had I entertained such thoughts when there was a deafening eruption of fire. It had the unmistakable bass punch of a DShK heavy machinegun, which is basically the Russian equivalent of our own Browning .50-calibre HMG. *Thud-thud-thud-thud-thud* went the opening burst, after which the echoes from the fire reverberated like thunder back and forth across the airfield.

Our convoy came to a sudden halt. I could see where a Technical had skidded onto the apron and opened up, the DShK's muzzle spitting gouts of thick flame like some enraged dragon. I flicked my eyes across to the C-130, fearing it was the target. But whatever the gunner seemed to be unleashing upon, it didn't appear to be our means of getting out of there. Not yet, anyway.

A swarm of airport staff rushed towards the Technical, trying to drag the gunmen bodily from its rear. Amidst all the yelling and the screaming and the chaos, I could get the gist of what they were saying: *What the fuck are you up to? Can't you see the big cheese from Britain is here?*

I wondered what exactly we would do if the guys in the Technical refused to play ball. Would we six execute some kind of fire-and-manoeuvre from here to the C-130, with only our pistols to put down the rounds? Or would we take out the Technical and its occupants first, before making our move? Either way, there was nothing like being outgunned.

Finally, the firing from the Technical petered out, with us being none the wiser as to what exactly had been the cause of all the rumpus. Meanwhile, The Douglas was sitting in his vehicle, seemingly utterly unperturbed – probably finishing off The Times crossword, as he waited for everything to 'settle down'. Word was given to move again and we made a dash for the C-130, at which point we began our hurried goodbyes.

But as we went to mount the aircraft's open ramp, there was another, fiercer eruption of fire. This time it was met by a retaliatory burst, leaving none of us in any doubt that this was a

Yours truly, Des Powell, having a natter with the boss. We're conferring on tactics. The WWII founders stressed the concept of 'merit above rank' and that the SAS would be a 'classless' institution. True to form, you can see by the body language that this is a conversation of equals.

Left: A and D Squadrons deployed first, overland. But then Saddam Hussein started lobbing Scud missiles into Israel, in an effort to trigger World War III. Overnight, the Scuds became the number one target, leaving only B Squadron free to be rushed into Iraq.

An Iraqi Scud. The massive MAZ-543 transport-erector-launcher (TEL) truck is cloaked in camouflage netting, making it extremely hard to find. Saddam could launch the Scuds from practically anywhere, and his missile scientists had massively boosted their range. Our mission was to hunt them down, before a chemical warhead hit Israel when all hell would be let loose.

Problem one. When we hit the desert, flying into Iraq on Chinook twin-rotor helicopters, the terrain was nothing like our briefing. It was rock-hard, billiard-table flat and devoid of even the slightest scrap of cover – hence our patrol's decision to 'hide in plain sight.'

Not for the first time, 'Murphy's law' – if it can go wrong it will – seemed to be in play. With A and D Squadrons having nabbed the best vehicles, we were forced to deploy in ones that looked not a great deal different from the Russian-made GAZ/UAZ jeep, which was used widely by the Iraqi military. In the greatest of ironies, it would enable us to hide in plain sight, making like the enemy.

When adverse weather hits the desert, it can prove catastrophic, largely because it is so unexpected. As SAS blades fought against torrential downpours, the rain turned to sleet and snow, the worst weather in living memory to hit Iraq. The eight men of our patrol were in the midst of it all, the furthest Coalition forces behind enemy lines.

My nickname in Air Troop was 'Kamikaze'. I'd earned it because of the THREE 'parachute malfunctions' I'd suffered – in other words, my 'chute failing to open properly. The wild confusion and high-octane chaos of such jumps can be sensed in these photos (I'm in the white helmet and suit). It's so easy for something to go wrong. But as a result, I'd grown accustomed to such near-death experiences, which come with the territory when serving in the Regiment. That made our freezing, snowbound Iraq sojourn just another survival challenge.

British and American warplanes headed into Iraq, as Saddam torched the desert oilfields. They were directed onto Scud missiles and their TEL launchers by SAS patrols on the ground, taking them out with pinpoint air-strikes. But due to the horrendous radio malfunctions our patrol suffered, we'd only learn how successful we'd been in eliminating such targets upon our return to headquarters.

The perfect end result of *Bravo Three Zero*'s mission: one nicely-fried and mangled Scud – this one being inspected by US forces, May 1992, at the end of the Gulf War.

Above: US General Norman Schwarzkopf shaking hands with members of the SAS, after the action was over. Fiercely opposed to special forces operations at war's outset, he was a total convert by war's end.

Left: Home for tea and medals. Prince Charles shortly after the Gulf War, paying a congratulatory visit to our Hereford base. I'm centre photo, wide-eyed and bushy-tailed, awaiting the Royal handshake.

Hereford, two years after the Gulf, assembling a team for a task in Malaysia, training their special forces and anti-terrorist units. Yours truly, Des Powell, is 'No. 7', with *Who Dares Wins* TV personality, author and good pal, Mark 'Billy' Billingham, on my shoulder, at No. 8. (*Below*) Myself, far left of photo, about to board a US Air Force Galaxy C17. After the Gulf War I'd spend another 14 years in the SAS, completing 19 in total. Happy days.

two-way firefight now, with us sandwiched bang in between. More and more vehicles started darting this way and that, most of them boasting some kind of large weapon bolted to the rear, as the tempo of fire stiffened.

'Everyone aboard! NOW!' we yelled, jerking thumbs at the open ramp. 'Mount up! Mount up! Mount up!'

Smart cookie that he was, the pilot already had the C-130's blades turning and burning. As figures dashed up the C-130's ramp, the six of us fanned out forming a thin cordon of defence. We hadn't quite drawn our SIGs yet; we hadn't quite shown our hand. But any second now . . .

The two Special Branch guys paused halfway up the ramp, seemingly torn between sticking close to their HVT and joining us on the cordon. They gave us a look, which seemed to say: *What the hell are you lot going to do against all of them?*

By way of answer we told them to get the fuck aboard, and seconds later they too were gone. One last look around the airport and it was clear that mayhem was about to ensue. On a word from our team leader we collapsed the cordon, dashed up the ramp and gave the loadie the *go, go go!*

Even as the tail began to lift, the pilot got the C-130into motion, accelerating down the runway. The accompanying thud and rattle of gunfire was just about audible, above the deafening roar of the four turboprop engines, and then we were clawing our way into the skies over Mog. Moments later we felt the whirlybird swing around and we began to power out across the open sea, the pilot all but hugging the wave-tops.

All six of us glanced at each other, with the same expressions: *Yeah, that was interesting . . .*

Four hours later we touched down in Nairobi, and Douglas Hurd made a point of coming around to personally thank each of us. I was massively impressed by how he had never once looked to any of us for help or support all the time that we had been in Mog. Self-possessed, cool, collected, he was the epitome of what a world statesman should be like.

'In spite of our somewhat hurried exit, I think we achieved quite a lot back there,' he remarked, with a chuckle. 'All in all, a very good day's work. Of course, you can't hang around for too long on these kind of trips, for obvious reasons, but all too short though it was, I enjoyed your company immensely. Please will you pass on my warmest regards to the Regiment.'

We reassured him that we would.

With that, the foreign secretary was gone, no doubt flying off to some other important assignation. As for us, we had a task or two still to achieve in Africa, as we'd decided to tack on a bit of specialist training to the end of this one. When all was said and done, we felt pretty good about the Mog mission. We'd pulled it off with barely a mishap. Hiding in plain sight had actually worked a treat.

But whether it would do so here in the Iraqi deserts was anyone's guess.

CHAPTER ELEVEN

APOCALYPSE NOW

Come nightfall there had been no alarms of any sort, so we broke down the cam netting and moved off, aiming to execute a repeat of our previous night's road watch. But something was very different now. The weather had most definitely turned. There was a bitter, biting wind blowing from the north, and we could feel a frost cutting the air. It was hard to believe it – this was the Iraqi desert after all, which we had been reassured would be like 'England in springtime' – but a cold snap seemed to be creeping in.

It was well below freezing, and the conditions were made all the worse in the open wagons. Rumbling along in the Dinky, it felt like the Brecon Beacons in the middle of a bitter January. We stopped to layer up, putting on whatever extra clothing we had, which was precious little. I handed around the Gore-Tex kit the SEAL sergeant had given us – a few pairs of gloves and hats – which right here and now could prove a lifesaver.

It had been each man's decision what cold-weather kit he would bring, and with the appalling weather briefing, plus the restricted space on the Dinky, some of the guys had opted for one fleece, and nothing more. We each had the tight, World

War Two-era Para-smocks we'd been issued with, but in truth they were pitiful bits of kit, and for sure Chewie wasn't about to squeeze into one of those. Without a proper Gore-Tex windproof at the very least, the cold cut through you like a knife.

Desperate times called for desperate measures. It was Driller who had the brainwave. He delved into the rear of the Dinky and broke out his NBC kit. Cumbersome though it was, the NBC jacket-and-trouser combo was made of a closely woven outer layer of poly-cotton, with a thick inner layer of polyurethane foam impregnated with charcoal. It was the latter that was supposed to soak up any chemical agent and prevent it from reaching your skin and killing you.

But in the darkest of ironies, it wasn't sarin nerve agent or mustard gas that was proving to be our greatest enemy right now. It was the cold. Our NBC suits offered one extra line of protection from the life-sapping chill. Designed to guard against killer agents, they were the windproof extra layer that we all craved. But there were several downsides, of course, chief amongst them being that the charcoal tended to rub off, and in no time any exposed skin would stain black. The noddy suits were also cumbersome to move and to fight in, but frankly, we were desperate.

As we nosed onwards into the freezing night, bulked up like a bunch of abominable snowmen in our NBC gear, I pondered just where we were at. The terrain didn't seem remotely different, no matter how far we moved from the DZ. It was all flat, featureless, rock-hard desert. I didn't doubt that come sun-up we'd find ourselves hiding in plain sight once again. We'd survived for two days doing just that, in our makeshift LUPs. But who knew for how much longer our luck would hold.

We were still a good distance from the MSR and moving at a crawl when we heard it: the grunt of a powerful diesel engine. Vehicles meant people and around here in the open desert at this time of night that had to signify the enemy. We pulled to a halt. The noise was coming from the far side of a low rise, and as we listened it seemed to be getting louder, which meant that some form of vehicle was approaching, moving off-road.

We needed to get eyes-on whatever it was, and we needed to do so without the Pinkie and the Dinky getting spotted. I volunteered to head to the top of the nearby rise, to take a butcher's. It was Joe, the RAF slipper queen, who offered to come with me. Two-up – you never went anywhere with less than two – we scrambled towards the ridge, not that it really warranted being called that: it was more just a blip in the landscape. Even so, bulked up in our noddy suits as we were, in no time my pulse was pounding with the exertion, and with the tension of the unseen and the unknown.

As we neared the high point we dropped to our knees, topping out crawling on our bellies. Up here, the wind was utterly punishing, as it sliced across the open desert like a knife. It cut through the NBC suits as if they were made of paper, chilling us to the marrow. As we eased our heads over the lip of land, all of a sudden we spotted it. To the west, further away from the MSR, there was a massive halo of light illuminating a vast expanse of terrain. It reminded me of the kind of effect made by ranks of arc lights, when road crews work on the motorways at night. Beneath the lights it was a veritable hive of activity. Dark, ant-like figures dashed hither and thither, moving between trucks, jeeps and other vehicles.

It had to be Iraqi military, but was this the big one – the launch site for a Scud?

Keeping low, I broke out my pocket night-vision scope from my belt kit. I studied the scene for several long moments, sweeping the lenses this way and that. I could see a lot of men in uniforms, but very few weapons. They didn't strike me as being a force preparing for some kind of a battle or sortie. It looked more like they were technicians – engineers? – preparing for some kind of military-engineering tech set-up.

But were they readying a Scud site? Was this what a Scud team in action looked like? What else might they be doing out here?

'What the hell d'you think it is?' Joe hissed.

I kept my eyes glues to the scope, as I shot back a reply: 'Bunch of RAF rock apes getting ready for their annual ball.'

'Yeah. Real funny.' Pause. 'But d'you think it could be a Scud crew? Preparing for a launch?'

'Dunno. Let's keep looking.'

I swept the scope this way and that, scanning for the smoking gun: the erect form of a V2-like missile, or a similar shape lying prone on its carrier. But no matter how hard I searched, I couldn't see anything remotely resembling a Scud. Of course, that didn't mean a thing. In the intel briefings we'd been told how Saddam had ordered the actual missiles to be delivered at the last moment, when the launch site was 100 per cent ready: that would minimize the risk of any being spotted and taken out.

Lying on our bellies in hiding, there was something mesmerizing about watching the frenetic preparations. Part of me was tempted to wait for as long as it took to actually witness the arrival of a Scud. Part of me just wanted to see one being jacked up to vertical on its launcher, as the entrails of the exhaust fumes began to curl around the fins at its base, menacingly. But it made far more sense to get the coordinates radioed back to HQ, so our fast jets could arrow in, take a look, and if necessary hit them.

After spending a good thirty minutes on that ridgeline, the two of us were chilled to the core. Decked out in our noddy suits, I'd sweated profusely during the climb, and the congealed sweat was now freezing to my body, with embedded grains of sand for extra comfort. Much longer and we'd be like blocks of ice, welded to the ground. Forcing our limbs into motion, we scrambled downslope, moving back towards the vehicles.

Once we got there, we gathered everyone for a rushed conflab. Our mission was clear. It was not to attack; not to hit the enemy. It was to radio back intel on key targets. Trouble was, we didn't know if our messages were getting through. So, did we take matters into our own hands and launch some kind of assault? Even if we did, we had to wonder what our chances were with a target like this one.

There were eight of us, in a Pinkie and a Dinky. We had no heavy weapons and nothing to engage at long range. The beauty of the .50-cal and the Mk 19 grenade launchers was that you could lob in the rounds from a good 1,500 metres away and do some real damage. If the wagons were carrying that kind of armament, we could remain where we were and arc in the fire, with a spotter on the ridge calling in the shots. The enemy would be hit by utter surprise, and with a devastating barrage of fire.

As it was, even if by some miracle we managed to shoot up the enemy with the weapons we had to hand, what were our chances of making a getaway? Unless we disabled all their vehicles, they were likely to be as fast as we were across such ground, and very likely a lot swifter. Big six-wheel-drive trucks of the types I'd seen would doubtless crunch and bust their way across the stony desert, whereas we had to feel a way through.

But the clincher was Chewie's take on things. Somehow, he was certain his signals were getting through. It was just the return messages that were proving somewhat elusive. In that case, if we could radio the enemy's coordinates to HQ, we had to presume there would follow the mother of all air missions.

Decision made.

Using our Magellan GPS, we worked out that the enemy position was around 2 km west of us. By extrapolating from our own grid, we were able to give an accurate fix on its location. That done, Chewie broke out the Clansman, rigged up his antenna and sent the burst message winging into the skies.

One of the biggest problems with the radio was the amount of time it took to set up and to crank out the message. In the briefings at Camp Victor, we'd been warned about the skills and the technological competence of the Iraqi military's DF – direction-finding – units, electronic warfare specialists who were able to trace the source of any signal. So once Chewie's burst had been sent, we packed up as fast as we could and got motoring.

When the F-16 Fighting Falcons – about the fastest warplane in the US arsenal – got over that target, their strike mission would render that convoy and the surrounding desert into fire and ruin. We did not want to be anywhere near here when that happened. If nothing else, you didn't need the brains of a rocket scientist to work out what a high-flying pilot might make of two GAZ-like jeeps trundling across the nearby desert.

Whoopee. Time for extras.

We set off, aiming to melt away into the open and to seek out a new LUP. It had taken a good while to find, scope out and report in that enemy position, and first light was but a couple of hours away. We wanted to be well hidden come sun-up. Once again, the race was on to find a half-decent place of hiding.

But barely had we covered 500 metres when the desert right on the noses of our wagons dissolved into a wall of seething flame. Out of absolutely nothing and the raw darkness, the terrain 100 metres ahead of the Pinkie just erupted into a paroxysm of flaming, fiery ruin. We ground to a halt, as the rock and sand simply transformed before our very eyes.

It was like a scene from the movie *Apocalypse Now*, when the US warplanes tear overhead, unleashing napalm, the cloud of fuel mixed with gelling agent igniting into a deadly writhing hellstorm. The massive burst of boiling orange fire rose high above us, tinged with a thick pall of black oily smoke, spreading a good 100 metres across the desert to our front.

The deafening roar of the inferno washed over us, rocking the Dinky on its springs, as the flash of the conflagration lit up a huge swathe of sky. I was so shocked, I was rendered utterly speechless. As the burning heat tore into my exposed skin, I was also shit scared. We tried to shield our faces from the whirlwind of blasted grit and rocks, as I wondered what in the name of God could have caused it. It looked to me as if a string of bombs must have tumbled into the desert, followed by the mother of all firestorms.

Obviously, Jim had pulled to a halt in the Pinkie, but his position in the lead had put him a good few dozen yards closer to the fire. Once the worst was over, we pulled up alongside his wagon. For a good few seconds we just stared at each other in a totally stunned silence. We were lost for words. Just ahead of us, the desert was still smoking and blackened from end to end, with licks of flame still crackling hungrily, and the unmistakable smell of burning gasoline lay thick in the air.

One hundred metres. It had been so damn close. Had we set off a little earlier; had we been driving a little faster; had the pilot's aim been a little more accurate – then we would have been toast. *Roasted.* That was if it *was* an airstrike. I'd not heard the slightest whisper of any warplane in the skies above us, either before the explosion or after.

'Fuck, that was close,' Jim whispered, breaking the silence, his voice laced tight with adrenaline. 'Another few yards and we'd have been in amongst that.'

'Don't I know it.' I breathed out a long exhale, releasing just a little of the pent-up tension. 'What the fuck d'you think it was?'

'No idea.' Jim paused, shaking his head in wonder. 'One thing I do know, though: we need to get the hell out of here.'

'Too right. Let's get out of here, Jim. Let's sod right off and live to fight another day.'

'Yeah.'

'So, where to?'

'You know what – anywhere that isn't here.' Jim glanced around at the others. 'Everyone okay? Anyone injured?'

Miraculously, we had come that close to getting seriously smoked and not a soul amongst us had suffered much more than a scratch.

'Right, let's get going,' Jim announced.

We gunned the engines and jolted into motion as fast as we could manage, longing to be swallowed into the night – to hide.

As we pushed ahead, I tried to make some kind of sense out of what had just happened. Had that 'napalm strike' hit us – and I didn't doubt we were the target – we'd have been completely annihilated. I could just imagine what Emily would have been told: *Your husband is missing in action and his remains have not been found.* Maybe in months to come some technical wizard would manage to scrape up a few DNA fragments from the twisted, blasted remains of the Dinky, from which they'd prove that was where the four of us had met our maker. But that would be small consolation.

These were dark, dark thoughts, and as we pressed onwards into the freezing night I couldn't seem to shake them off. Facing that napalm strike, we had come that close to getting wiped out, as I had done on countless other occasions when serving in the Regiment. But how many times could you keep cheating death, I wondered?

Three times during my time in the SAS I'd suffered a 'parachute malfunction', which is a formal term for saying that my chute had failed to open. *Three times.* With most guys in Air Troop, that never happened even once. With me it was so often that my Air Troop buddies had given me a nickname: the kamikaze. You could argue that wasn't particularly fair, because the Japanese kamikazes of World War Two volunteered to fly their warplanes into Allied targets, taking their own lives, whereas I didn't choose to suffer a parachute malfunction, not even once. But regardless, the name stuck.

The first time had been during my HALO training, which we'd been undertaking from the British military base in Cyprus. We'd been executing a jump from 12,000 feet. I'd pulled my chute at 3,500, as intended, but I sensed right away that something wasn't right. I'd glanced upwards, only to realize it was taking too long to deploy. The rigging lines were strung out above me and the expanse of silk was half-trying to inflate, as a voice yelled in my head: *Come on! Come on! Open! Open!*

I was doing what's known as a 'Roman candle' – plummeting to earth like a firework, before – *blam!* – the earth would arrive at my feet. As our instructors had stressed time and time again: *It's not the freefall that kills you, it's the ground when it hits.* We'd had it drilled into us that if you didn't like what you saw above your head, you had to cut loose and switch to your reserve. The decision to do so had to be made more or less instantly, as the ground was rushing up to meet you very, very fast.

I made the call to 'pull and punch', thinking: *Fuck, here we go – hero time.* But in the back of my mind there was a fearful voice saying: *What happens if the reserve doesn't open?* I had to force myself to ignore that voice, and to pull and punch anyway. With one hand I hit the release, to cut free from the semi-inflated chute, while the other triggered the reserve.

Momentarily I felt a surge of sickening panic, as the main chute disappeared high above me, taking all its drag with it, and sending me plunging into the freefall once more. But then the reserve snapped into shape and all of a sudden I was floating down to earth nice and easy, but with my pulse hammering away like crazy. I drifted down the last thousand feet and made a reasonable landing, all things considered.

The instructor came over for a word. 'Right then, Des: what was the problem up there?'

'I didn't like what I saw above me head.'

'Fair enough. Good drills. It just shows you, the system works. You're here to jump another day.'

Indeed I was. Thank fuck for that.

A few days later, we were doing another jump from 12,000 feet, as we worked our way up to over twice that height, jumping with oxygen and all the works. A different instructor – a highly experienced RAF free-faller – had joined us for the day. He was one of the last to jump, by which time I was already on the ground. The first I knew that something was wrong was when the guys to either side of me started pointing skywards and yelling out warnings.

I looked where they indicated and I could tell the instructor was in trouble. He'd clearly suffered a similar kind of malfunction – his main chute had failed to open properly. For some inexplicable reason he never managed to trigger his reserve. We watched, aghast, as he plummeted down in a Roman candle and piled in. He died upon impact.

We aborted the remainder of the course, and returned to the UK, while an investigation got underway. It sure brought home to us how easy it is to die in this line of work. That guy had been a highly experienced parachutist, but still something had gone wrong and he had died.

What quirk of fate had left me alive, but him very, very dead, I wondered? Either way, it had proven hugely unsettling. That was one of the first times I'd looked into the face of death, and while not exactly laughing, I'd got away scot-free. There would be other times, two more parachute malfunctions included. Too many times, for my liking. You can't keep beating the odds.

Yet now here we were in Iraq, trying to do just that.

We'd moved a few dozen kilometres away from the napalm-strike point, when we stumbled upon a sad excuse for an LUP – a dip in the landscape. As it was all there was, we crawled into it, totally exhausted and frozen to the bones. The irony didn't escape us. On the night that the Iraqi desert had decided to turn Arctic, we'd very nearly got ourselves fried. As we set up camp, freezing hands trying to unroll the icy cam nets and get them mounted on the ice-cold steel tubes, there wasn't much being said by anyone.

The few words shot back and forth were all about what in the name of God the firestorm might have been. The consensus was that it had to have been 'friendly fire'. Any which way we looked at it, no way could we conceive of the mighty US Air Force being alert to the presence of eight dirty-looking Brits dressed in noddy suits, and driving a couple of crappy local-looking jeeps. If they spied us here, some 300 km inside enemy territory, we were going to get whacked.

It was really that simple.

But then again, maybe it had been the Iraqis. Maybe when we'd stopped to send the radio signal we'd been detected by their DF units. Maybe that had been a volley of rockets, such as were fired from a Soviet GRAD, a truck-mounted 120 mm multiple-rocket launcher, of which the Iraqi military had shedloads. Fuck knows. All we were sure of was that none of us had seen anything like it before, not in all the training nor all the wars in all the theatres that we had ever known.

All we could do now was hunker down and get into our LUP routine. We had the cam nets up. Hopefully, they'd render us reasonably hidden. But not even they could hide us from the kind of thermal imaging kit that the American pilots boasted. Those sophisticated sensors sought out the hot points in any terrain – like the warm engine blocks of recently used vehicles.

That night – our third in Iraq – was one plagued by nerves and a series of false alarms. After the napalm strike, we were edgy. Jumpy as hell. The slightest noise of an aircraft in the heavens sent our minds spinning back to the moment when the mother of all firestorms had erupted before our eyes. At one point, Jim got us to unfurl our Union Jack flag, and to weight it down with stones on the edge of the LUP, where we just had to hope it would be visible to any passing pilots.

Plus we were so unbelievably *cold*.

A while before sun-up, Jim made the suggestion we get on the move. No one was against it. I felt colder than I could ever seem to remember. Convinced we were deploying into a balmy English springtime, due to the weather briefings we'd been given, even our doss bags were the standard two-season jobs, fit for an English meadow in March.

Thank God we'd brought some waterproof bivvy bags with us, which you could stuff your green maggot into, to form a windproof cocoon. But we only had one per two of us, the reason being with our stag rotation only one of any pair should be sleeping at any one time. With the weather turning Arctic, even a shared bivvy bag was better than nothing.

All this just went to show – *Never trust the intel*. More to the point, this place – this moment – had us seriously unsettled.

Spooked. In fact, we were dead right to get moving early; to shift from our present position, which offered bugger all cover. Jim's instinct would prove unerringly prescient. For the eight men of our patrol it would prove a matter of life or death.

We got rolling, heading northeast, back towards the MSR. But we had a steady wind blowing into our faces now, and making any headway proved a nightmare. The breeze whipped up the desert surface, driving it into eyes and face. Frozen, cracked skin was getting sand-blasted, adding insult to misery, but more importantly it made it all but impossible to keep to proper driving procedures. If we stuck rigidly in the Pinkie's tracks, its tyres kicked up a barrage of dust, which was batted right into our faces.

After a short while Driller pulled offline by a few dozen yards, moving upwind of the Pinkie, and we were free of its dust trail. As was only to be expected with Driller, fine mobility drills. Now we were cutting our own swathe through virgin terrain, we would have to remain extra vigilant. The Pinkie might avoid any trouble, whereas we might drive right into it. But as luck would have it, the kind of danger that awaited us could hardly be avoided, no matter what path we chose to steer.

We'd moved about 3 km northeast of our LUP when we spotted it: in the far distance, vehicle headlamps were probing the gloom. It was around first light by now, but a cold fog was hanging low over the desert, adding a surreal, ghostly tinge to the scene. The mystery column of vehicles materialized out of the freezing mist, heading southwest – so in the opposite direction to us. For some reason – sheer chance, or because they were on the hunt – they were making a beeline for where we'd just spent the night in our LUP.

I alerted the guys on my wagon: Driller, Geordie Trev, Quiet Alex. We got our eyes and our weapons trained on the inbound convoy. Even at this distance, it was clear from the way they were moving that they had to be military. They were driving fast and with their headlamps full-on, making no effort to hide their presence from any marauding warplanes. It was either a very ballsy move or a decidedly suicidal one.

For a second it crossed my mind that they might be one of the squadrons. Maybe A or D Squadron had advanced this far? But I dismissed it more or less instantly. No way could they have pushed that quickly 300 km into Iraq. They were good – no doubt about that. But not even two squadrons of SAS blades driving hordes of tooled-up war machines could fight their way that far that quickly. More to the point, they would be moving tactically, proceeding on 'black light'. No way could this be them.

For a second I pondered whether we should turn around and run. But from what I could see via my scope, these guys looked to be driving Toyota-type pick-ups, and I didn't doubt they could move way faster than us. More to the point, if we opted to flee, it would give the game away and the chase would be on. I figured we had no option but to try to bluff it out. As Jim hadn't so much as slowed or altered his course one jot, I reckoned he felt likewise.

I pulled my shemagh tighter around my face, gesturing for the others to do the same. Thank God they'd actually had the foresight to get a job lot of these into stores back at H. For once, someone had actually done their research – realizing there were different styles of shemagh worn by different nations. In Saudi, they wore distinctive red and white check. In Iraq, black and white or brown and white would both pass muster.

As I glanced at the others, for a moment I almost burst out laughing. We were all wearing the right shemaghs alright – very authentic-looking. But what made the look all the more convincing was the bastardizing of our NBC suits as DIY cold-weather gear. After several hours of use, any exposed skin had been stained a dirty blue-black by the charcoal. No one in their right minds would ever conclude of us lot that we were 'white-eyes', as the Arabs tend to refer to Westerners.

It was classic: saved by some totally messed-up intel and a bit of lateral thinking. Only we weren't saved yet. Far from it. We were heading into a shitstorm – our second in less than twenty-four hours.

'Yeah, so tell me – how do I look?' Driller demanded, from where he was hunched over the wheel, shemagh flapping in the slipstream.

'Tops, mate. Like you should be riding a camel. Lawrence of Arabia eat your heart out.'

He glanced at me. 'We're bluffing through, right?'

By way of answer I gestured at the Pinkie. Jim wasn't slowing down and he certainly wasn't shying away. If anything, he was steering us on a bearing that would bring us to within a hair's breadth of the approaching convoy. It was still barely light, and in these conditions Jim had to be gambling that we could pass ourselves off as friendlies.

'You think he's made the right call?' Driller ventured.

'No other option.'

'Death or glory and all that yada-yada.'

'Concrete Reg, all the way.'

We carried with us Motorola encrypted radios, which were

good for line-of-sight comms between vehicles, but with all the wind noise and the racket from the wagons, they were rarely of much use. In any case, there was little need right now to communicate: wherever the Pinkie went, the Dinky went too.

With bluffing it, the one thing on our side was the plethora of Iraqi specialist and irregular units. Other than the Republican Guard – who I had a sneaking suspicion these guys might be; they were driving exactly the right kind of vehicles – Saddam had raised a number of paramilitary forces. Exploiting allegiances within his Al-Bu Nasir tribe, plus his political apparatus, the ruling Arab Socialist Ba'ath Party, he'd raised militias, armed tribal chiefs and bankrolled any number of other shadowy outfits. Then there was the Special Security Organization, the much-feared Iraqi secret police. We just had to hope that with our charcoal-stained features and our crappy wagons, we could pass ourselves off as one or other of those.

Five hundred metres. Four hundred. Three hundred. The gap was closing fast. I could feel my adrenaline starting to spike big time, my teeth grinding against each other with the tension of the coming showdown. On our present line of march the convoy would pass to the left-hand side of us, which put Jim and I on point.

'Keep your weapons well hidden, lads,' I hissed between gritted teeth. One glimpse of an M16 or Minimi and the game would be up.

If the enemy rumbled us, I wondered how they would react. Other than simply hosing us down, they might try to funnel us into some kind of a trap. As we'd all been repeatedly warned back at Victor, Saddam would love nothing more than to capture some special forces types alive. Anyone who allowed that to happen should expect to get paraded in front of the world's media, before the really nasty stuff started to happen. At Camp Victor we'd been briefed about what had been done to captured Iranian prisoners – including having electrodes attached to their private parts, and worse.

The easiest way to trap us would be to use the Toyotas to form a makeshift road block. Back at H, I'd been put in charge of counter-roadblock training – or 'ramming' as we call it. At Bridgend they had a race track, which came complete with the Glue Pot corner, the Devil's Elbow and the Runaway straight. It was rough and ready, but perfect for our needs, especially because right next door was a very handy scrapyard. I got into the habit of giving the scrappy £50 a piece for six cars, the only prescription being that they had to be drivable.

A bog-standard roadblock is two cars forming a V-shape. You might imagine the best way to ram through was to accelerate to 60–70 mph and smash through the centre of the V, but that only creates a potentially fatal accident. Ramming is a refined skill, as I used to demonstrate. We'd climb aboard the clapped-out Ford Escorts or VW Golfs or whatever the scrappy had flogged us, decked out in neck braces, knee and elbow pads and helmets, and strap ourselves in, making sure we had just enough fuel in the tank to execute a few ramming runs, for obvious reasons.

Most vehicles have a heavy end and a light end – the former where the engine is, the latter where it isn't. The trick to ramming was to approach at a relatively slow speed, accelerate at the last moment to around 30 mph and to punch through, aiming to keep your own vehicle drivable. You'd target the light end of the blocking vehicle, aiming to create a pivot effect where you spun it on its axis. Conversely, if you hit the engine with your engine, you'd very likely finish off both sets of wheels, and very possibly the occupants.

Even at 30 mph it causes one hell of an impact. One day I'd managed to get eight rams out of the one car – a VW Golf. For two days after that my head was spinning and I felt nauseous, but it had taught me a lot. Counter-intuitively, it isn't the big heavy wagons that are the best for ramming. Big cars with wide bodies have great crumple zones, but when a wing gets properly stoved in, it collapses against the wheel and makes the car undrivable. The best 'rammers' are the simple, tried and tested models – Ford Escorts, Vauxhall Astras and the VW Golfs.

After my time at Bridgend, I still didn't know much about what went on under the bonnet, but I knew how to handle most vehicles. I'd learned that 4x4s have added strength and traction to be able to punch through. You can use a 4x4 as a makeshift weapon, for they're built to take punishment, but in a roadblock situation the same rules apply: slow it down, aim for the pivot point and accelerate into the impact, driving through.

I reminded myself of all this now. If the enemy tried to con-figure a roadblock up ahead, we'd aim for the rear of one of the Hiluxes, preferably one not carrying a heavy DShK, and use the tried and tested technique to punch through. By rights, the Pinkie had more weight and oomph than we did, so Jim should take the lead, and as he'd done a stint at Bridgend himself he should know the drills.

We were 250 metres apart now, which meant that Jim's wagon was about to draw level with their lead vehicle. I could sense the tension in the air – of us watching them and of them watching us, and both sides waiting for the other to make the first move. I tried to calm my mind and to think logically, reassuring myself that we had the big advantage: we knew who they were, whereas they would have little idea about us. This far into Iraq, it would make sense that we were their brother warriors. That was unless A and D Squadrons had seriously started to kick ass, and word had gone out to all Iraqi units: *Be on the lookout for a few white-eyes dressed strangely and driving . . . Land Rovers.*

With that in mind, I made a grab for my dog tags and mouthed my mantra: *Let's fucking do this, Des, and let's get home for tea and medals.*

No sooner was I done, than almost as if in answer I saw a charcoal-blackened arm snake out of the front passenger's side of the Pinkie and it started to . . . wave. It was Jim, and he was gesticulating at the Republican Guard or whoever it was riding in the approaching convoy, as if Saddam was his Great Leader too. As if we were all on the same team.

Shit. What a ballsy move.

Utrinque Paratus – ready for anything. It is the motto of the Parachute Regiment. If we got through this, Jim would have proven it a thousandfold.

We followed suit, hands waving in greeting and teeth glinting in the friendliest of smiles. If any of us had known any Arabic, we'd no doubt have called out a suitable welcome. But in another indication of how rushed and bastardized was our deployment, we'd not had even one basic Arabic lesson. Normally, at the very least you'd be taught the key phrases, if nothing else to help win some hearts and minds.

230

We were 150 yards apart now and waving like lunatics, but still those in the oncoming convoy seemed disinclined to reciprocate. Hell, did Iraqis even greet each other by waving? Maybe in Iraq it was the equivalent of showing the middle finger? As no one had thought to brief us on any of the local customs, we just didn't know.

By now I was shitting myself, my breath coming in heaving gasps as I tried to control the panic rising up from within. I forced myself to focus, making sure I had a golden egg slotted into my M203 grenade launcher. At this range and against these targets, it was the perfect weapon. One 40 mm round on target would lacerate those thin-skinned wagons, shredding the occupants. More reasons to thank the SEAL team sergeant, if we ever made it out of here alive.

All of a sudden I saw a hand snake out of the lead Toyota.

It was grasping an AK-47.

For a moment I figured that we were done for, before the figure started to brandish it at us, seemingly in sign of brotherhood. *Unbelievable.* The bluff seemed to be holding. Other figures started to follow suit, as all along the convoy the Iraqis started to wave around their guns and to yell and cheer. While I couldn't make out a word of the Arabic, I had a good idea of the gist of what they were saying.

Yeah! Go get 'em.

Let's whoop the Yankies' arses.

Long live the Great Leader Saddam.

As vehicle after vehicle roared past, I tried to keep my pulse down to something like normal. I could not believe this was working. Of all the bluffs I'd ever seen pulled, this took the biscuit.

The last Hilux rumbled past the Dinky, its occupants waving and cheering, and all I wanted to do was to keep my eyes glued to our wing mirror, but of course we didn't have any, because we'd removed anything shiny or glittery back at Camp Victor. Instead, I risked a quick swivel of the head and a swift glance behind, but the convoy of Toyotas didn't seem to be stopping. They just kept barrelling off into the distance, trailing a thick cloud of dust, without the slightest hesitation or deviation.

It really did look like we had pulled it off. *Shit, that had been close. Shit, that had been epic.*

Up ahead, Jim's wagon slowed to a halt. We pulled up alongside. I noticed that every man amongst us had eyes wide as saucers. Fear; excitement; adrenaline; pulse-pounding gut-wrenching balls and bluff – it tended to do that to a bunch of guys like us, having just pulled off such a manoeuvre 300 klicks behind enemy lines.

Jim breathed out a big long *Fuuuuuuuuuck*.

There was a chorus of similar expletives. Some moments just call for a good communal venting. I knew exactly how everyone was feeling. It had been a near-range, in-your-face, up-close-and-personal confrontation with the enemy. In many ways, it had proven just as unsettling as the fearsome napalm firestorm of just a few hours before. All in all, it had been one hell of a wired few hours.

It struck us then how the wagons had been the saving of us. With convoys of Iraqi vehicles – regular military, irregulars, Scud crews disguised as civvie transport, the works – skating this way and that across the desert, we were just one more in amongst the mix. But eight men moving as a patrol on foot – that kind of thing just didn't happen around here. If Bravo Two Zero and Bravo One Zero had deployed and been spotted, their chances were . . . not good.

Jim suggested we go find an LUP, to hide up for the remaining hours of daylight. We'd survived. *Twice.* But both times had been so damn close.

We needed to lie low, keep ourselves hidden, reassess and recuperate.

CHAPTER TWELVE

RUNNING THE GAUNTLET

When I'd made my HALO jump over the Norwegian–Russian border, my hands had been so numbed with cold that I'd had to keep whacking them against my sides, just to try to get some of the blood flow and the warmth back into them. I was so cold now as we hurried to set camp that I found myself having to do the same – whacking my hands repeatedly against my sides.

By luck we'd found our first patch of semi-decent cover since driving down the Chinook's open ramp at the DZ. We'd nosed the wagons into a steep-sided wadi – a ravine that would flow with water like a raging torrent, but only on the rare occasions when it rained. God knows we'd had our share of bad luck, but none of us figured it was about to pour with rain any time soon here in the desert.

My hands and feet had been so numb for so long, I just couldn't seem to get any life back into them. It was then that I remembered the MREs. US military rations contain *self-heating* meals. It wasn't the food that I was dying for, but the warmth. If I wrapped my hands around a food sachet as the chemical-driven reaction was triggered, I'd have fashioned for myself a DIY hand warmer. Thumbs up again to the SEALs at Al-Jouf.

All I was hoping for was to breathe enough life back into my pinkies so as to be able to function and to set camp. As I was rooting around in my Bergen, my mind flipped once more to the other two Bravo patrols. Going in on foot, they would have taken less kit. And in an elite soldier's mindset, when he's told he's deploying into an 'English spring', cold-weather gear is the very last of his priorities. I shuddered to think what state those guys would be in. It simply didn't bear thinking about.

As if by some weird, spooky coincidence, it was now that Chewie managed to get our first news of how the other patrols were faring. He'd managed to decipher one of today's burst trans-missions, making it – at least partially – readable. It was an 'advisory' from HQ, and a good part of it remained jumbled. But at last there was news of Bravo One Zero and Bravo Two Zero which Chewie had been just about able to figure out.

We gathered, aghast, as he delivered to us the long and short of it. We had one patrol, Andy McNab's Bravo Two Zero, com-promised and all eight men were reported MIA – missing in action. As for the second patrol, Patrick Johnson's Bravo One Zero, the message regarding that lot was seriously garbled, but from what we could make out it seemed as if they might not even have deployed.

In truth, the Bravo One Zero guys had walked down the open ramp of the Chinook, surveyed the terrain and decided that no way were they heading into all of that. They'd got the pilot to fly them to an alternative DZ, but when they'd found it no better than the first, they had made the decision to return to Al-Jouf.

Doubtless, the call made by Patrick Johnson and his patrol had been the right one, but it had taken real balls. Had Bravo One Zero deployed on foot, it stood to reason they would have suffered the same fate as McNab's lot, which would mean we'd have sixteen men missing in action right now.

Patrick Johnson's actions had very likely saved all on his patrol, but for sure there would be those who would slag him for making a 'bad call' and for 'cowardice'. In due course I'd make a mental note to myself: I would seek out Pat, just as soon as I was able to and tell him exactly what I thought – that he had done entirely the right thing. In fact, that was the kind of decision that a medal should be given for. It must have taken incredible bravery, self-possession and presence of mind to make such a call.

But for now, we sat in a stunned silence, as we tried to make sense of all that had happened.

Chewie had more. As he worked his way through the advisory, we began to get a sense of just how deeply the Regiment was in the shit. As far as we could tell from the fragmentary message, both A and D Squadron had taken hits. A Squadron had crossed the Iraqi border and ended up recceing an Iraqi military outpost at night. One of the Pinkies had snuck through the defensive perimeter, only to blunder into a tangle of barbed wire. The noise of the impact had alerted the enemy and all hell had let loose.

The guys in the wagon had let rip, while at the same time endeavouring to drive out of the contact. In the process, their vehicle had gone into a ditch and got hopelessly stuck. As the guys de-bussed, one of their number, Staff Sergeant Baz Matthews, had taken rounds in the thigh and lower leg. The other blokes on the wagon had picked him up and begun to carry him across the desert, but trading fire with the enemy and laden down with an injured man, their position had looked hopeless.

With the enemy closing in, they'd prepared to make their final stand. Most of their spare ammo was in the wagon, and they only had what they had bugged out with, in their belt kit and chest rigs. It was then that Baz Matthews had done an exceptionally brave thing. Although barely conscious, he'd ordered the others to leave him, so he could hold off the enemy and they could make their getaway.

Reluctantly, they'd done as he'd asked. They'd left Baz Matthews with their 66 mm LAW, so he might give the enemy the good news. With him providing covering fire, the others had managed to escape, after which they'd made contact with a Coalition warplane, the pilot of which had managed to guide them to a rendezvous with the rest of the squadron. But of Baz Matthews, there was no further news.

It was a given in the Regiment that details of casualties were shared with the men as soon as possible. It was about up-front honesty and integrity and maintaining the esprit de corps. But this news really hit me hard. I felt devastated. I knew Baz Matthews very well. He was one of the old and the bold, but more importantly he was one of the main guys who'd first inspired me to go for SAS Selection. I sat there in the desert feeling numbed to the core, unable to comprehend that he was very likely dead.

When I'd first made it into Para Reg, Baz Matthews had been my instructor. I could tell even then that he was different – there was an aura of invincibility about him. A couple of years later he went for Selection, and sure enough word came back that he'd broken the records for the time to complete the infamous

Pipeline and the Point-to-Point sections. A while later a close mate of mine in 1 Para told me he was trying for Selection, and that Baz had offered to take him out for a beer and to tell him what it all entailed.

He asked me if I'd like to go too. I said I would, so the three of us met up. After talking to my mate about Selection, Baz had turned to me. 'So, Des, what about you? You interested in coming up to H?

'Err, probably not, no.'

'You sure? I think it might be just the job.'

'No, no, I don't think it's for me.'

'Never say never, Des. Listen, if you ever change your mind, get in touch, eh?'

Baz had left it at that, but of course the seed had been well and truly planted. Over the next year or so word of his exploits filtered back to me, and the fact that he was doing exceptionally well in the SAS not only left me feeling proud, but of course it inspired me to try for Selection myself. When I finally made it into Hereford, I ran into him on the base.

I told him straight out: 'You know what, Baz, you were instrumental in inspiring me to get up here.'

He grinned. 'Fuck me, Des, if I'd known that I'd have avoided you like the plague.'

Now, after Chewie's news, I sat there in the freezing darkness feeling totally at rock bottom. If a legendary figure like Baz Matthews – a superlative soldier and a true athlete – had been taken out, when serving as part of a squadron-size deployment and just a few score kilometres inside Iraq, what possible chance did we stand?

According to Chewie, D Squadron had had their share of dramas too. At around the same time as Baz Matthews was making his last stand, D Squadron had got attacked while in a desert LUP. As the men went to bug out, one of the Pinkies had refused to start. I wasn't entirely surprised. This kind of cold sapped battery power and turning over cold engines was never easy. The guys from that lifeless Pinkie had legged it, but not before one of them had taken a burst of rounds to the body.

We were just days in, and already it didn't sound good. We had two guys injured and one of them, Baz Matthews, very possibly dead. Plus we had eight other blokes from B Squadron missing, presumably on the run. That meant that somewhere in the desert not so far from us, the Bravo Two guys were out and about in conditions like these, with no vehicles, nor the shelter, the cover or mobility they provide. Even if they weren't killed in a shootout with the enemy, they'd have less cold-weather kit than we had, for everything had to be carried on their backs. It was a horrific proposition.

No one was saying very much right then. There was a dark feeling that had descended across the lot of us. Even Chewie and Joe, the two standout cheerleaders of the patrol, had fallen ominously silent. And if I'm honest, the news had hit me probably the worst of all.

Jim called us all together for a heads-up, and in an effort to galvanize us. He talked us through the obvious – that if Bravo Two Zero were in such serious trouble, then that should have triggered the lost comms procedure, and the SAR helos should have come in to extract them. But they'd been reported as MIA, which had to mean that the lost comms procedure and the helo extraction had failed. Nothing else made any sense.

'I've got a feeling no SAR helos came,' Jim remarked, ominously. 'I've got a feeling we're on our own. Which means we've just got to get on with it. We've still got the wagons. Whether the head shed think we're in a lost comms situation or not, with the radio playing up there's no way of us knowing. And if no SAR helos came for McNab's lot, they ain't coming for us either. So, no choice: we've just got to crack on.'

'Can't see any other option,' I volunteered. Someone had to say something, and as patrol 2iC I felt I had to lend Jim some support.

'But I tell you what,' I added, 'we've got to get a warning to the head shed that no more patrols get sent in on foot. We may be saying the bleedin' obvious, but I'd rather be hanged for a sheep as a lamb. In a way, us lot have done what the Regiment should have done, which is recce the ground before going in, only we've done it the wrong way around. It's that old saying – time spent in recce is never wasted. We've got to let the head shed know.'

Joe nodded. 'Agreed, mate. Chewie, let's get words to that effect into the next sitrep.'

'Got it,' Chewie confirmed.

'Right, we need to decide upon a cover story,' Jim continued, 'just in case we do get bumped and . . . taken captive.' He was dead right. With all of McNab's patrol compromised and on the run, it brought it all home to us how real was the threat. 'I know no one likes talking about it much, but anyone got any bright ideas if we do go in the bag?'

'Tell you what,' I volunteered, 'what if we claim we're a search-and-rescue team looking for downed pilots? I mean, we're driving bog-standard RAF wagons with no weapons on 'em – so let's use that to our favour.'

'Good idea, let's do it,' Jim confirmed. 'If we're forced to E & E on foot, the best route is north to Syria. If we're in the wagons, we stick to heading south to Saudi. Either way, we go for that cover story – we're an RAF search-and-rescue party. Are we all agreed?'

While no one liked it very much, there were a series of nods. After all, what other options were there?

'But you know what, I don't think we're going to get caught,' I said. 'Think about it. We're two crappy wagons with no weapons to speak of, trundling about in the desert. We've been sat up on the MSR for three nights now, and I don't doubt we've been spotted. But what did anyone see? Us lot, in shemaghs, skin stained black, going about our business. This far behind the lines, they're going to take us for some of their own. We look purposeful, we're here for a reason, passing through everyone else's lives.'

'Hiding in plain sight,' a voice piped up. It was Quiet Alex. 'Know it well. Tried and tested. Bulletproof-reliable, as long as you get it right.'

'Yeah. Exactly.' That was the most I'd heard Alex say since we'd deployed, and he had it bang on the nail. 'That's exactly my point, only you said it in a lot fewer words, mate.'

Laughter.

'After all,' I continued, 'if we were a fighting force we'd be shooting stuff up left, right and centre and the wagons would be bristling with weaponry. We aren't, and they're not.'

'Yeah,' Driller snorted, 'more's the pity.'

'Yeah, mate, but that's probably what's kept us alive so far, or at least prevented us from getting bumped. If everyone sees us just motoring through their lives waving at them and smiling, we don't give the profile of being "enemy". If they do notice us at all, they probably think we're Iraqi SF or maybe one of their sneaky-beaky outfits.'

'Yeah, that's until someone decides to drive over for a chinwag and to get a brew on.'

'So what next?' I ventured. 'Time's running out and we need some kind of a plan.'

'Simple.' Jim eyed each of us in turn as he continued speaking. 'We move off to get eyes-on the MSR. We hide in plain sight. We find some Scuds. We report them in. The mission hasn't changed.'

Jim was right. We were here now, deep in the crap, and no one was going to get us out of this but ourselves. No option but to crack on. Not that I rated our chances very highly, after the grim news about McNab's patrol and Baz Matthews. But you know something? When you think you're as low as you can get, Murphy's Law – *If it can go wrong it will* – always seems to come into play, just to prove there is somewhere lower you can get to.

Barely had Jim finished speaking when it started to snow. Flurries of big white snowflakes started to drift down from the skies. In the freezing conditions the snow began to settle, blanketing everything – wagons, camo nets, desert – in a thin crust of white. This was beyond belief. This was the weirdest, most outlandish kind of shit any of us could ever have imagined.

As we went about breaking camp, the weather just kept worsening. The wind stiffened and the snow thickened, and soon it was close to blizzard-like conditions. Some kind of 'England in springtime'. This was beyond desperate. Even as the snow kept falling, Driller pulled me aside for a quiet word.

'Didn't like that stuff earlier, about the cover story, Des,' he remarked. 'If we're bumped I say we fight to the last man and the last fucking round. And I tell you another thing: if it comes to it – you save a bullet for me, and I save a bullet for you.'

It was dramatic kind of stuff and I figured I needed to lighten the mood a little. 'Yeah, for sure we'll make a good account of ourselves. But mate, once we've killed every fucker in sight, you and me have a long tab ahead of us, 'cause all the money we've saved up while we're here in Iraq, well – we've got stuff to do with it, remember? You're gonna go buy yourself an Itchy-Fanny 1000, and I'm taking the missus to California.'

Driller was big into his superbikes, and he was saving up to buy a Kawasaki something-or-other, slang for which in my book was an 'Itchy-Fanny 1000'. And I had promised Emily the holiday of her dreams on the west coast of the USA. But chiefly, I was trying to get his mind off the dark thoughts of topping ourselves, if we were about to get captured.

But mostly, right now I was worried sick about the way the weather had turned. That was our real worry, not the Iraqis. If we tried to make a night move up to the MSR, I didn't doubt that some of us at least were going to be in serious trouble. Guys would be going down with hypothermia. Some of us might die.

Teeth chattering and lips smarting with the cold, I sought out Jim to tell him exactly what I thought. One entire Bravo patrol MIA in conditions like these. A and D Squadrons compromised and with men injured and on the run. Thickly falling snow.

Sod-all visibility. Practically a whiteout. No way were we about to start waltzing about in the desert, with all that going on. If we did, guys would start going down fast.

As part of learning my medic specialism in the Regiment, I'd spent several weeks 'embedded' at a hospital trauma unit, back in the winter of 1989–90, and I'd grown used to seeing homeless guys come in. At first I thought they'd had too much to drink, as they staggered about like drunkards and mouthed off at the hospital staff, slurring their words. At first I'd wanted to step in and show these blokes how to behave. In my book, getting pissed and bad-mouthing the nurses just wasn't on.

But it was then that one of the doctors took me to one side and explained what was really going on. The homeless guys weren't pissed: they were hypothermic. Or at least, they weren't chiefly pissed. They were suffering from acute exposure to the cold, and they'd used alcohol to try to numb the effects, but that was a vicious circle. Alcohol actually hastens the onset of hypothermia, because it makes the capillaries dilate, which makes you lose more body heat, which in turn makes you succumb to the cold more rapidly. In short, they were dying from prolonged exposure to the cold.

One of the earliest signs of hypothermia is intense, uncontrollable shivering. The US military has a great term for it: they call it 'jackhammering'. The next stage is a crushing feeling of fatigue – the sense that you just want to lie down and rest. That's followed by ever-growing confusion, as your core body temperature plummets, and the associated effects – slurred speech, vagueness, erratic behaviour and aggressiveness. In the final, terminal stages, the brain starts to tell you you're actually burning up with heat, when the opposite is true. That's why people who go down with hypothermia are often found naked, having ripped all their clothes off before they die.

The way to treat a homeless guy was to strip him out of his wet, frozen clothes, get some hot drink and food into him and to get him warm. In extreme cases, you had to try to get him into a steaming hot bath, to kind of drag the body back from the brink. Often, the same guys would turn up at the hospital time after time after time. They were drinking too much, which only made it worse. They were eating too little, which only made it worse, as food produces heat. A couple of times we even picked up guys dead from the streets.

All of that had made an indelible impression upon me. It was one hell of an eye-opener. Hypothermia is deadly and it can kill quickly. More importantly, it can creep up on you and by the time it's really starting to take effect, your brain is so scrambled you just don't realize the danger you're in. And by then, of course, it's too late.

I explained all this to Jim as the snow continued to flurry about the wagons, and to gust beneath the camo netting. By the time I was done, he was in complete agreement. Tonight, we had no option but to hunker down where we were and to focus all our energies on trying to stay alive.

We'd have to try to share bivvy bags and use each other's body heat to stay warm. Stag duty was going to suffer, but no one bar a lunatic would be moving in the desert in such conditions. Even so, neither Jim nor I were kidding ourselves that we weren't in dire straits. We had sod-all cold-weather kit, no usable comms with HQ, and no way to make contact with A or D Squadrons. It was a very lonely feeling right then.

Desperate times call for desperate measures. I can't remember who first suggested it, but we decided to commit a cardinal sin on such missions – to break hard routine. When you're freezing cold, as we were now, a hot drink can be a lifesaver. As the snow began to pile into drifts and we shivered beneath the pathetic shelter offered by the camo nets, we decided there was only one thing to do – to fire up our tiny, foldable 'hexy' stoves and get a brew on.

We did so in pairs. Soon Driller and me were warming our hands over the flame given off by the hexamine solid fuel blocks, which are similar to firelighters. By now I reckoned I'd got his measure. His reaction to the bloke who'd gone berserk with the machete in the Belize jungle pretty much defined the man. He was feisty and up for it. In fact, we were both fiery characters. It meant there was a special bond between us.

'Driller, we'll get the brew on with my cup, not yours, okay,' I suggested.

We'd share the brew, 'sippers', and I had a very specific reason for favouring my mug over his. Back in Al-Jouf I'd managed to blag one of the SEALs' water-bottle-cum-mug combos. The large metal 'mug' came with a foldout wire handle and it fitted snug over the water bottle, the whole lot slipping into one of the pouches of my webbing. But most importantly, you could put the mug direct onto a stove, boil a good pint of water, and drink from it without burning your lips, because it had a special, heatproof covering.

'What's so wrong with mine?' Driller challenged, but I could tell by the glint in his eye that he was up for a bit of fun.

'Look, mate, I'm not drinking from yours, 'cause it has a thick rim of maskers all around it, which makes the coffee taste like liquorice. So, we'll use my nice clean Yank mug and not get us lips burned, okay.'

Pretty much every British Army canteen – mug – looks the same: it's bastardized with a lip of tape, to stop it scalding the user. That's why my US mug was such a find, as Driller well appreciated. There was another upside to brewing up with Driller. We both drank coffee and we took it exactly the same: scalding hot, black, one sugar. Brewing up is like a religion in the Brit military, and some of the others on the patrol had turned out to have decidedly dodgy habits when it came to making their brews.

Top of the list was our resident Hobbit. Trev viewed a brew a bit like his breakfast porridge – it was all about boosting his energy, fitness and time on the triathlons. He'd take a standard tea bag, add three sachets of whitener and heaps of sugar, and then pour on the hot water, with the result his 'tea' ended up more white than brown.

I'd take one look and remark: 'You want some more milk with that?'

Shortly, Driller and I were squatting with the stove between our knees, warming our hands over the steaming mug and feeling just a tad more cozy. Once it was ready, we passed the precious brew back and forth, sippers, savouring every drop. After a while I could feel Driller eyeballing me. I could tell he had something on his mind.

I let him know there was no time like the present. 'Go ahead, mate, I'm all ears.'

'Look, Des, it's like this: we've got to get the rounds down the fucking range,' Driller growled. 'All well and good waltzing about in the desert looking for Apollo space rocket launches, but when all's said and done even if we see Scuds going up and we send back a message saying what we've seen and here's the coordinates, so what? We've still not taken out anything ourselves. And we still don't know if they're hearing our comms.'

'Go on, mate, I'm listening.'

'Plus they can send up a Scud from anywhere – they're mobile. Yes, we've had some luck, but they can send a Scud airborne from anywhere. We'd be better off going on the offensive, hitting 'em when we see 'em. Plus it might warm us up a bit, getting into some action. This desert is as cold as a witch's tit. It's Baltic. That's my bent on it, anyways.'

'Right, I hear you.'

'I dunno about you, Des, but I don't want to go back to camp with full mags and all bombed up and we haven't actually done anything. If we go on the offensive we seize control and we can be sure we've hit the enemy.' Driller paused for a second. 'Plus there's this: it's only a matter of time before we get compromised by something bigger and nastier than us. Which means we're either toast, or it's endex, and either way that's a case of – *For you, Tommy, the war is over.* Time is running, mate.'

I paused, thinking through the ramifications of what Driller had said. If we did go on the offensive, the team would face its baptism of fire, which made me wonder how all of us would stand up to the test.

'Okay, Driller, just on a similar front . . . How do you think the guys are doing? How're they bearing up? How's Mr Quiet doing?'

He eyed me for a long second. 'Look, Des, anyone is fucking quiet to you. Just 'cause you live on Coronation Street and go down the Rovers Return with your whippet and drink stout and wear a flat cap, if people don't talk and act like you doesn't mean they're funny buggers. Anyone who's quieter than you is a funny bugger in your books. Only, they're not.'

By now – and despite everything – the two of us were laughing, the shoulders going up and down as we tried to stifle the chuckles. I knew exactly what Driller was driving at: I do tend to talk nineteen to the dozen. I could see Jim eyeballing us from where he was brewing up with Scouse at the Pinkie, as if to say – *What the hell are you two laughing about?* For now I chose to ignore him, especially because Driller wasn't done.

'Look, Des, the only reason he's quiet is 'cause he's only just come to us. He's a decent bloke, his drills are good, he knows his way around his mobility skills, which are key right now and he's doing what's been asked of him. Just 'cause he's quiet doesn't mean he's a shit operator.'

I nodded. 'Yeah, fair one, mate.'

'If you're concerned if he'll perform well in a contact, I don't think you've got anything to worry about. Today I spotted him with Chewie helping him on the comms, and no one had asked or said a word. He just got stuck in. I like that. Plus you know what you were like when you first came to the Reg. Everyone is quiet to start with.'

'Okay, fair one.' Pause. 'So what about Trev? Little Trev?'

Driller burst out laughing. 'Tell you what, did you see him today? Did you see him today?'

I knew what Driller was driving at. With the desert sand getting into everything and no washing, Trev's flame-red hair was sticking out in all directions, as if he'd just been electrocuted. Combine that with his extremely pale, chalky complexion, massive blue-green eyes and big conk of a nose, and he was starting to look distinctly like an alien life form.

'He's got that shock of hair all matted up,' Driller added, 'those big eyes wide as saucers, and he bounded up to me and was chatting away in his broad Geordie accent . . . I can't understand a word even when he's talking at full volume, so what chance do I stand when he's whispering and hissing at me in the Iraqi desert?'

'Yeah,' I agreed. 'Trev the Terrier. Always on the fucking go. Fit as fuck. Never stops talking. Can't understand a word he says.'

'All you can do is nod and say "yes".'

We were laughing outright now.

'Yeah, but Little Trev is sound, mate,' I added. 'He's our secret weapon.'

Driller nodded. 'If anything, in a contact you'll have trouble holding him back. Can't sit still. The Duracell Bunny. Once we set him going – he's our secret weapon. A ninja. Des, on the whole the patrol is sound,' Driller continued. 'And by the way, we've got the airborne contingent on our wagon – that's me and you. So what can go wrong?'

We were still passing the coffee back and forth, trying to make it last. I don't think a hot drink had ever tasted so good or felt as cheering as it did then. I figured I ought to let Driller know.

'You know what, Driller, you made a decent cup of coffee at long last.'

More merriment. More shoulders going up and down. Jim was staring at us now, and I could tell what he was thinking. *What are those schoolkids up to? Immature gits. Having a laugh at a time like this.* But in my book, letting off steam and having a good squaddie's whinge and bellyache is crucial to keeping up morale.

'What about the others?' Driller ventured.

'You referring to Uncle Chewie? Chewie is not like anyone else in the SAS, mate. He's like your uncle, instead. Uncle Chewie – has he showed you his puppy?' We were cracking up now. 'Truth is, I'm well pleased. If he can't get through on the comms, no one can.'

'Too right,' Driller agreed. 'All you have to do is give him two bean cans and a piece of string and he can talk to God. He's an all-rounder, Des; a wizard on comms, good in mobility, a steady pair of hands.'

We nodded. Chewie was tops. After a longish pause, Driller piped up with this: 'Tell you what, Des, you don't think they've given us the wrong freqs, do you?'

By 'freqs' he was referring to the frequencies given to the patrol by the head shed prior to departure, without which communications to and from HQ simply would not be possible. It was inconceivable that they may have given us the wrong frequencies. Such a schoolboy error on a mission of this magnitude just didn't bear thinking about.

'Well now, that would be a gargantuan fuck-up, wouldn't it?' I mused. 'No, mate. No way can they have done that. There's got to be another reason. Either the Iraqis are jamming us, or the signals are getting screwed by the ionosphere.'

'For fuck's sake, Des, everything with you is "the ionosphere". If the wagons don't start, it's the ionosphere. If the coffee's not right, it's the ionosphere. If you go for a dump and you're all bunged up, it's the ionosphere.'

'Look around you, mate.' I gestured at the thickening snow-drifts. 'There's six inches of snow on the ground and it's falling thick and fast. With the weather out here, anything's possible.'

'Okay, yeah, the weather is all messed up. I have to agree with you on that. Whoever heard of it snowing in the desert? But in a contact, Uncle Chewie is the guy we want. He's rock solid. He'll take a contact in his stride, no bother with him, mate.'

'What about the RAF?' I ventured. Driller spluttered into his coffee. I pretended to go all serious for a moment. 'You know Joe's having an operation when he gets back to H?'

'Really. Shit, I didn't know that. What for?'

I glanced in the direction of the Pinkie. 'Yeah, he's having that fucking sleeping bag surgically removed.'

Driller couldn't help it – an explosion of pent-up mirth burst forth. 'Yeah, I've noticed that. If he's not in his sleeping bag, he's got a bivvy bag wrapped around his ankles.'

'Yeah, the reason is he's still got his bedroom slippers on. It's to hide his bleedin' slippers. If a contact does come, there'll be no problems finding the RAF. He'll still be in his doss bag putting down the rounds from there. When I start giving battle control orders he'll be in his green maggot and slippers, giving it root-ie-tootie in comfort.'

We were falling about now. I could see Jim scowling in our

direction, like a school teacher who wanted to scold some naughty pupils. But it felt to me like this was the first time we'd downed tools since the mission began. It was a release, and boy did we need it.

'I tell you something else, Des, for morale, Joe's fucking brilliant,' Driller volunteered. 'He's been smiling ever since we left H. All through training in the UAE – smiling like a Cheshire cat. The same out here. I'm pleased he's here – just to get the chance to slag the RAF. He's a sound guy, Des. Nowt to worry about with Al.'

We paused, trying our best to savour the last dregs of the brew.

'What about Scouse?' Driller ventured.

'Scouse is the equivalent of Trev on their wagon – he's their secret weapon. On the Minimi and giving it hell, it'll be all about holding him back.'

'Agreed, pal.' His expression turned serious for a moment. 'You know, Des, I get the feeling Scouse had a rough upbringing.'

'Why's that?' I asked.

Driller shrugged. 'Just a gut instinct, you know.'

'Yeah, I hear you. I reckon maybe he has. You know what that's about, don't you?'

'No, Des, what?'

'Well, you know what Scouse families are like? You know how big their families are? You heard that joke about the Scouse family? It was that big, when they got a dog they patted it to death. Well, Scouse's family was that large they lost him when he was just a little 'un.'

The two of us were chortling away now. I saw Jim make a gesture, like – *What are you two laughing at?* I shook my head at him – *Tell you later.*

'Good bunch of guys here, Des,' Driller concluded. 'If we go for it we can make a good account of ourselves. If we get the two secret weapons in action, we start doing left and right flanking on the enemy, we're going to be unstoppable.'

'Fair one, mate. I hear you.'

'Look, have a chat with Jim, will you?' Driller suggested. 'Tell him what we talked about. Put what I've suggested to him. You know I'll back you all the way.'

'No problem. Leave it with me.'

'You know with Jim, he's airborne brotherhood. He's the airborne contingent on their wagon. We'll have three Paras giving it wahoo, rockall and whatfor. What can go wrong?'

'Yeah. Got it,' I confirmed. 'But what d'you think of old Jim though? I mean, as a commander?'

'Des, he's just the same as us – he's Concrete Reg. But he realizes he's a sergeant now, so he's all about holding us back. That's what it's like when you start going up the ranks. We've got it easy, as we're not up there yet. But when that day comes, it'll be harder for us to get seriously down and dirty. That's just how it is.'

'I reckon Jim's already got in mind what we're talking about,' I told Driller. 'Think about it. We're running low on rations, water, fuel. He's got to be thinking along the same lines as us.'

I promised Driller I'd raise it with Jim, and push to take the fight to the enemy. First opportunity I got, and before they got the jump on us.

Having chewed the fat with Driller, I figured I'd go do the same with the guys on the other wagon, just to see how they were bearing up. First stop, Chewie. What drew me to the BFG was that he liked his brews the same as Driller and me.

'Hello, Des, you had some coffee?' Chewie greeted me, as

I crunched through the snow and ducked under the Pinkie's camo-netting.

'No, mate, that was Driller's.' I reached out and grabbed Chewie's mug, taking a good gulp. 'Tell you what, you make a fine cup of coffee. Are you sure you're not my uncle, Chewie?'

He looked down at me, grinning. 'Typical fucking Yorkshireman: pinch all the grub and neck all the coffee. And no, I'm not your uncle and I don't want to be.'

I fixed him with a look. 'Shame. Tell you what, a lot of the guys have been wondering – have you got a puppy, Chewie?'

He gave me a suitably expletive-filled response, after which I figured Chewie was all good. His spirits seemed high. It still seemed impossible to wind him up. Chewie could rip off your arms and legs and beat you with the soggy bits, but nothing ever seemed to rile him.

I moved on to Joe. Joe was also a coffee man, but he bastardized it with lashings of sugar and creamer. He was Trev's equivalent on the coffee front. Still, I'd always try and neck some, just to twist him. I tried to grab a gulp now, before he could stop me.

'Eh, get off!' Joe objected. 'Go get your own.'

'Don't be like that.'

'I've fucking sussed you, Des.'

'What d'you mean?'

'I've sussed you. You don't make any brews, do you? You let Driller make the coffee, go drink his, then go around everyone else's until you're full.'

'Yeah, he's just been all over mine,' Chewie cut in. 'Fucking sussed you.'

I put up my hands in mock surrender. 'You got me, lads.'

'Yeah, piss off, you Yorkshire monkey.'

There was no point starting on Scouse, 'cause he was a standard NATO tea man – milk, two sugars – and I do not like tea, period. In any case, he'd watched me scrounging Chewie and Joe's brews, and I could tell he'd enjoyed every minute of it. Jim was also a tea man, so no joy to be had there.

Either way, it was mission accomplished. After running the brew test, I could tell that despite the murderous weather, no one on Jim's wagon was losing it. Not yet, anyway.

Come first light, no one had died. But our water bottles had frozen solid and there was a thick layer of snow and ice covering everything. Our doss bags cracked and hissed as we shook off the worst, disengaged ourselves, prised our eyelids apart and tried to get our limbs to move. The bizarre thing about such conditions is that you can actually die from dehydration as much as you can hypothermia. Cold, icy water is the last thing you feel like drinking when you're chilled to the very bones.

The cam nets crackled as we tried to get a brew on with painful, cracked hands. With the charcoal effect from the NBC suits our skin was blue-black, but even so I didn't doubt that we were suffering from frostbite. Intense cold kills flesh; the more exposed the skin, the more rapidly it succumbs. Fingers and toes are the first to go. The symptoms are a complete loss of feeling in your extremities, before the skin starts to change colour. I knew for sure that I had frost nip, for I'd lost all feeling in my feet and hands.

It was still snowing, but not quite as heavily. The desert seemed eerie, cloaked as it was in a silvery white blanket. In every direction it looked utterly godforsaken and deserted. If I hadn't known better, I'd have thought we were on Arctic operations. The Pinkie appeared distinctly odd, roofed over with camo netting and a thick carpet of white. I guessed the Dinky must look equally bizarre. Question was, what were we to do now?

What we desperately needed – apart from shelter and cold-weather gear – was *information*. We needed to have words with HQ, and to get a sense of our options. We had one other means to try to make contact – our TACBEs, a small, compact rescue beacon, which could also be used for line-of-sight communications with overflying aircraft. With its pin still inserted in the top, the TACBE serves as a transmit-and-receive radio set; with the pin removed, it becomes a tactical beacon, sending out a pulsed distress signal – something for a search-and-rescue team to home in on.

We decided to give the TACBE a whirl. We knew the Americans had AWACS aircraft in permanent orbit, coordinating airstrikes. Making contact should be a breeze. Chewie stepped a short distance away from the wagons, us watching anxiously as he made the call.

'Hello any callsigns, this is Bravo Three Zero, radio check, over. Hello any callsigns, this is Bravo Three Zero, radio check, over.'

After a few seconds Chewie shook his head: no response.

'Hello any callsigns, this is Bravo Three Zero,' he tried again.

Again, nothing. Just a faint hiss of static filling the void.

'Any callsigns, Bravo Three Zero, over.'

Still zilch.

No matter how many times he tried it, all he got back was a

wall of silence. Like Chewie had said, comms always works until the shit hits the fan.

Jim called a Chinese Parliament – a Chinese for short – so we could consider what the hell to do. Apart from the snow, and the terrible news about the other patrols, for us nothing much had changed. It was hard to see how the weather could get a whole lot worse, and somehow we'd lasted the one night. We could probably survive one or two more. We'd yet to take casualties, we were still covert and we still had our mission to execute. Jim figured we should lie low for the day, resting as best we could, then head towards the MSR come nightfall.

The snow would serve to mask the terrain, so we'd have to proceed at a dead crawl, feeling our way. The absolute key thing was to not lose a vehicle. Without the Pinkie or the Dinky, we were done for. Of course, we'd been sleeping in the shelter of the wagons, to help shield us from the snow. Tactically, you're supposed to doss down somewhere you can get away from the vehicles swiftly, for they are invariably the bullet magnets.

But as was painfully clear to us, our main enemy wasn't the Iraqis any more – it was the weather.

CHAPTER THIRTEEN

SNOWBOUND

We set out at last light, moving at a snail's pace with tyres crunching through a thick crust of snow. As the wagons nosed ahead cautiously, trundling through the freezing chill of the gathering night, the crescent moon glimmering eerily off the snow, I reflected on our predicament. With no reliable comms, we had no idea of the bigger picture. For all we knew, the failure of the Bravo patrols could have caused the conflict to spiral out of control. For all we knew, the Israelis could have lost patience and their paratroopers might be already on the ground.

I say 'failure' because, of the three patrols intended to be at the tip of the spear, one was missing in action and one had turned around and – rightly – refused to deploy. So I didn't doubt that neither of them had found any Scuds. We had radioed in a good deal of reports, but we had no idea if our intel was getting through or being acted upon. In short, the Bravo missions were in danger of becoming an out-and-out disaster.

I was dragged back to the present – to the icy cold of the snow-bound desert – by a sudden pitching forward of the Pinkie. Up ahead I saw the lead vehicle break through the crust of snow, and kangaroo across what had to be some kind of massive crater. One moment it had been trundling along, and the next the wheels just plunged through and went down hard. This was the big challenge of night driving in such conditions: the snow filled potholes and gullies, and blanketed boulders, masking the terrain. The Pinkie might have made it across that monster crater, but the Dinky wouldn't stand much of a chance.

'WATCH OUT!' I yelled at Driller, worried he was frozen stiff and half-asleep at the wheel.

I'd done him a disservice. He'd seen what was coming and even now was wrenching the wheel to one side, pulling out of the 110's tracks and putting our overloaded wagon into a tight turn. But the crater must have been seriously large. Though we veered hard right, as sod's law would have it we ended up hitting the very deepest part of the depression.

BANG! The front end punched down through the snow and came back up again like a bucking bronco, by which time I was on my feet and preparing to vault clear.

The fucking vehicle's going to flip, I was thinking.

I tried grabbing hold of anything I could, while behind me I could see Quiet Alex and Trev jockeying for positions and readying themselves to leap. As the second set of wheels went down – KERBANG! – I saw Trev lifted up and practically catapulted free of the Dinky's rear. How he held on I'll never know, but that was the Duracell Bunny for you – Power On; he never ran out of strength or gas.

We pulled up on the far side to inspect the damage. Trev had cracked his chin, and it was a right bloody mess; I'd scraped my elbow red-raw; even Quiet Alex admitted to having banged his head pretty damn hard. But the real worry was the Dinky. As Driller went to crawl under the wagon to check for damage, pushing the snow aside as he went, I broke out my medical pack, and with dressings and bandages I patched us all up as best I could.

By feel alone Driller could tell that the underside of the Dinky had taken a proper hammering, but without light he couldn't assess how bad it was. We were in the middle of a dark, snow-bound wilderness, and the last thing we wanted was to start flashing around torchlights. We figured we had no option but to press on, and say our prayers that the wagon would hold together for the rest of the night hours.

We set off, nosing ever closer towards the MSR, and as we did, an incredible sight met our eyes. A way to the east, Coalition air-strikes were pounding Baghdad. We were close enough to see the aircraft going in, and the searing flash of the explosions reflecting across the frozen snowscape. It was the first time we'd seen direct evidence of the air war – barring the mystery 'napalm' strike – and the very sight of it stopped us dead in our tracks.

We watched as laser-guided munitions plummeted into ammo and fuel dumps, causing almighty great explosions. Fierce spurts of tracer arced up in return, as the Iraqi military fought back. As we watched I thought to myself: *Shit, the people living in that city – the non-combatants – they have to be taking one hell of a pounding.* They were doubtless getting hit, and all because they had a power-crazed maniac for a leader. My mind drifted from thoughts of that to the task in hand – Scud-hunting. A lot of innocent people were going to die in this war, and all because of Saddam Hussein.

We got motoring again, and Jim steered us to a position where we could keep one eye on the MSR and one eye on the pounding that Baghdad was taking. That way, we could keep a watch out for Scud convoys, while also drawing up a BDA – battle damage assessment – of the airstrikes, which we could radio back to headquarters. No one else could be anything like as far forward as we were, with eyes-on the airstrikes. It gave us a unique perspective. Our eyewitness report would be a one-off, and hopefully useful.

No matter how we might search the length and breadth of the MSR, it seemed to remain utterly deserted. It cut through the desert snowscape like a ghost highway. Upon reflection, it was hardly surprising. Who else but lunatics like us would be out in the desert, moving around in conditions like these? But if we couldn't spy any Scuds, what hopes did we have of preventing this conflict from spiralling out of control?

As we fought to remain alert and to keep scrutinizing the utterly inhospitable terrain, my mind flipped back to the last time I'd been on the cusp of triggering World War Three. I'd been a young lance corporal serving in 1 Para. We'd deployed to Hong Kong, then a British colony, to help police the border with China. We'd been briefed that the main problem was the illegal immigrants – 'IIs' in military speak – sneaking across the border from communist China, drawn by the bright lights and freedoms of Hong Kong.

The frontier was marked by the Sham Chun River, a waterway no more than a hundred feet across at its widest. The IIs would try to ford it at night, under cover of darkness. On the Chinese side, patrols of the People's Liberation Army (PLA) would do all they could to catch them. On our side, we had to try to intercept them before they made a dash for Kowloon, the lights of which could be seen glinting in the distance.

Trouble was, the PLA were hardly renowned for their easy-going approach to those who turned their backs on the glorious People's Republic of China. Pretty quickly we started finding the bodies in the river. Many of the IIs consisted of entire families – men, women and children. The corpses showed all the signs of having been beaten half to death, before being dumped in the Sham Chun. It made the stomach churn.

One night we heard sounds from the far bank of someone being subjected to a horrendous beating. We flicked on our Dragon Light – a portable, battery-powered searchlight – and in the beam that shone across the river we nailed three PLA soldiers, who were kicking the living daylights out of an II. Being an aficionado of martial arts, I could see that they were using him to practise some of their favourite moves on.

I was in command of three young Paras who epitomized the Concrete Reg mentality. We decided we'd had more than enough. I told our interpreter to yell across to the PLA thugs to stop the beating, or else.

The reply we got back was basically: 'Screw you. Or else what?'

As I've said, I don't like bullies. By way of response, I cocked my SLR, the superlative L1A1 Self-Loading Rifle, with which all British troops were then equipped. The beauty of the SLR was that it was squaddie-proof. You could drop it in the Sham Chun, leave it for a month, drag it out and it would still work.

I raised my weapon to my shoulder and told the 'terp' to let the PLA guys know exactly what the 'or else' was going to be. It was nice to see the lads under my command following suit: *If Des is going for it, we're fucking going for it, too.*

The PLA soldiers reciprocated, and all of a sudden we had the three of them with AK-47s, facing four of us with SLRs, and the bullets were about to fly. We were all in the ready position, and apart from the gurgling of the river and the groaning of the II the PLA heavies had beaten to within an inch of his life, there was a deadly silence.

As we stared each other down, I was willing them to open fire. If they did, I had no doubt we'd take them out. I figured we would be engaging each other at around 150 feet, and in terms of accuracy the SLR beats the AK-47 hands-down.

Of course, the thought was going through my mind: *This is going to be the flashpoint for World War Three.* But I didn't particularly care. We were Paras and we had a code: *What we'd started, we'd finish.* And not another blow or a kick was going to be unleashed upon that II. *Next move,* I told myself, *I'm fucking slotting the lot of you.*

Still, in my mind's eye I could see how the conversation would play out with the colonel of the Regiment: 'So tell me, Corporal Powell, why did you open fire on the PLA?'

'Well, they were beating the crap out of an II.'

'That does not give you the right to open fire on the PLA and now we are at war.'

But sod it, no backing down.

Perhaps fortuitously, the interpreter managed to talk the PLA guys out of opening fire. I'm not sure exactly what he said, but eventually they lowered their AK-47s, yelled across a few final insults and dragged the II off into the shadows.

After that, everything changed. We talked about it amongst ourselves in my patrol. Any IIs caught on our side were getting bussed back across the border – women and children included – and it was obvious what kind of fate awaited them upon their return to the so-called motherland. Horrific.

A couple of nights later we caught three young women – sisters; bedraggled; exhausted; half-starved – clambering onto the riverbank on our side of the Sham Chun. We wrapped them in blankets and gave them sandwiches and flasks of hot tea. Once they had recovered a little, I pointed towards the distant lights.

'Hong Kong. *Hong Kong.* You go Hong Kong.'

At first the girls thought I was playing some kind of sick trick on them. Maybe I'd let them go and shoot them in the back, the kind of thing the PLA would no doubt find highly amusing. But finally, they realized this was for real. They broke down in tears. Then they did that Chinese thing of bowing low, with their hands clasped together in front of their tear-stained faces, to show their gratitude. With that, we ushered them on their way.

From then on, I never sent another II back to China. Instead, we showed them the way to Kowloon. We must have let a good hundred go during the remainder of our posting. That was a hundred souls saved from savage beatings, rape and murder. If we'd been found out I'd very likely have faced a court martial, as commander of the patrol. But frankly I didn't give a damn. That was the Para Regiment mentality: when faced with a bad, bad situation you had to make it right, no matter if it would trigger a Third World War.

In a way, Saddam's Scuds were the equivalent of those PLA heavies. Saddam was using his missiles to beat up on blameless parties – first the men, women and children of Kuwait, and now the same with Israel; all innocent civilians – in an effort to further his own megalomaniacal ends. I didn't want that happening on our watch. Trouble was, as we failed to spot the slightest thing moving on the MSR, right now I felt that we were failing.

By the time we'd decided enough was enough, and to search for an LUP, the wind was up and it had started to sleet, which if anything was the worst kind of conditions yet. Driving through such weather with no windshield or roof, the ferocious gusts tore into us. In no time we were soaked to the skin. With the wind-chill factor I could feel the sleet freezing to my skin. I was cold like I had never thought possible. My hands and feet were like blocks of ice. My limbs were aching and numb. Even my mind felt sluggish and unresponsive.

These, I knew, were the early symptoms of hypothermia. We needed to find some shelter fast and to get a brew on. The visibility had dropped to no more than 30 yards, so we squeezed the wagons up to that kind of distance as we crawled ever onwards. My one consoling thought was that no enemy troops would be mad enough to be out in such conditions, and even if they were, they stood little chance of seeing us, conditions were so bad.

The further southwest we went, moving away from the MSR, the less challenging the terrain seemed to become. It was smoother underfoot, so less punishing on the wagons, and we were especially mindful of the damage to the Dinky. But the hours hunched in the exposed cabs, as the sleet and snow cut into us, had proven hugely debilitating. Finally, Jim called a halt. He'd found us a shallow, snow-filled wadi and we eased the wagons inside.

First thing I did was force my frozen limbs into motion, going around each of the lads in turn, doing a sense check, my aim being to gauge how close they were to shutting down. Guys with severe hypothermia might wander off into the snow, their brains telling them they were heading into paradise. With a smile on their face they would rip off their clothes, lie down and die. I'd witnessed as much a year or so after getting into the SAS.

I was assisting on Selection, when an officer went down with advanced hypothermia during a night march. As he was being led away to thaw out, he broke free and dashed into the storm. We chased after him, but in the blizzard-like conditions we lost him. We didn't find him until morning, by which time he had frozen to death. Utterly tragic.

The British military had carried out exhaustive tests on pilots who'd been forced to ditch in the sea. They'd found the best way to bring someone back from the brink was to get them into a scorching hot bath. There was no chance of doing that out here, but we could do the reverse, by getting some scorching hot liquid inside us.

While we got busy getting the brews on, Chewie got on the comms. It was the measure of the man that despite the freezing conditions and his numbed mind, he was trying to keep religiously to the scheds – sending his daily messages to HQ. Having got a hot drink down us, it was time to take a look at the state of the Dinky. Driller crawled underneath to get a butcher's, but reappeared looking troubled.

'No doubt about it, she's taken a serious pounding,' he remarked. 'Can't say how bad it is, or how it's going to play out.

One consolation: far as I can tell she's not losing any oil, or not too much. Best you take a look, Des.'

I did as suggested, sliding myself under the wagon using the patch of compacted snow left by Driller. I could see where the underside had grounded out, smashing into the rocks and boulders of the crater. The impact had been triply hard, due to all the excess weight she was carrying. When I'd left school at fifteen I'd gone straight into the Sheffield steel mills, working as a smelter, being the youngest in the factory doing what was a real man's job – hammering red-hot, molten steel. So, while vehicle mechanics wasn't really my thing, I understood metal, and I doubted whether the Dinky could weather many more such hits.

I dragged myself out, covered in snow and dirt. 'It doesn't look good. Last thing we need now is to lose a fucking wagon.'

Jim called us in for a heads-up. One by one we moved into the lea of the Pinkie, our single biggest patch of shelter. It was then that I clocked RAF Joe. From somewhere he'd produced this 'Deputy Dawg'-style hat – the type with the furry ear-flaps, which you can either fix up on the top of your head, or let down to tie under your chin. Right now Joe had the flaps roped firmly around his chops, giving him the appearance of some redneck from *Deliverance* country.

'Joe, what's the score with the Deputy Dawg hat?' I needled him. 'If the Iraqis catch you in that, you're in rag order, mate.'

'Take a look at yourself,' he fired back. 'You're not at 25,000 feet any more, Des. Didn't know there were any DZs around here.'

It was a fair one. Being an Air Troop boy at heart, I'd long got used to wearing my freefall goggles 24/7 when on operations. Strapped tight around the head, they provide great eye protection, and have vents at the side to prevent them from steaming up. Ever since it had turned Baltic and started to snow, I'd kept them on more or less permanently, plus my shemagh pulled tight around my face.

Driller joined us, and the last to wander over from our wagon was Trev. Somehow, he'd managed to perfect the Hobbit look 100 per cent by now. From somewhere he'd produced a black woolly hat, but it was one that had lost all its elasticity. As a result, he'd been able to pull it right over his head on top of his shemagh. In fact, it was so loose it kept dropping down over his eyes.

I nudged Driller. 'Have you seen Trev?'

'Yeah. Looks like a sodding Smurf.'

I had to admit, Driller had it nailed. Dressed like that, Trev was more Smurf than he was Hobbit.

Jim called us to attention. 'Yeah, so a few hours earlier we hit that monster crater,' he began, as he tried to blow some warmth into his cupped hands. 'Not good.' He glanced at me. 'What's the state of the Dinky, mate?'

'She's taken a real pounding. Can't say how she'll hold up.'

'Right, well, lessons learned. We don't know what damage we may have done, which means we've got to be more careful, especially in these kind of conditions. Could have lost a vehicle, and then we'd be totally screwed. Got to be a lot more careful.'

'What d'you mean, *got to be more careful*?' I demanded, my temper starting to spike. I wasn't exactly warming to Jim's schoolmasterly tone. 'We're on our chinstraps, freezing cold in a Dinky, we see your wagon go down, we take evasive action, but the crater's a big one, it's full of snow and we hit the worst part. There's nowt anyone could have done about that.'

'Look, Des, I'm just saying we've all got to take more care. I'm just saying let's learn the lessons. I'm not accusing anyone of anything, am I?'

We locked eyes. 'Dunno. Are you? 'Cause if you are, best come right out and say it.' A beat. 'And I tell you another thing – Driller there could not have acted more quickly. He was on it like a tramp on chips.'

'Leave it, Des,' Driller cut in, but I could tell he was simmering now. 'Look, Jim, it was me in the driver's seat and I'm big enough and ugly enough to fight my own battles. So, you got something to say, say it to my face.'

'Fuck me, what's got into you two?' Jim fired back, his gaze swivelling from Driller to me and back again. 'You're like a married fucking couple. I'm just trying to make sure it doesn't happen again, at which point we'll be right royally screwed. Let's learn the lessons, that's all I'm saying.'

'What lessons?' Driller challenged. 'Like lesson one: blame me.'

Jim let out a string of curses. I could see his breath pooling in the still and freezing air. 'Well, like what about this: we reduce our speed when driving across snow-covered desert at night. Like that, for starters.'

There was a difference between how we operated the two wagons on the patrol. It was subtle, but it spoke volumes. With the Pinkie, Scouse was the main driver, but Joe would take a turn, to give Scouse a break. In the Dinky, Driller was always at the wheel. At one stage I'd suggested that he allow Trev to take a turn, to give him a much-needed rest. But Driller was having none of it. He was first class behind the wheel, and he didn't trust anyone else. Hence any criticism of his driving got Driller seriously riled.

'We were sticking in your tracks and following your lead,' I told Jim. 'You chose the route and you set the pace.'

It was Scouse's turn to bridle now. 'So, what, I'm to fucking blame, is it?' I could see him balling his fists.

'Fuck off, Scouse,' I snapped. 'No one said anything like that.'

'Dead right,' added Driller. 'Fuck off.'

The two of us were in 'Para Mafia' mode now – shoulder to shoulder, closing ranks. I could sense a drying-room moment was almost upon us. A great deal more of this and we'd be scrapping in the snow.

'Easy, boys, easy,' a voice cut in. It was Chewie. 'Maybe you're forgetting something, but we're all on the same side. Fucking Para Reg mentality – I thought we were here to fight the Iraqis, not each other.'

'Fair one, Chewie, but you know what us Para Reg blokes are like,' I countered. 'We love a good old-fashioned argument and a brawl.'

'Tell you another thing,' Joe volunteered. 'You'd never hear this kind of language in the good old RAF. Shocking.'

A few choice expletives were thrown in Joe's direction, before things began to simmer right down.

I glanced at Jim. 'No hard feelings, eh, mate?'

'Got a bit heated there,' Driller added. 'Best shake hands and make up.'

Jim shrugged. 'Sod it, we're all on edge.' He glanced at the thick flurries of snow swirling around the wagons. 'Just look at this shit. No wonder we're getting at each other. Jumping down each other's throats.'

In short order we were slapping each other on the back and the altercation was halfway to being put behind us.

But the crater thump in the Dinky wasn't going to be so easily forgotten. Already, I could feel a familiar sensation, the same as I had felt after putting the VW Golf through eight ramming sessions, at Bridgend race track. My neck and lower back were seizing up, and no doubt the whiplash effect would be with me for a while now. I didn't doubt that the others felt the same, and with whiplash nothing in the medical pack would make the slightest bit of difference.

As I manipulated my neck this way and that, trying to ease the tension a little, I stole a glance at the others. Eyes rimmed with red stared out of frozen, blackened features, above lips that were dry and cracked and turning blue. With several days' growth, our beards had frozen to our skin, and in places the stubble formed dark, dirty icicles. No doubt about it, we looked like a bunch of half-starved, half-mad, half-dead desperadoes.

'Right, if you Para Reg lot have kissed and made up,' Chewie announced, 'who wants to hear the good news?' A forest of hands shot up. 'When I sent the sitrep, I got a half-garbled confirmation that our signals *are* getting through.'

'About bloody time.' Jim punched Chewie playfully on the shoulder. 'Only joking. That's fucking great news.'

'Yeah, marvellous, mate. But what does "half-garbled" mean?' I asked.

'It means as far as I can tell HQ knows roughly where we are and that we're still on task.'

Despite the murderous weather and the uncertain fate of the other Bravo patrols, there were no orders to abort the mission, as far as Chewie could tell. In fact, it seemed that HQ were keen to send us more intel, so we could continue with our tasks, only very little of it was getting through, at least not in a way that Chewie could interpret.

'So, are they getting our target coordinates?' Jim asked. After all, that was the million-dollar question.

Chewie nodded. 'I think so. I can't guarantee it, but yes, I think they are.'

There were a few seconds of silence as we tried to digest this news. It was a step in the right direction, certainly. And knowing Chewie as well as I did, I didn't doubt that he was right. He was a total pro and he was certainly no bullshitter. Quite the opposite, in fact. He tended to err on the side of caution, especially where comms were concerned.

'Right, this is where I figure we're at,' Jim announced. 'We've still got problems with comms, though from what Chewie says we are being heard. The messages may be garbled their end, like they are ours, but we've got no indication they want us to withdraw. So, options. One: we keep doing what we're doing – hunting for the Scuds and sending back target coordinates. But it's only a matter of time before we either freeze to death or get bumped. Two: we head west, and try to link up with one of the squadrons.'

We all knew the problems with option two, highly attractive though it might sound right now. With no reliable comms, we had no way to warn either A or D Squadron that we were coming in. That meant there was a very real danger of getting brassed up by our own side. After the near-miss of the napalm strike, none of us fancied being shot to shreds by one of the squadrons. We reminded ourselves of our mission: it was to remain covert and to hunt for Scuds.

Despite everything that had been thrown at us, we were still on task. If we could hold out for a few more days, the weather had to turn and maybe we could get a resupply in by helo. We were doing a daily health check on water, food and fuel. Fuel especially was running low, for this terrain and these conditions tended to burn through it fast. But all things considered, we figured we could keep on mission for a few more days.

As the morning wore on I tried to get some sleep, but the hardest thing turned out to be remaining static during the hours of daylight. Movement draws attention, but lying on the freezing ground for hours at a time, in wet kit and in a thin doss bag, was sheer hell. The cold reached up from the ground, like fingers of ice. The snow and sleet blew in from all sides. I'd fall asleep, only to wake up a few minutes later to find myself jackhammering. As I lay there, teeth chattering uncontrollably, I wondered just what part of me was still alive. I felt as if every molecule of my body was slowly giving up the ghost.

I'd drift into a dreamlike semi-slumber, only to 'hear' Emily talking to me. It felt so real, I could imagine her lying next to me, both of us warm and cosy in our new Peterborough home. We'd long had this dream of heading for California. We'd hit Los Angeles' Venice Beach, then motor up the coast nice and slow, visiting Santa Monica, Monterey and San Francisco. From there we'd branch off to the Napa Valley, do the vineyards and fly home. Two weeks, done and dusted.

I'd promised to get it organized once I was back from the Gulf, and I swear I could hear her voice now, talking through our plans. Of course, when I came back to consciousness with a crash, Emily was nowhere to be seen. Instead, the wind had got up and we had 30 miles-per-hour gusts tearing through the wagons, which meant the real temperature had to be into the double figures below zero. The desert was so flat the wind just sheared across it, and the wadi offered precious little in terms of a windbreak.

I glanced around. I could see guys huddling together to try to keep warm. Sharing body heat. I remembered talking to some of the guys in Mountain Troop about how at high altitudes the greatest single challenge was the windchill factor. But at least on the hills you had the advantage of being able to keep on the move: exercise creates warmth. Conversely, when you have to stay still, windchill becomes one of the biggest factors in taking guys' lives.

At one stage someone asked Scouse to give us a song. We were freezing cold, horribly isolated, scared to death – keeping up morale was key. If we lost our collective spirit we'd be in danger of losing the will to go on. Scouse was second only to Quiet Alex in not saying very much, but as we all knew, he loved to sing. It was hardly very original, but seeing as he was from Liverpool we used to slag him about that city's most famous band.

'What was it like, Scouse, being the Fifth Beatle?'

'What was it like, being in the Cavern in them days? Come on, you must have some stories.'

'By the way, Scouse, them silly haircuts – they really don't work.'

The Cavern Club was a famous central Liverpool music venue, situated in a converted cellar under a five-storey fruit warehouse. It was where the Beatles had first started playing and where they had been discovered. Generally, Scouse took the slagging in a stoical silence, but he never seemed able to resist the provocation to sing.

'Hey, Scouse, give us a Beatles song,' RAF Joe suggested.

It may have sounded utterly bizarre, considering the parlous state we were in, but we were desperate for something – anything – to lift our spirits. Scouse shook his head: too cold by far to sing.

'Come on,' Joe needled him. 'It's been a hard day's night . . .'

Joe started to croon the Beatles classic, if you could even call it crooning. A few others joined in, cracked voices drifting, muffled, through the thick snow.

'Lads, lads, give it a rest – you're slaughtering it,' Scouse objected.

'Well, come on then, show us how it's done,' Joe countered.

So, as the wind howled and the snow swirled all around, Scouse started to sing.

CHAPTER FOURTEEN

SCUD ALLEY

It was somewhere around last light when I was jerked awake from a frozen slumber. For a second I had no idea what had wakened me, before my eyes were drawn to the most awe-inspiring sight imaginable. From the desert just to the west of us a massive column of vertical fire burst forth and tore apart the silence. An immense roaring, whooshing sound washed over us, as a blinding white light arced skywards at an unbelievable speed, cleaving through the heavens.

Whatever it was, it powered onwards and upwards, rising to impossible heights, before the angry light of the exhausts faded and was gone, dwindling into the gathering darkness. As the hush descended over the desert once more, the four of us at our wagon locked eyes. From the others' expressions, it clearly hadn't escaped their notice that the fiery projectile had disappeared into the skies to the west of us – *in the direction of Israel.*

We rolled out of our doss bags and gathered for a hurried heads-up. I knew for sure what we'd just seen. That was a Scud launch, and where there was one missile there were bound to be more, plus there would be the TEL – the launcher – and the Scud crews. We needed to mark the position with the Magellan and to get an urgent report radioed into HQ.

But others seemed less convinced. Jim eyed me for a long moment. 'Not sure, Des,' he ventured. 'Not sure at all. It could be an AA gun firing.'

I did a double take. 'AA' stands for anti-aircraft, but no way was that any kind of gun. That was a missile. If nothing else happened on this mission, radioing in this Scud launch would make all the angst and suffering worthwhile. Freezing cold and half-dead though we were, this was it. It was what we were here for. We'd dropped into Scud Alley to find and stop the missiles; to help prevent World War Three. We needed to have the courage of our convictions and to seize the moment. To win the day.

'Jim, if it's AA what are they shooting at?' I retorted. 'Do you see any aircraft in the sky, 'cause I don't. Baghdad's not under attack, and there is not a single plane anywhere. Plus that thing took off like the bloody Apollo rocket.'

'Maybe it is, maybe it's not,' Jim countered. 'Can't say for sure it's a Scud.'

I was getting somewhat irked. 'Looks like a rocket, lights up like a rocket and sounds like a rocket. Has to be a Scud, Jim. Let's mark it as a Scud launch.'

'Maybe it is, maybe it's not,' Jim repeated. And just kept repeating.

In response, I certainly wasn't budging, and Jim wasn't either. The eyes of the others were on us now – two former Paras, about to head for the drying room, though you'd have to go a long way to find anywhere remotely warm or dry around here. Fortunately, it was then that good old-fashioned democracy intervened. We held a vote, all eight of us, and this time the boss was very much *not* having it his way.

Everyone but Jim was convinced it was a Scud. Using the Magellan, we configured an eight-figure grid for the launch site, giving an accuracy to plus or minus 50 metres. With that, Chewie sent the burst message, getting the target coordinates winging through the skies.

Still Jim didn't seem particularly happy. I wondered if he was hypothermic; I made sure to get a hot brew into him, and tried to strike up some kind of a conversation, but still he seemed morose and downbeat. Borderline defeatist. It was not like him at all.

Despite everything, I felt totally ecstatic. We'd caught a Scud team with their proverbial trousers down, and I didn't doubt they were going to get hit. This is what we were here for. It was snowing heavily again, and Jim appeared to have his mind set on pulling out, no matter what.

'We've got to bug out, Des,' he declared, darkly, 'before all eight of us die of exposure. We're freezing our nuts off, we're going down with frostbite and our only option is to link up with one of the squadrons, or to head for the border.'

Jim was worried whether the wagons would hold up for much longer, especially in these conditions. The vehicles had taken a real pounding, plus there was the report we'd heard of the D Squadron wagon that had refused to start, leading to its occupants getting shot up and going on the run. We'd been living amongst the enemy for days now, Jim pointed out, and it was only a matter of time before we got compromised. And if we lost the vehicles, we were as good as dead.

The more I listened, the more I realized a lot of what Jim was saying was basically right. Maybe *I* was the one turning hypothermic? Maybe we *should* make an about turn and execute a dash for friendly lines? Maybe we'd all end up very, very dead otherwise?

But maybe there was an option 'A-plus', as I liked to think of it. What about if we struck out to whack a target of opportunity, and then made a dash for the border. That way, we could go out all guns blazing, executing a typical SAS hit-and-run raid at a time and place of our choosing, before high-tailing it back to safety. We were still full of bombs and bullets. We could do one final spectacular, before bugging out – the kind of thing Driller had argued for, forty-eight hours earlier.

I outlined my idea for the A-plus option, and Jim's spirits seemed to lift. I figured that as patrol commander he'd been wrestling with a horrible conundrum: did he order a retreat, to save the men under his command, but in doing so pull us out of the war without a man amongst us ever having fired a shot? For a soldier of Jim's standing – Concrete Reg through and through – that would have been a hellishly tough decision to make. The burden of command. Rather him than me.

But now he had the A-plus option: we could bug out, but do so in a blaze of glory.

Jim gave it a solid thumbs-up. That's what I liked about him. I didn't agree with all that he said. His take on the Scud launch had been inexplicable; truly bizarre. We'd flashed over it big time. But he'd been outvoted, he'd accepted it and we'd moved on. And whenever the ballsy option presented itself, Jim was up for it. Considering the state we were in, that was saying something.

To go on the offensive after everything – that was the mark of a true leader commanding an SAS fighting patrol.

We broke camp and set forth. Now the decision had been made, we were all in a more upbeat, positive frame of mind. We were heading home, but we were also on the hunt. Even better, we hadn't been driving for an age when we saw the horizon to our rear dissolve into a burst of flame. Hopefully, that had to mean that there was one fried TEL launcher and several Scud missiles incinerated in the process.

As we drove on I was hoping and praying that the intel Chewie had radioed through had been received by the head shed and acted upon. It would be great to receive confirmation, but with the dud comms we'd all pretty much given up hope of that by now. Yet something in my bones was telling me that Chewie's message had been heard and had scored results, which was a great feeling right then.

It began to snow more heavily, though now it was interspersed with blasts of freezing rain, which turned to ice as soon as it landed. Miserable conditions. Utterly life-sapping. It was painful even to hold my weapon, it was so iced up. I'd taken to sleeping with the M16 inside my doss bag, so as to keep it from seizing up with the cold, but you can't do that when you're on the move. Any exposed skin stuck to the bare metal of the vehicles and tore when you tried to pull it away. I wondered how we could fight like this, even if we could find a suitable target.

As we pushed ahead into the swirling darkness, it was only the thought of causing maximum havoc and mayhem that was keeping my spirits up. I was determined to go out fighting, as I always had been growing up on the streets of the Steel City. We had a saying in Sheffield: *Iron doesn't become steel until it's forged in fire.* That ethos had a big influence on me, in a working-class area where the future was all about the steel mills, or going down 'the pits' – the coal mines. And when the going got really tough, I put my father's behaviour on his death bed – his courage, his compassion and his resolute determination – before me, as the example that I should aspire to.

I did so right now, as we battled through that Iraqi snowstorm. No giving up. No breaking down. No turning back. This was where we would dig deep. This was where the rubber would hit the road, and where we'd finally get to show our mettle.

But only if we could find a target.

Progress was at a snail's pace, visibility terrible. Over such terrain in such conditions and driving such vehicles, we had no option but to proceed at a dead slow. With first light barely an hour away, we'd come across nothing remotely feasible in terms of a target of opportunity, and we'd pushed only a few dozen klicks towards the Saudi border. At this rate, it would take us a good week to get there, and we'd be all out of food, fuel and water long before then – never mind going out in a blaze of glory.

More worrying still, we seemed to have developed a problem with one of the vehicles. Sod's law – it was the Pinkie. As we'd crawled through the frozen darkness the 110 had started coughing and spluttering. Towards the end of the night the engine had begun cutting out. We didn't think it was a problem with the fuel. It had to be something integral to the motor or the electrics. But we were painfully aware that for a hit-and-run

282

spectacular we needed the speed of the wagons. We weren't about to go out with much of a bang, with a Dinky and a stop-start Pinkie to hand.

We found an LUP of sorts, and those not on first sentry got our heads down and slept like the dead. I awoke to take my turn on stag, with Driller as my watch-buddy. We managed to squeeze the two of us into the one bivvy bag, pulling it up to our waists in an effort to keep our legs at least warm, our weapons sheltered in there with us. Driller broke out a bar of Hershey's chocolate – one of the last from the US MREs. He cracked it in two, and we munched away in a frozen but companionable silence.

We were in rag order and we knew it – barely capable of putting up a fight. To one side, poor Chewie was tinkering under the bonnet of the 110, with freezing hands. The poor sod doubled as the patrol's signaller and the mechanic on that vehicle. Eventually, even the easygoing Uncle Chewie cracked. He slammed down the bonnet in disgust.

'Fucking piece of crap.' We guessed he'd had no joy getting to the root cause of the problem.

We were under no illusions as to what losing the 110 would signify. Disaster. You couldn't squeeze eight blokes onto a Dinky, never mind their kit. We'd have to either abandon both vehicles and head off on foot, or maybe keep the Dinky piled with our gear, and try to march beside it. Neither was a particularly attractive proposition, to put it mildly.

I realized how strong was my own desire to get out and survive. But in light of the problems with the Pinkie, it was hard to keep upbeat. It was 28 January, our seventh day in Iraq, and none of us was in any fit state to make a run for the border on our pins. Little did we know it, but the decision as to what we should do was about to be taken right out of our hands.

It was last light and we were preparing to move out of the LUP when I heard it: the distant beat of rotor blades cutting through the air. At first it was so faint I figured I had to be imagining it. The noise seemed to come and go tantalizingly, riding on the icy gusts of wind. I stopped dismantling the freezing camo netting, to better listen. I could see other figures to left and right doing likewise, so clearly it wasn't me alone who had heard something – the question was, what exactly?

The beats came and went. Louder-softer, louder-softer. The noise seemed to be coming from the southwest, so from the direction of the Saudi border. Gradually, we realized it was growing in intensity, drawing closer all the time. We locked eyes. Surely it had the signature beat of a CH-47. Was there a chance it could be coming for us? Had the head shed decided that after so long in such conditions, we needed extracting? If so, how did they even know where to find us? Were Chewie's sitreps getting through loud and clear?

It stood to reason that it was either a search-and-rescue mission, or maybe a resupply for one of the squadrons. We listened to the familiar, thudding beat of the wocka-wocka's rotors drawing closer and closer, barely daring to believe it might be coming for our patrol. But eventually the sound faded away again, until all settled back to a windblown, empty silence. The disappointment felt crushing.

'That was a CH-47,' a voice remarked, ruefully.

'Resupplying one of the squadrons,' someone added. 'Got to be.'

'Too right,' I piped up. It was exactly what I'd concluded. 'And you know what that means. If we head out on that bearing, we'll find them. We'll find A or D Squadron, whichever it might be.'

I felt a kick of adrenaline – of hope – even as I said it. Sod the risk of friendly fire – the wagons were dying on us, we were dying a slow death from exposure, and we needed to make contact with one of the squadrons. That was our ticket out of this hellhole and back into the war. With the squadron having just had a visit from a CH-47, they'd have enjoyed a major resupply, and it was inconceivable that it wouldn't have included cold-weather gear. We could link up with them, get ourselves properly kitted out, refuel, replenish and refresh. Surely that was our best chance of staying in the war.

I said as much to the others.

Then a voice piped up: 'Could be a Chinook, could be the enemy. We can't be 100 per cent certain.' It was Jim, urging caution as always.

'Hand on heart, Jim, that was definitely a CH-47,' I told him. 'And it has to be resupplying one of the squadrons.'

'Yeah, Des, it could be. Could be a Chinook. But it might just be an Iraqi helo. They do have 'em, Des.'

'Yeah, but not Chinooks, Jim. Not fucking Chinooks.'

'Could be a SAR helo. Could be the Yanks. No way of knowing it was British even.'

'Listen, it was a CH-47 resupplying one of the squadrons. Got to be.'

'Des, there's no way of knowing,' Jim insisted. 'No way of knowing.'

We flashed. The argument went back and forth, getting more heated with every exchange of words. It was looking like the drying room part two, before some of the others intervened.

'Des, mate, we just can't be certain either way.'

'Plus if it is the squadron and they see us in the distance, they're just as likely to brass us up.'

'Remember it's a full-on Sabre Squadron we're talking about here. Anything will be fair game. Chances of getting shot up are very, very real.'

I wasn't having any of it. As far as I saw it, this was our chance. Still full of bullets and bombs, we had everything to play for. I continued to argue for linking up with the squadron and sod the risk. We had a saying in the Regiment: analysis to paralysis. Basically, if you looked at every conceivable angle and every possible danger, you'd end up doing nothing. This was one of those cases, as far as I was concerned, but it didn't seem as if a lot of the others were with me.

'Tell you what,' Jim suggested, in an effort to calm things down. 'We'll put out a patrol to probe the terrain, and see if we can find signs of either the squadron or the helo. How's that?'

'Great. I'm game. Who else is going?' I said it through gritted teeth, because I still believed we should all mount up and head for that rendezvous regardless. But if this was the best Jim could manage, so be it.

'Yeah, not now Des,' Jim demurred. 'We thunder out of the snow and the darkness, the lads are going to take us for the enemy. No. We lay up here for the rest of the night, and half the patrol heads out at first light.'

'That's all well and good, Jim, but the squadron could have moved by then. We could miss our chance.'

'We could. But better that, than dead.'

'But that means—'

'Des, it's over,' Jim cut in. 'I've made my decision and I'm in command. We stay here for the night. We push out come first light.'

Jim may have signalled that the discussion was finished, but I was seething. I stomped over to the pathetic shelter provided by the Dinky, to vent and to lick my wounds. This was our one and only chance to stay in the war, and we were very likely going to miss it, and all because Jim didn't have the balls to go for it, or so I reasoned.

But as I sat there, stewing in my darkest mood yet, I remembered a salutary lesson, one it seemed I was in danger of forgetting here in Iraq. After I'd failed on my first Selection attempt, I had been called before the sergeant major of the Training Wing. He told me that I had to go before the OC, Major Dominic Pitman, the guy who'd been my company commander back in Para Reg. It was for the OC to say if they'd have me back for another shot.

'But one thing before you go,' the sergeant major added, his face darkening. 'I heard you had a fracas with Lance Smith in the drying room. Is that right?'

'Yes.'

'You know something, I'm disgusted. You fail, you take it on the chin. You don't take it out on those who've done better than you. We do not do that kind of thing up here.'

'Yes. You're right. Apologies.'

He dismissed me, telling me to go see the OC. Major Pitman

and I talked about how I'd come to fail, and how they were willing to have me back again if I fancied another go. We agreed I could try for that winter's Selection, if I really had my heart set on it. It was then that I decided to confess to the major – known to all as JC, for obvious reasons – my misdemeanour. Better he heard it from me, now, than from someone else second-hand.

'One more thing, boss. I need you to know I dragged one of the blokes into the drying room. I want you to hear it from me. I just smacked Lance Smith in the teeth.'

JC had been filling out some paperwork. He paused, pen poised over the form, before glancing up at me. I could see the doubt that had crept into his eyes. I wondered if I had blown it.

'Not very clever, Des. Not how we do things around here.' Then he kind of shrugged. 'But hell, he's a crap hat, so you can come back and try again anyway.'

The subtext was this: 'crap hats' are how we airborne types tend to refer to any regiment that isn't airborne. In other words, JC would allow me back as we were Concrete Regiment brotherhood. But otherwise, I'd have been out on my ear.

'Thanks boss.'

'But Des, make no mistake – you won't survive if you bring that kind of attitude up here. Are we clear?'

'Yes, boss.'

Only now, I wasn't convinced that I had taken on JC's advice at all. Here in Iraq, was I being too much Concrete Reg and not enough Hereford; not enough the thinking man's soldier; the grey man? Jim's cautious approach – maybe that was the right way to deal with this. He was commanding a patrol of eight men, and he was hellbent on bringing them out alive. We had one

Bravo patrol MIA, and in these conditions I didn't doubt that all had been captured or killed. Even worse would be us lot getting wiped out by our own side.

Here in the Iraqi desert A and D Squadrons had been allocated completely separate swathes of terrain in which to operate. One lay north of a certain demarcation line, the other south of it. This was to avoid any accidental contact between the two squadrons and a blue-on-blue. Neither would ever stray outside the borders of its area of operations, not without first making radio contact to warn the other what it was about to do.

There had been blue-on-blues within British special forces before, most recently in the Falklands. A member of the Special Boat Service (SBS), the sister regiment to the SAS, had been shot dead by an SAS patrol. A firefight had started when the two units had strayed into each other's territory at night. Only when voices started yelling out in English did the firing peter out, but by then the SBS guy had been tragically killed.

As I thought all of this through, I figured that maybe I was being too gung-ho. Too much of what JC had warned me to leave at Hereford's gates. I was desperate to stay in the fight here in Iraq at all costs, but sometimes you had to temper pure aggression with reason. Plus my inexperience was doubtless showing. By contrast, Jim had very likely made the right call tonight, and that was why the rest of the lads had been on his side.

The more I thought about it, the more I realized that I was the aggressor here, and why? What was I trying to prove? I'd come here hoping to finally prove that I was fit and proper material for the Regiment, but right now I was at risk of doing the opposite. Sometimes the bravest, most courageous option was not to stand

and fight. It was to take the path less travelled, just as Patrick Johnson had done, when he'd got the Bravo One Zero patrol to walk back up the Chinook's ramp and return to Al-Jouf.

That had taken real balls. That was the true mark of a man. In doing so, he'd saved his patrol from a fate that didn't bear thinking about. He'd chosen not to deploy and to fight a hopeless battle, so that he and his patrol could live to fight another day. And he'd had to make that decision, knowing full well he'd get slagged for it behind his back, and by worse men than he was.

I am generally the first to speak up and voice an opinion, but I like to think I'm also the first to concede and to apologize. I went and sought Jim out and told him exactly what I thought. He'd made the right call. I was in the wrong. And that was all there was to say about the matter.

Typically, Jim was pretty good about it. He'd been fairly similar to how I was, before he'd taken up a position of patrol command. Tonight, he didn't need or seek any apologies.

'You know what,' he ventured, 'hearing that helo made me feel kind of vulnerable. Not sure exactly why. But what d'you reckon to putting out some of the Elsie mines around the perimeter? Just for the night hours.'

In my view there had been far too many accidents caused by mines in the SAS. But tonight was different. If the enemy came looking for the source of the noise made by the mystery helo, they might blunder across our LUP by accident. At least the mines should give us a bit of early warning and slow them down a little. I told Jim I was all for it.

'Right, keep a close eye,' he said. 'I'll take Scouse and go get the mines out.'

I did just that, as the pair of shadowy figures flitted this way and that, crouching down to ground level to set the mines. That done, they came back and briefed us on the locations where they had all been placed.

Otherwise, you might wander off for an early-morning crap and end up blowing yourself to pieces.

CHAPTER FIFTEEN

ON THE RUN

At first light we forced stiff limbs into motion and prepared for stand-to: all of us awake, eyes down our weapons sights in all-around defence. After a week's solid driving and trying to survive in such horrendous conditions, we were exhausted, and not only physically. Being always on the alert, always on edge, was mentally draining. We were plagued with fatigue. The very idea of linking up with one of the squadrons and being able to drop our guard, even for a short while, was tantalizing.

As the thin light of dawn crept across the frozen terrain, there was no sign of either A or D Squadron anywhere. But then we heard it: the grunt of an engine. Despite the pitiful state of us, the adrenaline started pumping. This could only mean one of two things: an Iraqi vehicle, or one of the squadron's forward wagons. Either way we could be in real trouble.

Something hove into view. A truck. Not a Pinkie or a Unimog, that was for sure, which only left one option: the enemy. It was around 300 metres away, trundling through the snowscape in a slight dip in the terrain. As it came closer, I could make out more details. Six wheels, yellow cab, rust-encrusted bulbous orange rear. A water bowser.

I stole around to the rear of the Dinky and grabbed the familiar form of a 66 mm LAW. Such water tankers tended to accompany the regular Iraqi military units, keeping them topped up with supplies. If there was the one vehicle, there were bound to be more, and maybe even armour. I flipped the LAW out into its extended firing mode, and brought it to my shoulder. It was the one weapon we had that could take out such a target, or something even more substantial, like an Iraqi T-55 tank.

I was willing the truck driver to pass on by. We were still roped under the camo nets, with a good thatching of snow, so there was every chance he wouldn't see us. I saw the truck pull to a halt not 150 metres away. Maybe he was halting for a fag break. Our wagon was closest to the threat, and it was from one of our guys that the alert was given.

Trev gave the signal: we had one guy on foot moving towards us. Despite all the camouflage, somehow we'd been spotted, though I couldn't for the life of me imagine how. My mind started racing. First light was the best time to launch an ambush. Your enemy would still be rubbing the sleep from his eyes, and there was just enough illumination to see and to kill by. Was this the trigger for some kind of a planned attack? Was the bowser guy some kind of come-on? Were we surrounded, and about to get whacked?

My eyes darted everywhere, as I tried to keep the truck covered with the LAW. No way of telling how many more there were riding in the cab. The seconds ticked by, before Trev's hand signal changed again: the guy had reversed course and was heading back towards his vehicle . . . *at speed*. I got eyes-on and I could see that he was practically running. It was obvious what must have happened. He'd got close enough to realize we weren't Iraqi forces waiting for an early-morning water delivery.

As a result, he was now making a dash for his vehicle.

I brought the 66 to bear. I glanced over my shoulder to make sure the area of the back blast was clear. I had the truck cab bang in my sights, as my finger started to gently take up the pressure on the trigger. Then a thought struck me. *Hang on a minute, the guy is dressed in civvies*. Sure, he was providing water to the Iraqi military, but did that make him one of the enemy? A combatant? Could I really blow the hell out of him and his bowser and live with myself afterwards?

More to the point, what might the ramifications be? With some of our own – Baz Matthews, the entire Bravo Two Zero patrol and maybe others – very possibly captured, they would likely bear the blowback from any Iraqi civilians getting killed, especially if it was British special forces who were responsible. Anyone who found himself a captive was in a bad, bad place anyway. The last thing he needed was us making it any the worse.

After a long moment's indecision, I lowered the LAW. As I did so, I saw other guys doing the same with their weapons. Seconds later the Iraqi driver jumped back aboard, fired up the truck, dropped the clutch and started chugging out of there as fast as a heavily laden water bowser could go. We stood up, eyeing each other uncertainly. Had we done the right thing? Had we bottled it? Should we have blown him away regardless?

We had no idea if the truck was fitted with a radio, but it made sense that it would be. How else would Iraqi commanders call in water supplies? In which case, how long did we have before the enemy gave chase?

It was Jim who broke the silence. 'Right, lads, that's it – fucking decision made. Cam nets down and let's get the hell out of here. We know we've been compromised. In no time this area will be crawling with the enemy. We're no longer covert. We're no longer putting a patrol out to look for the squadron. Only one thing makes sense now. It's time to run for the border.'

No one was about to argue. We all got busy and in record time we had the LUP broken down and kit stowed away. We fired up the Dinky and waited impatiently for Jim to take up the lead. Trouble was, something was keeping him. Finally, he hurried over, his face like murder.

'Fucking wagon won't start. Fucking thing's died on us.' He slammed a fist into the wing of the Dinky. 'Pieces of shit!'

This was not good. Every second was precious now. But with a dead Pinkie, what options were there? We were condemned to bugging out on foot, and whatever direction we tried to head in we faced all but certain death or capture. We reckoned we were over 200 km from the Saudi border, and we'd be hunted all the way. We'd have to pile all the kit onto the Dinky and tramp beside it in the snow.

Dead men walking.

It was then that Driller had a brainwave. He eyed Jim and me for a second. 'You know what? Fuck it. Time for a good old bump-start.'

After a rushed explanation, he manoeuvred the Dinky until it was nose to tail with the bigger wagon. The rest of us got into positions, half in all-around defence, the remainder ready to shove. No way were the few of us about to push a heavily laden 110 through this kind of terrain thick with snow, but with a little help from the Dinky . . .

'Put her into second!' Driller yelled. Second gear.

With barely a glance behind Scouse gave a thumbs-up. 'Ready!'

'Right, when I give you a bump, drop the clutch and pile on the gas!'

'Got it.'

We strained at the ready, Driller gunned the Dinky's engine and moments later we were stumbling through the snow as Driller nudged the heavier wagon into motion. Scouse dropped the clutch and there was a coughing and kangarooing from the Pinkie, before a gout of choking fumes shot out of the exhaust and the engine fired into life.

A ragged cheer went up, as we leapt back aboard the wagons. We set off, bucking and bouncing across the frozen terrain going as fast as we could manage. We didn't even pause to gather up the Elsie mines from where they had been sown, just beneath the surface of the snow. If Water Bowser Guy did lead the enemy to our LUP, they'd have a nasty little surprise waiting for them. Even if they arrived in vehicles, the mines were powerful enough to blow out a tyre. The enemy would find themselves in the middle of a minefield, which would very likely slow them down a little, which should buy us a few minutes, and every moment was precious now.

To add a layer of subterfuge, we pushed west-northwest for a few kilometres, as if we were making for the Jordanian border, before executing a diversionary manoeuvre the details of which remain classified, but which got our vehicles onto a bearing for

Saudi Arabia instead. That manoeuvre is normally executed by a column of vehicles moving at night, when their tyre-tracks will be hard for the enemy to follow, the idea being that any force in pursuit was unlikely to anticipate it and would lose the trail.

Of course, right now it was almost fully daylight, but we were relying on the falling snow to cover our tracks, so that by the time the bad guys reached the manoeuvre we'd just executed, they'd miss it and lose us completely. Hell, right now we'd give anything a try.

I got up on the passenger seat of the Dinky, so I could look back along the length of our march, checking for how far our tracks were visible. *Where the hell were the blizzard conditions when you needed them?* I wondered. This was some way to bug out, having just been compromised a good 200 klicks behind enemy lines. I made a visual scan for the enemy, running my eyes across the terrain in all directions. Nothing. I did a sweep with my scope. Still nothing. Where the hell were they?

There was little chance of my falling off the seat, we were moving so slowly. I didn't blame Driller. He was nursing the Dinky along, as the engine grumbled and the suspension groaned and she ploughed through the snow. But still, and for reasons I was utterly unable to comprehend, we didn't seem to have anyone haring after us. Why? Why was no one in pursuit? Maybe Water Bowser Guy hadn't been believed. *A force of the cursed enemy, camped up in the snow, here, in these conditions. Who was he kidding?*

After an hour or so we stopped to perform a listening watch. We felt certain that A and D Squadron had to be somewhere to one or the other side of us, and we hadn't completely given up hope of making contact with them, and somehow avoiding being shot so we could execute a joyful reunion. The terrain around here was utterly flat and featureless. It reminded us of the kind of ground we'd been dropped in, nine days earlier, by the Chinook. Difference was, now it was encrusted with snow.

We'd been stationary for a good few minutes, when I spotted the dull glint of sunlight off glass. We had vehicles to our rear, moving in our general direction. It could only be the enemy, for A and D Squadrons would be pushing the opposite way, further into Iraq. I figured they were maybe a kilometre and a half distant, which would put us within range of their heavy weapons – that was, if they'd spotted us.

I passed the warning around and the consensus was that Water Bowser Guy must have talked. Our hearts were racing as we began to contemplate the worst. Our diversionary manoeuvre must have failed. Water Bowser Guy and his buddies seemed to be hot on our tail, and very possibly with light armoured vehicles and even tanks in their number.

'Bastard,' Driller growled. 'Should have captured him when we had the chance.'

'Yeah,' I agreed. 'Could have took him with us and let him go at an appropriate time. Still don't think we should have slotted him though. Imagine if we'd shot that guy and put a 66 through his water bowser. Bit overkill. Only option was to take him with us.'

'And his truck,' Scouse piped up. 'I can just see it – a Pinkie, a Dinky and an Iraqi water bowser. *Convoy*.'

'Yeah, at least we wouldn't have run out of water,' Jim added, jokingly.

There was a brief pause. That was the first time since we'd deployed that Jim had actually cracked a funny. We were almost too surprised to laugh.

As we eyed the enemy vehicles, they seemed to be criss-crossing this way and that, executing some kind of search pattern. It looked as if they'd lost our tracks, but we didn't figure that would fox them for long. Jim ordered us to mount up. We climbed aboard our trusty steed and sat there, waiting impatiently for him to take up the lead. But the Pinkie just didn't seem willing to budge. Finally Jim jumped out and kicked the 110 in a fit of sheer rage, before dashing back through the snow to us.

'Bastard wagon!' he hissed. 'This time it really is finished.'

In desperation, Driller tried the bump-start manoeuvre again, but there was not a spark of life from the 110. This was not good. With a dead Pinkie, we were condemned to bugging out on foot and just one look at the terrain told us what that would mean. East and north, we'd run into Iraqi forces. West and south, either Iraqis or the squadrons. In short, there was nowhere left to run. Either way we were screwed.

Suddenly, I had a brainwave. We had a chain in the Dinky – the one with which we had been supposed to rip out the innards of Saddam's fibre-optic cables, if we'd found any. Destroying them had been of secondary importance, for our key mission had been Scud-hunting. Yet right now, that chain might prove an absolute lifesaver.

I explained to the blokes what I had in mind. If we lashed the chain to the Pinkie, surely we could load it with Jim and his team and use the Dinky to tow the bloody thing out of there. It was batshit-crazy and very far from standard operating procedure, but it was maybe the best – the only – option that offered up any chance of survival.

As a mark of the guys' quick-wittedness – our collective ability to think outside the box – all were on for it pretty much right away. Then again, we were totally desperate, so what were the alternatives? Stay here and die. Stomp off into the snow and die. Or chain the Pinkie to the Dinky, get rolling and say our fucking prayers.

Jim added a gloss to the DIY-tow-truck escape plan. Checking our maps, he figured we should make directly for the open road, the one that led from somewhere around here right to the Saudi border. No way would the Dinky make it, if it had to drag a crippled 110 loaded with blokes and kit across the snow-encrusted desert. But on the highway we might just pull through – as long as we avoided the Iraqi military, our SAS brethren, plus the scores of high-tech US warplanes quartering the skies.

We manoeuvred the Dinky into pole position, broke out the chain and laid it in the snow, paying the length out between the two wagons. The time when you have to resort to one vehicle towing another is a moment of huge vulnerability, and we were all on edge. With the chain attached, Scouse got behind the wheel of the Pinkie, with Driller taking the lead. At first, he did his best to try to keep the engine noise down, as he eased up the revs and tried to nudge both wagons into motion, but that just left us going nowhere.

'Listen, mate, just fucking go for it,' I told him, 'and screw the noise.'

Taking that cue, Driller piled on the power, the 90's 2.5 litre engine howling as he put pedal to the metal. For a moment the

Dinky's sand-tyres spun and wrestled with the snow and dirt, as they struggled to find enough traction to drag the dead weight of the Pinkie free, before finally we lurched forward, the two wagons moving as one.

We set out at a painful crawl, sounding like some kind of mobile scrapyard. The Dinky was bucking and plunging over hidden obstructions, the chain shaking and clanking then going horribly taut, as the two vehicles tried to wrench themselves free of each other. The noise felt as if it must be audible to every Iraqi from here to Baghdad, but at least we were underway. Moving in daylight like this, a Dinky towing a Pinkie, it couldn't be long before we started taking hits. It was a horribly exposed feeling.

No matter how much the enemy vehicles to our rear kept closing the gap, Driller couldn't nurse any more speed out of the Dinky, with the weight she was being forced to drag through the snow. We tried executing a few evasive manoeuvres, but these were designed for a column of SAS war wagons moving at speed through decent terrain, not for us, creeping along in tandem through this desert snowscape.

Finally, I called a halt. By default, as the Dinky was taking the lead, I'd shouldered some of the burden of command and decision-making. That was always the role of the lead wagon, and that vehicle's commander.

In tense and heated tones, we tried to work out what the hell we were to do. From the looks of things, the enemy were not so many minutes behind us now. I argued that we needed to stand and fight – and to do so here, at a time and a place of our choosing, or at least as good as we could make it. Others were adamant that we should keep running. Thankfully, those amongst us who knew the futility of that course of action won the day.

We parked up where we could best conceal the wagons, de-bussed, and moved a good 200 yards away from them. That way, when the bullets started to fly, at least the enemy mightn't lay eyes on the vehicles. If they did spot the Pinkie and the Dinky, they were sure to mallet them, just to make triply sure we were trapped. We got into a snap ambush, the two Minimis, our handful of LAW 66s and the M203 grenade launchers primed and ready to let rip. Then we lay in the snow on our bellies, burrowed in as best we could behind the odd boulder and rock, and waited.

'Fuck, seems like they're going to do a left and right flank on us,' Driller warned.

From what we could see of the enemy manoeuvres, it looked as if he was dead right: rather than coming at us head-on, it seemed like they were going to try to get behind us; to surround our position, ensuring there was no avenue of escape. My mind flashed back to Driller's comments about saving a final bullet for each other, to avoid getting captured. Dark thoughts.

When facing imminent combat, the mind does strange things. Time slows, so that a second seems to last a lifetime. Actions play out in tortuous slow motion. I seemed to have aeons in which to think; to reflect. Here we were facing imminent death, as I had done so many times before in the Regiment, but all those times I'd somehow managed to survive. So maybe there was a chance that even now, death could be cheated one final time.

Three times I'd suffered 'parachute malfunction'. The first was the Roman candle, when HALO training on Cyprus. But not a year later I'd been in Switzerland, jumping with the Fernspäher, that nation's nearest equivalent to the SAS and experts in high-altitude mountain parachuting. I was there to learn some tricks from them. We did a jump over the Eiger, diving out of a Pilatus PC-6 Porter, a Swiss-made aircraft with an incredible short-take-off-and-landing capability. We leapt out high above the peaks, pulling the chutes at around 12,000 feet, due to the mountains towering all around us. But unbelievably my chute malfunctioned again: *Roman candle number two.*

Of course, I was shitting myself. Who wouldn't be? But I managed to do a repeat performance as before, executing a cutaway and punch, and at 7,000 feet I triggered my reserve. I got down safely, but not to any great accolades from the Fernspäher boys. I'd done the right thing, but I'd been too slow, they cautioned. By the time I'd triggered my reserve, I'd near as damn it ploughed into one of the flanks of the Eiger, for it drops down in a series of steps. As they pointed out to me, I was very lucky to be alive.

They say trouble come in threes. The third malfunction was the worst. Not long after the Eiger jump I was in a country in East Africa, the location of which remains classified, training with that nation's special forces. We did a series of HALO jumps, on one of which I felt my chute deploy, but somehow not fully. I had guys to left and right of me screaming: 'Des, cut away! Cut away!' As I tried to work out what the hell was going on, I realized I had a line trapped over the canopy, which basically cut it in two. One side held far more air than the other, so it was skew-whiff, making me highly unstable.

The chute threw me into a spin, something I had absolutely no control over. If the rotations became too severe, the G-forces would make me black out, at which stage I was finished. As the deformed chute slammed me around the sky, I fought with it like it was some kind of thing possessed. It cannoned me one way and then the other, flinging my legs out almost at right angles. Of course, I knew in my heart that the chute was screwed, but I just didn't want to cut away – *not for a third time.*

How many lives did a guy have? If I'd stuck with that chute, I wouldn't be here now. Finally, I managed to conquer the fear and to cut away. It wasn't a nice landing, but I survived.

The point was, the lesson was, you had to master your fear. In fact, you had to *channel* it. To be able to step foot into the valley of the shadow of death time after time, and to fear no evil, you had to harness your fear. That was the essence of soldiering in the Regiment. I never once refused to jump, even after those three malfunctions had earned me the 'kamikaze' nickname. You had to harness the fear and use it to give you absolute self-belief; the confidence that you could win through almost anything.

Like now, facing an Iraqi army – eight blokes lying on the open desert snows.

CHAPTER SIXTEEN

DESPERADOES

We waited. I put my hand to my dog tags and repeated my mantra. Over and over, and if the truth be told with more urgency than I had ever done before. And for some reason – one that I will never be able to understand, not until the day I die – the enemy failed to close on us, so as to wipe us off the face of the earth. There was little point speculating as to why. It made not the slightest sense to me nor any of the other guys. But somehow, those in pursuit just didn't close right in, to annihilate us.

Muzzles sparked. Probing bursts of fire laced across the landscape. Rounds from heavy machine guns skittered and whined horribly, as they ricocheted off the frozen terrain. To left and right there were the snow-muffled pops of impacts. But the enemy seemed to have gone static. They kept standing off, lobbing in the odd burst of fire from afar.

Maybe Water Bowser Guy had let his imagination run riot: maybe he'd reported that there were thousands of us armed to the teeth. Somewhere around here A and D Squadrons were raising merry hell, so maybe that had added to the enemy's reticence, their lack of hunger to properly whack us. Maybe they'd mistaken us for one of the Sabre Squadrons, which underscored their reluctance to close for the kill. Once bitten, twice shy.

After an hour or so, we figured we could wait no longer. When you've lain on frozen ground for too long without any form of insulation, your body starts to freeze to the surface. Literally. You actually have to peel yourself away. And the longer you remain, the more the ice-cold earth will suck away whatever strength remains. Eventually, your screwed-up mind starts to tell you, *This feels nice. It's warm and it's comfy here, so why don't we stay?*

We forced ourselves to move; peeled away; clambered to our feet, limbs screaming. We kicked others into life, wherever we had to. If the Iraqis weren't going to come and finish us off, we had to get moving. Keep pushing on. Stay here, and one way or another we were going to die. Stop moving and we were dead. Stasis equated to death.

We stumbled to the wagons. Driller fired up the Dinky. God bless the little beauty – she wasn't inclined to give up on us, not yet. In a stop-start pantomime we got moving, chain clanking as we crept onwards, pressing southwest across the benighted landscape, eyes peeled, searching for that metalled road. But the snow carpeted everything – warping contours, features, landmarks. It was the most horrific and exposed feeling ever. Where was that bastard road?

I still couldn't understand why we hadn't been smashed. I could still see the glint of sunlight on windscreens to our rear. But we also heard the odd, distant burst of heavy weapons firing to either flank, so maybe the squadrons were out there right now mixing it and causing merry hell. We knew they'd been in action from that burst message we'd received. We knew they were advancing in strength and that they packed a real punch. Maybe that was what had saved us? Who knows?

I also couldn't understand why we hadn't been hit from the air. Surely the Yanks could see us? So why hadn't we got a few barrels of napalm or a maverick missile up the Pinkie and the Dinky's backsides? Nothing made any sense. It was as if we were moving in a dream. But the cloud cover was thick and glowering, so maybe it was shielding us from the eyes in the sky. We pushed on. No point stopping. We weren't Scud-hunters any more. We weren't hunting anything. We were the hunted.

We were like rats, and we were crawling towards the sanctuary of the border, praying that against all odds we might make it.

It was mid-afternoon and we were still creeping towards the border, the Dinky dragging the dead weight of the Pinkie, when I spotted it. From the passenger's seat of the lead vehicle, I detected the glint of sunlight on metal a way up ahead. It had to be the enemy. Sure enough, they'd got in front of us and were lying in wait.

I dragged out my scope and got a butcher's. As I pulled the image into close-up focus, it wasn't what I was expecting at all. This was no Iraqi battle tank or BMP, hull-down and monster gun swinging in our direction. Instead, it had the sleek, glistening, curved lines of some kind of an aircraft. Or maybe even a missile. Could it be a Scud, lying this far out in the desert and apparently abandoned?

'What in the name of God is that?' I muttered.

We crept closer. The nearer we got, the more concrete shape and form the mystery object took on. Eventually, we could see it was either the fuselage of an aircraft that had been shot down, or maybe some kind of 'drop-tank' – extra fuel tanks that warplanes carry slung under their wings, when executing long-distance sorties. When the fuel is exhausted the tank is jettisoned, hence the name.

We skirted around it without stopping. There were a couple of the objects, each looking like a giant silver pod. As we pushed onwards, there were more and more of them scattered across the terrain, but the beguiling glint they gave off just served to add to the sense of disorientation and confusion we were feeling. We knew we had the enemy at our backs. We could sense it. But were the flashes of sunlight to left and right enemy vehicles, or more of the pods?

No way of knowing.

We drove on through the final hours of daylight, fighting exhaustion. Towing a wagon like this, frozen stiff, hounded by the enemy, we were all utterly finished. Several times my forehead smashed into the Dinky's dashboard, as I fell asleep at my post. God only knows how Driller was keeping awake. If we carried on like this, we were bound to crash into a boulder, or worse still drive over some unseen, snow-choked ravine, as Driller – or Scouse – dozed off at the wheel.

Eventually, with dusk almost upon us we called a halt. We pulled up close to a couple of the discarded pods. We stayed in the vehicles as we studied the terrain. The light began to fade, as the snow-heavy, glowering skies seemed to sink down and merge with the darkening desert. We scanned our arcs. There seemed to be no movement and no sign of any vehicles in any direction now. The desert was like a ghost land.

'Can you see anything, mate?' I asked Driller, as he executed a 360 scan, using a pair of binos.

'Yeah, what's that to the left of us?'

I looked where he indicated. 'It's unmoving, mate, so could be a drop-tank.'

'Could be. I'll keep eyes-on.'

We did this for several long minutes, before something extraordinary happened. It was Chewie who first noticed it, and as the wagons were pulled in close we could all hear.

'Don't see that very often,' Chewie remarked. 'At any other time, we'd be enjoying that, you know.'

We glanced in his direction. Chewie had an arm outstretched towards the west. By some quirk of the weather, the Iraqi sun had managed to emerge from the thick cloud cover, even as it sunk towards the earth, going down in a blaze of golden red. Fingers of sunlight lanced through the belly of the clouds, dusting them a fiery pink. As the sun slipped lower and was swallowed by the earth, the effect seemed to spread, until the entire sky was etched in pink, from horizon to horizon.

As if by some unspoken understanding, we'd stepped away from the wagons to watch the show. The wind had dropped. It was noticeably less icy. We were still cold, wet and miserable, and in rag order, but for a few seconds we were transfixed by the setting sun.

In my mind I was thinking: *Bloody hell, we've survived everything that's been thrown at us these past few days, but is this a good or a bad omen? We're still together, still alive, the trucks are bruised and battered and half-dead, but we aren't beaten yet.* Even as I entertained those thoughts, and the sun slipped out of sight completely, I felt my spirits lift. *Yeah, we're going to get through this.*

I turned to Driller. 'What d'you reckon, mate?'

'Nice. Great sunset.' He glanced at me. 'And you know what, we're still here.'

'That we are, pal, that we are.'

It was an emotional moment. I knew exactly what Driller meant. No one had managed to capture or kill us. Not yet they hadn't, anyway.

'You know what they say, mate,' I added. 'Red sky at night, shepherd's delight. Maybe it's a good omen?'

Driller snorted. 'Yeah, maybe in Yorkshire they do. More sheep than people. I bet your first date was with a sheep.'

'No mate,' I countered, 'my first date was with the wife, Emily. The one and only.'

'Bullshit. I've see your tats. How many names did you have to have blacked out, just so she can't see them when you're on the job? Just short of a footie team, wasn't it?'

I laughed. Humour. If we still had it, no one had managed to beat us yet.

In my teens, I had had a few tattoos done, including one or two girlfriends' names. I was done with that by the time I was in the Paras. At one stage I'd talked to Emily about getting them all properly removed, in part because the Regiment isn't keen on tattoos, especially any overtly military ones. But her take on it was simple.

'Des, you've had them since you were sixteen. They're a part of you and you're too old to get rid of them now. I know you're thinking about work, but it's simple – just keep them covered.

Wear a long-sleeved shirt. At the end of the day, I don't even notice them.'

It was nice of her to say so, and I listened. I didn't have any removed. But I did have the girls' names blacked out, for obvious reasons.

I went to grab a quick heads-up with Jim about what was next with the patrol, as we slipped into the night hours.

'Mate, I reckon if we press on in the darkness there's a good chance we might lose a wheel, or worse,' I remarked. 'I reckon we've made enough distance between them and us, so how about we stop right here?'

Jim was in full agreement. We figured we'd remain in the wagons, good to go if we had to suddenly get on the move – not that you could make a 'sudden' move, with a Dinky towing a Pinkie. We'd keep some guys on stag, while the rest tried to doze in the wagons. And that was exactly what we did, all night long.

Come first light, there was not the slightest sign of any other forces in the area – hostile or friendly. We got moving, thanking whatever gods there may be that the Dinky, at least, agreed to start. But with the road still nowhere to be seen, we began to argue amongst ourselves about whether we should change course, and head for where we figured A Squadron had to be. When we stopped for a listening watch, we could hear the odd distant grunt of a diesel engine in that general direction.

The other guys reckoned that had to be the squadron. I figured that was maybe wishful thinking. It could just as easily be Water Bowser Guy and his buddies. Once you've been seen by the enemy deep behind their lines, and when they know your warplanes have torn seven bales of shit out of their mates, you were hardly likely to be given an easy ride. No, the enemy would not want a target like us to slip through their hands. We'd been lucky, but they were out there, searching, of that I felt certain.

The consensus was that we press on for the border. The risks of changing course on a wing and a prayer were just too great. Driller got the Dinky rolling, and an hour or so later, from out of absolutely nowhere, a concrete road appeared. We pulled up so we could survey its length. It seemed utterly deserted, from end to end. Gently nursing the Dinky, Driller eased us up onto the hard, smooth surface, dragging the 110 on its clanking chain behind it.

It was still very early in the morning and a cold mist blanketed the desert, the road rising just above it. It was eerie, to put it mildly. We turned onto the road, still taking it real easy, in case the Dinky was feeling inclined to give up the ghost. After days in the desert, it felt utterly bizarre to be driving down a smooth patch of tarmac, and even more unsettling to not have every turn of the wheel accompanied by a deafening chorus of jolts, bangs, clanks, groans and thumps.

As we trundled along that exposed stretch of highway, I had never felt so exhausted or so chilled to the bone. We had to be approaching the Saudi border, but what a cruel irony it would be if the Dinky gave up on us now, or if our bodies packed up on us. All of a sudden we emerged from the mist to arrive at a crossroads. Before us lay two highways, intersecting each other, complete with lamp posts and road signs. They, of course, were all in Arabic, so we were still none the wiser.

After nine days in the blasted wilderness, to us this appeared like an utterly absurd – almost impossible – apparition. Then, through aching, smarting eyes, we spotted something even more bizarre lying further up ahead. It was a police car, parked up just beyond the junction. It looked like an everyday NYPD cop car, complete with black and white chequered decals and a big set of blue and red lights atop the roof.

Driller and I glanced at each other. *What the hell?*

'Fuck, that's a New York cop car,' I muttered, my voice hoarse and cracked. 'Fuck, you don't see that every day in the Iraqi desert.'

Driller replied with something equally bizarre and we lapsed back into silence. It was like a Mexican standoff. Here we were, eight blokes frozen solid, riding in a Dinky towing a Pinkie, and there they were parked up in their New York-style cop car, nice and toasty. And between us lay what we could only presume was the Iraq–Saudi border.

From what we could see, the cops looked like your typical Saudis, with close-cropped dark beards, pristine white head-scarves atop smart uniforms. After nine days of deep desert operations, we looked like ... well, what exactly did we look like, I wondered. A bunch of the evillest cutthroats from the dirtiest souk in all of Arabia? To a man we were bearded, skin stained black, wearing a hodgepodge of combats, NBC suits, Arab shemaghs, mixed with a smattering of civvie gear. Basically, anything that might offer a modicum of warmth.

We were also filthy, unwashed, stinking to high heaven, and on top of all that we were armed to the teeth. 'Piratical' was the word that sprang to mind. And if the Saudi coppers only knew it, stuffed in our Bergens we each had nine days of frozen excrement – another reason to absolutely refuse us entry into the Kingdom of Saudi Arabia, if this was the border.

Of course, the Iraqis had been waging war against the Saudis, for the Saudis had provided the main bases for Coalition troops, and that had to mean that any Saudi border force was bound to be more than a little nervous; on edge; trigger happy. Driller had slowed the Dinky to a little above walking pace. I signalled for him to stop completely.

I got out of the wagon on frozen-stiff pins. I glanced back at Jim in the Pinkie, then forward to the cop car, my eyes like saucers. Telling the blokes to cover me, I took a few tentative steps, forcing my legs into motion. I had my M16 held in my hand, but down by my side, adopting the most non-threatening stance I could muster.

I turned back to the wagon, and gestured for Trev to join me. 'Listen, we're going to go forward and hopefully have a chat with those guys,' I rasped. 'But all non-threatening, okay?'

There was still no movement from the cop car, and this early in the morning I figured the guys had to be kipping. I felt edgy as hell, for although this had to be the border, and they had to be Saudis, there was still just that tiny nagging doubt in the back of our minds. We closed the gap, warily, moving in from where we'd stopped, a hundred yards or so from the cop car, until just a fraction of that distance separated us.

Finally, I saw movement. One head, and then two, turned in our direction, the cops' eyes wide with shock. Finally, they cracked a window, staring out at us like we had just beamed down from planet Zog.

'British troops,' I announced, through cracked lips, the words sounding so weird after so long fighting and running behind enemy lines. The cops looked decidedly unimpressed.

'British troops,' I tried again. 'Iraq. Coming from Iraq.'

Then I had something of a brainwave. I unwound my shemagh, which after so many days was half-frozen and half-glued with dirt and sweat to my features. Maybe that might convince them.

'British troops,' I repeated.

Getting a butcher's at my features, the cops seemed to relax just a fraction. One started speaking, though neither of them had yet to step foot outside their vehicle.

'It is okay, I speak good English,' he told me, in what sounded like a pukkah Oxford accent.

Trev and I almost laughed with relief. I asked if he could take us to his leader, to which the guy confirmed that he could.

Then I paused for an instant, and, as if in afterthought, I added: 'You *are* Saudi police, aren't you?'

The guy cracked a smile. 'We are. There is nothing to worry about. We are. Follow us.'

I said we'd be happy to, but we'd have to go very, very slowly, 'cause we were a Dinky towing a Pinkie. To avoid any confusion, I gestured at the umbilical linking the two vehicles. They stared at the tow-chain. I could read the expression in their eyes. How in the name of almighty Allah had we managed to emerge from the war-torn Iraqi desert . . . like that?

Just goes to show you, the Lord works in mysterious ways.

They shrugged. No problem. We'd take it nice and easy.

CHAPTER SEVENTEEN

DELIVERANCE

We limped our way across the border, and from there we headed to the local Saudi cop shop. Once we reached it, Jim managed to put a call through to Al-Jouf, using the Saudi cops' phone. Several hours later one of our officers turned up with fresh vehicles, and together we towed our battle-scarred wagons back to Al-Jouf. By the time we got there it was obvious that some of us – all of us, truth be told – were knocking on death's door.

We stumbled to the showers. I got under the showerhead, turned it on and collapsed into a squatting position, and for a good hour I just let the hot water gush over me. Thawing out my hands and feet was sheer bloody agony. I had frostbite alright. Eventually, I got a bit of food down me, but what I craved more than anything was sleep. I had never felt so utterly finished.

Incredibly, one of the head shed started banging on about the possibility of us deploying again – in other words, heading back into the Iraqi desert. Apparently, we were the only patrol to have pulled off anything remotely like what we had. As we clearly knew what we were doing, they might need us to head back in again. We could lead patrols to some of the Scud sites we'd identified, to ensure they'd been properly smashed. We might even be able to seek out some of the missing guys.

Words failed me. *Unbelievable*. Right now, and for some time to come, none of us were going anywhere.

They'd managed to get a few tents flown into Al-Jouf. I crawled into one, feeling half-dead, found myself a dry doss bag and was instantly asleep. I awoke many, many hours later, having lost all track of time. After a quick feed, we had a first proper debrief and I started to appreciate why the head shed were so keen to get us to turn around and venture back into Iraq. At that moment, we had as many as forty-three blokes missing and on the run. Apparently, because our patrol had been so 'successful', they figured we might be able to buck the trend.

The story of our successes went like this. While we had faced insurmountable problems getting clear comms from HQ, they had suffered no such issues with our burst signals. Every single one had been received loud and clear. The problem had been *one-way only*. As a result, they had put in scores of airstrikes. They figured we had enabled them to take out several key targets, along with 240 Iraqi troops manning those positions. How the hell they did the body count I had no idea.

I queried that very thing, asking how they could be so sure. Their answer: they'd got our target descriptions and coordinates, sent in the air recces and airstrikes, and the number of enemy dead was most likely in excess of 240. That was a conservative count. They had the intel and the reports to back it all up.

At all points they had been able to plot pretty much where we were, from the sitreps and the grids Chewie had been sending. Apparently, they had been amazed – gob-smacked – that under such conditions we had stuck with the task, dealing with garbled comms and the worst Iraqi winter in living memory, at the end of which we had got everyone out alive, not to mention the vehicles. Hence our patrol was an SAS success story, and right then that kind of thing was in precious short supply.

Hearing that gave all eight of us a real sense of achievement and a feeling of euphoria. Against all odds, we'd achieved our mission objectives – it had just taken the head shed to tell us that, before our exhausted minds could properly grasp it. We might be hobbling about on frostbitten feet and feeling like utter shit physically, but in terms of the mission, we'd pulled it off. And truthfully, despite the failure besetting the other patrols, that felt good.

Bravo One Zero we knew hadn't deployed, but there was more news about Bravo Two Zero. After an epic escape and evasion, Chris Ryan had made it to Syria, where he'd been handed over to the British consulate. He'd been able to reveal part of their story. Sure enough, they'd been dropped amidst impossible terrain. Compromised by a goatherder, they'd come under fire and been forced to go on the run. Like us, their comms had failed – both the Clansman and the TACBE. Like us, they'd been hit by terrible weather.

Unlike us, they'd decided to head for Syria, as opposed to Saudi Arabia, chiefly because they believed it was the only way to shake off the enemy. It was what the Iraqis would least expect. Hit by the snowstorms, they'd got split up. Andy McNab had led a group of five, who'd opted to hijack an Iraqi taxi and drive for the Syrian border. They'd run into an Iraqi military roadblock, and in the ensuing contact Bob Consiglio, my Blow Monkeys buddy – 'It Doesn't Have to Be This Way' – had got shot and killed.

For me, that news was a real body blow. But there was worse. Three men – Chris Ryan, Vince Phillips and Stan Jones – had marched into the blinding snow, facing the same kind of conditions we had endured, but minus vehicles. In the process, Vince had got separated from the others and he was very likely dead from hypothermia. Chris Ryan and Stan Jones had run into a second Iraqi goatherder. Stan had chosen to believe that man's offers of help, but Chris figured the Iraqi was hellbent on treachery.

Chris had pushed on alone towards Syria and after a truly epic journey he had made it. As for the rest of the Bravo Two Zero patrol, one man – Bob Consiglio – was definitely dead and the rest were either dead or very likely captured. I didn't doubt for one second that we would have suffered the same fate, had we not taken vehicles.

One of the things that Andy made certain to mention to the Head Shed was the mines we'd left in the ground, when we'd bugged out of our hide, after being spotted by water-bowser-guy. That way, when British forces did take possession of that area of Iraq, they would be able to mark off the minefield, to prevent any friendly forces from blundering into it unawares. In due course they'd lift the mines out of the ground. Otherwise, innocent parties might get injured by them.

Shortly, Chris Ryan was flown over to join us. He turned up looking seriously the worse for wear. He was dressed in a shaggy Arab goatskin overcoat and massive boots with the laces undone, and he was hobbling on his swollen feet, barely able to stand. His face was cadaverous and there was a haunted look in his eyes. He'd lost 38 pounds in weight, the skin had peeled from his feet, his toenails had dropped out, he had liver and kidney problems, and at one stage he'd ended up drinking radioactive waste, by accident. And by his own admission his head was right royally screwed.

Unbelievably, the head shed spoke to Chris and told him that once they'd got him kitted out again, they'd redeploy him into Iraq. It was the same as they'd suggested to us. What planet were they on? Chris and I talked through all that had happened with Andy McNab's patrol, one that I had originally been slated to be part of. He held out little hope for any of the others.

'Honestly, Des, I figure they're all dead. If any of them were still at large, they'd have made the border by now. That suggests they've all been killed or captured, and capture is as good as dead.'

Having spoken to Chris, I made a point of searching out Patrick Johnson, the commander of Bravo One Zero, to hear what had happened from the man himself.

'Yeah, Des, it's like this,' Pat began. 'We got off the Chinook first time around, took a good long look and thought: *Fuck, this is not what we were briefed at all.* It was flat as a pancake with not a shred of cover, and hard as rock underfoot.'

'That's exactly how we found it, mate.'

'Right, so we got back on, I got on the intercom and told the pilot: "Not a good area. It's not possible here. Can you fly us to an alternative DZ?" The pilot did just that and we tried again, but it was pretty much a carbon copy of the first. I said to Stan: "We will not get an OP in here. We will get compromised. As patrol commander I'm saying this is not possible. We will fail. We will get compromised and we'll be on the run with no vehicles." Stan agreed. So, reluctantly, we climbed back up the ramp and aborted.'

Stan Hardy was Pat's second-in-command, the equivalent of me on our patrol. As with Pat, he was another bloke I rated very highly.

'So, Des, what d'you think of all that?' Pat asked. 'What's your take on our decision?'

'Listen, mate, you did exactly the right thing, and do not let any other fucker tell you otherwise. Look at the Bravo Two Zero patrol. You guys would have ended up just like them. And you know what, we got compromised and had to go on the run, and the *only* thing that saved us was the vehicles.'

I told Pat he'd saved the lives of all on his patrol, and he should feel good about it. Typically, his decision not to deploy had gone down 'like a sack of shit' with the head shed, he told me. Again, what planet were those guys on? Sadly, the sniping would only continue, as men who had not been there on the ground accused Pat of cowardice. Eventually, Patrick Johnson, a great soldier, would resign from the military.

After forty-eight hours at Al-Jouf we were flown back to Camp Victor. We were taken to the local souk, to buy a bunch of UAE phonecards. Using those, we called our loved ones. I dialled the home number. Luckily Emily was there.

'Listen, lass, gotta be real quick,' I told her, 'but I'm fine and I'll be coming home. I know you've seen loads of stuff on the news, but I'm out of there now. Love you and see you soon. And that holiday to California – just as soon as I'm back, we're going!'

She told me she loved me and that she couldn't wait.

More than a little tearful, I have to say.

In the ensuing days the rest of the patrols filtered back across the border. We gathered at Camp Victor for a 'hot debrief' – something of a regimental tradition. At a hot debrief, anyone, no matter their rank, is free to say whatever is on his mind. Bryan

Clarke, the D Squadron bloke who'd been shot in the body when their wagon had failed to start, had survived his ordeal. He was there, strapped up in his bandages and seeking answers.

The hot debrief opened with each squadron being invited, patrol by patrol, to outline what exactly had happened. I heard accounts of the A and D Squadron patrols taking on some serious targets.

When Jim presented our patrol's achievements, there were more than a few raised eyebrows. Everyone in A and D Squadrons had heard about the Bravo patrol disasters, so this was something entirely unexpected. It took forty-eight hours for all the presentations to be complete, after which the CO got to his feet to take questions from the floor. Everyone was expecting him to take a real pasting.

The first question was the most obvious: why, when patrols went into their 'lost comms' procedures, had the SAR helos not materialized? Apparently, Bravo Two Zero was not the only patrol to have headed for a supposed SAR rendezvous, only to find no chopper there.

This was the CO's answer. At one stage he'd had forty-seven blades unaccounted for and very possibly on the run. He'd considered sending in SAR choppers, but he risked losing several airframes and their aircrew, not to mention the blokes who would be riding with them, to bolster the rescue teams. All things considered, he hadn't felt able to risk any more men.

It was getting decidedly heated by now. Someone asked him why there were lost comms procedures at all, if they weren't going to be adhered to. The CO countered by saying that it was his decision and his alone to decide what was appropriate at the time, and in war tough calls had to be made. Several figures told him they thought he was plain wrong. The CO retorted that they were entitled to their opinion, but he'd do the same thing all over, should the same circumstances arise.

People were steaming angry. They made the point that being special forces, they were old enough and experienced enough to be told the hard truth. If no one was going to fly to their aid, better to know that from the start, so they could act accordingly and get themselves out of the shit. The CO agreed that was something 'we all need to look at'.

Of course, calling in a SAR helo hadn't even been an option for us, as our comms were screwed. Jim raised the point: 'Right, so with the Bravo patrols, what was the problem with the comms?'

By way of answer, the CO turned to one of the officers from 264 Signals Squadron, the specialists who handle communications for the Regiment. The guy got to his feet and cleared his throat. 'Unfortunately the Bravo patrols were not supplied with the right frequencies. All three Bravo patrols.' Then he sat down again.

Jim and I glanced at each other in dumbstruck incredulity: *How the fuck does that even happen*? Not giving us the right frequencies was like handing someone your home telephone number, but forgetting to give them the area code. It was that simple an error. Chewie looked like he was poised to rip the guy's head off.

'And the TACBEs?' Jim asked. 'What about them?'

The same figure got to his feet again. 'The same thing – the wrong codes.'

Had Andy McNab's patrol been given the right codes, they would very likely have got through on their radio or their TACBE. They had tried with both and both had failed. They could have called in a SAR helo and no one needed to have got captured or killed. This single failure was utterly beyond belief. That, along with the crap terrain and weather pictures, had cost good men's lives. Short of dragging the 264 Squadron bloke into the drying room, what more was there to say?

By now we knew the full cost of the Bravo patrol screw-ups. After their taxi had got stopped at the Iraqi checkpoint, Andy McNab and his lot had been captured. Two men, Dinger Bell and Steve Legs Lane, had got away, but they made it only as far as the Euphrates River, which they had to cross to get to Syria. They'd tried swimming it, but Legs came down with hypothermia. Dinger managed to get him across to the far bank, but he was too far gone. Legs had died of hypothermia and Dinger was also captured.

Vince Phillips, the guy who'd lost contact with Chris Ryan's group, had also died of hypothermia. Stan Jones, the guy who'd put his trust in the Iraqi goatherder, had been betrayed. After a fierce firefight, he was also captured. Which meant that three men were dead, four had been taken prisoner and one, Chris Ryan, had got away.

None of this was pre-ordained. They could well have been pulled out safely, if only the right codes had been provided for the Clansman and the TACBEs. If we'd had proper vehicles, they'd have gone in with wheels, and very likely driven and fought their way out of there.

One bright point was the news about Baz Matthews, the A Squadron staff sergeant who'd been left for dead in Iraq. Baz had been found by the Iraqis, barely alive, and taken to Baghdad for surgery. By luck, he was operated on by one of Iraq's top surgeons, a man who had done his medical training in the UK. He spoke fine English and he told Baz that in saving his life, he was glad to be able to repay a little of the kindness he had experienced when in England. Baz Matthews would make a fine recovery and he would be repatriated to the UK by the Red Cross.

That night we went out on the town in the UAE, for the 'wet debrief' – in other words, a skinful of ale. As the beer flowed, tempers flared and there were more than a few punch-ups. But frankly, it was long overdue. We all needed to let off steam.

At one point one of the A Squadron sergeants sought me out. He told me that the Chinook we had heard flying in, on our eighth night in Iraq, had indeed been a resupply flight. On it were various packages for our patrol. Mostly they were Afghan-style coats, long shaggy garments made of goatskins. Apparently the RSM, Peter Radcliffe, had paid a visit to the Al-Jouf souk, to buy up whatever cold-weather kit he could find.

One of those parcels had had my name on it: 'Cold-weather gear for Des Powell.' Better late than never, I figured – not that any of it had ever got to us. If we'd managed to link up with A Squadron, it would have been a different story, of course.

After the hot debrief and wet debrief, we broke down into squadron-level groups, to drill down into any other issues. One of the officers told what remained of the Bravo patrols how we should have done this and how we shouldn't have done that, before I saw him turn in my direction.

'One last thing. There are reports of a certain spacing bar for a .50-calibre Browning having gone missing.' He paused. 'Well, Des, did you pilfer one of the SEAL team's spacing tools?'

I stood up. I was so livid I could have ripped the guy's throat out. 'What the fuck did you say?'

He blanched a little. 'Des, Des, calm down. I'm just asking about a spacing tool for a point-five-o.'

That was it. 'You fucking listen to me: in circumstances where we had no fucking kit, 'cause the mighty SAS couldn't furnish us with any, I'm big enough and ugly enough to go and get whatever I can wherever I can, especially as it's me who's heading 300 klicks behind enemy lines. I did what I had to, and I'd do it again. And by the way, I'm in the fucking SAS just like you are, so don't talk to me like some fucking kid. I'm not having it.'

Case closed.

As matters transpired, it would be the Bravo patrols – those sent in at the tip of the spear with the worst possible kit and the unusable comms – that would earn the greatest recognition from the Gulf War. There was a slew of medals, including – rightly – a Military Medal for Jim, the commander of our patrol. Chris Ryan also received an MM, in recognition for his epic escape and evasion, plus Andy McNab received the DCM, after he was released by the Iraqis and returned to the UK. There was a rake of other decorations as well. But mostly, 'we' grabbed the limelight amongst the public when Andy McNab published his book, in 1993, telling his patrol's story – *Bravo Two Zero*.

Despite the obvious shortcomings and challenges we experienced during the Gulf War, to me the Regiment remains the finest fighting unit in the world. I say that because, in spite of everything thrown at us in Iraq, we still pulled off some utterly incredible missions. For me, to have attempted Selection twice and to have made it into the SAS was one of the finest moments of my life. After Iraq I would go on to serve with the Regiment for a further sixteen years, every one of which was an honour and a privilege, something accorded only to the few.

As to the exploits of the Bravo Three Zero patrol, I remain proud of what we achieved in Iraq. Few know of us, due to the high profile and notoriety earned by our sister patrol, Bravo Two Zero. But we were also there, against all odds doing exactly what we had been sent in to do. The Israelis never did enter the war. Their paratroopers remained in their barracks, as the Scud threat dissipated. Special forces operations in Iraq reduced Saddam's Scud launches against Israel by more than 80 per cent, which is one hell of an achievement. In that, our patrol, Bravo Three Zero, played its part.

Of course, not a man in our patrol fired a shot in Iraq. We'd gone there hungry to mix it with the enemy and thirsting to get 'into the war'. We'd come away, nine days later, having escaped by the skin of our teeth, and to this day I do not know how we managed to evade the enemy and bring all of us out alive. I'd gone there hoping to prove myself fit for the Regiment. I'd imagined doing so by leading from the front, all guns blazing, Concrete Reg all the way. I returned having learned that another way entirely is possible.

While those who serve in the SAS have to be ready to take life when required and to fight tooth and nail when necessary, in Iraq I had had my eyes opened. I'd begun to realize that we were as much about saving life and preventing death – winning hearts and minds – as we were about being the killer ninjas or the 'death-dealers' that popular myth and imagination can tend to cast us as.

Just days after the last SAS patrol returned from Iraq, that nation surrendered. I'd like to think that we played a key role in minimizing the wider casualties and in bringing the war to a close.

EPILOGUE

After the Gulf War the Regiment was determined, as ever, to take care of its dead. Four men from the SAS had died on operations in Iraq, five had been injured and a number had been taken captive. Via the good offices of the Red Cross, the prisoners of war were repatriated, once the fighting was over, and the Iraqis also had the good grace to return the bodies of our dead.

One member of A Squadron had died. Just a few days before the cessation of hostilities David 'Shug' Denbury had been killed in a firefight with the Iraqi military. The dead man's family asked that he be buried at a private ceremony in Wales, and that is exactly what happened. The other three men killed in Iraq – all of whom were from Andy McNab's ill-fated Bravo Two Zero patrol – were buried by the Regiment, in Hereford. They were Sergeant Vince Phillips, Corporal Steve 'Legs' Lane and Trooper Bob Consiglio, my Blow Monkeys buddy from camp.

Their funerals were held simultaneously, on a Friday at St Martin's church in Hereford. At the end of the service, the funeral party, with the padre in the lead, carried the coffins at a slow march, escorted by a firing party armed with M16s. Behind each bearer party walked the bereaved families, including grieving widows and their young children, who had lost a father.

The funeral cortege halted at the plot reserved for the fallen of the SAS, where the padre spoke the closing words. As each coffin was lowered into the ground, the firing party let off their volleys – a crisp and fitting salute – after which the plaintive notes of the Last Post played by the bugler rang out across the scene. Thus our dead were lain to rest and we paid our respects, remembering men who in many cases we had known for years.

Some time after the Gulf War, several accounts of individual SAS missions were published, including Andy McNab's book, *Bravo Two Zero* and Chris Ryan's, *The One That Got Away*. There have been various criticisms levelled at these and other authors, accusing them of 'over-egging the pudding' in terms of the dramatics and heroics that took place on the ground in Iraq, especially with relation to the Bravo Two Zero patrol.

Chris and Andy were, and remain, good friends of mine, and as far as I am concerned our patrol could so very easily have suffered the same dire fate as did theirs. Thankfully, I wasn't on the Bravo Two Zero patrol as it was finally constituted, so I avoided getting wounded, killed or captured. As I wasn't a part of their patrol I don't feel qualified to comment on the authenticity of their accounts, but knowing both men as I do, they have my respect. I salute each of them for getting out alive, as I do all of the Bravo Two Zero patrol members, who survived the terrible trials and tribulations of Iraq.

Had proper SAS war-fighting vehicles been provided at the time, then I am certain that McNab's patrol would have grabbed them with both hands and deployed with guns and wheels. I am also certain that Patrick Johnson's patrol would have gone in driving vehicles, and that when they drove down the Chinook's open ramp, they would have surmised that even though the terrain was horrendous, at least with war-wagons they could run and fight their way to the border, if need be.

That is the real failure, in terms of the fate that befell the Bravo Two Zero patrol (and the Bravo One Zero patrol for that matter). Levelling criticism at those men who, in spite of everything did their very best to achieve their missions, is unacceptable in my view, and especially when the Bravo Two Zero patrol's dire fate – and the fate that befell Bravo One Zero - owed much to the failure to equip those fighting men properly for war.

As I've said, all the men of both patrols have my respect.

I went on to serve for another sixteen years in the Regiment, and I am proud of every year that I served. During that time I deployed across Asia, North Africa, East Africa, Southern Africa, the Balkans, across Latin America and to many other countries. Two years after returning from the Gulf I did have something of a fracas with one of the B Squadron sergeants, and the way that was dealt with entailed me transferring to D Squadron. In retrospect it was a blessing in disguise, as I got involved in far more stuff operationally with D Squadron than I would have done had I remained in B Squadron. So it's an ill wind that blows nobody some good, as they say.

In fact, I enjoyed my time with D Squadron so much that I did extended service for six years, after I'd completed my twenty-two years. During my time with the Regiment I was fortunate enough to become reasonably fluent in Spanish and Arabic, two key languages for the territories in which we operated. I also spent some of my time involved with missions carried out by The Unit. I ended my time in the Regiment having achieved Warrant Officer rank (WO2), and having been appointed 22 SAS liaison officer for 21 SAS (the territorial unit), and to elite units across the Five Eyes (FVEY), the alliance which unites American, Canadian, Australian, New Zealand and British military and intelligence functions.

In 2004 I left the British military to work in the private security sector, and I have continued to do so to this day. During that time I have acted as a close protection officer for a raft of VIPs and celebrities, including Christina Aguilera, Ricky Martin, Rod Stewart, Anastacia, Jeremy Kyle, Robbie Keane and Jim Davidson, to name but a few. As a private security contractor I worked for charities like Médecins Sans Frontières and for international media companies including CBS, ABC and NBC in Iraq, Afghanistan, Libya, Haiti, Kurdistan, Syria and elsewhere.

During a long and happy marriage Emily and I were able to have three children, two sons, Jake and Sam, and a daughter, Jessica. The boys are now both young men, and I am immensely proud to say that my oldest, Jake, is an accomplished boxer, and is poised to follow in my footsteps, going into the British military. Sam is an acclaimed professional dancer who most recently starred in the stage adaptation of the movie *The Bodyguard*, and I am overjoyed that he has found his path and is doing so well. My daughter, Jessica, is the youngest, and she's studying music and dance at college. Needless to say, she is talented and gifted beyond measure.

Sadly, a life in the British military elite, and thereafter in the private security sector, does tend to take a heavy toll on personal relationships. In 2020 Emily and I divorced, although our separation has been entirely amicable. We recognized that with all the time we had spent apart – mostly due to my being away in the world's trouble spots – we had drifted away from each other.

Desert Storm and the Gulf War are a part of (recent) military history. The defeat of a major force like the Iraqi military by a coalition of militaries, whose technological advancement ensured comprehensive victory and few casualties, was witnessed live and direct by the world's publics, as the TV pictures were beamed into people's living rooms. That made this perhaps the first war to unfold blow by blow, almost as it happened. Air power, stealth weapons, smart munitions and lightning-fast armoured operations were key to winning the war, and set the tone for future conflicts. But so too was the role of the SAS – and related American units – operating deep behind enemy lines on the ground.

Since the collapse of the Soviet Union and the dissolution of old certainties enshrined in the Cold War, the free world has faced a plethora of new foes. International terrorism, rogue states, narcotraffickers, people traffickers, mafia-type crime syndicates of stupendous wealth and power – in each of these cases the weapon of choice for taking them on is invariably special forces operators, working in close cooperation with the world's intelligence agencies.

In Iraq we had deployed with more or less the same kind of kit and weaponry that the LRDG and the SAS had used, in World War Two. Our missions deep behind enemy lines proved that not a great deal had changed in the interim, and despite the high-tech weaponry that the Coalition had been able to bring to bear. When it had come to hunting for, finding and eradicating the threat posed by Saddam's Scuds, no amount of state-of-the-art surveillance equipment or air power could do what was needed. At the end of the day it had all boiled down to a handful of lightly armed special forces operators, who, with a bit of grunt, good humour, spirit and savvy, had managed to do what was required.

In a sense, those are the defining aspects of special forces sol-diering. They were during World War Two and they remained so in Iraq, as they do today. As long as that is the case, none of those who wish to do us harm should be able to sleep easy at night, which is exactly how things should be.

Since the Gulf War, a number of rogue states have done their utmost to acquire, improve and perfect the Scud missile weap-ons-delivery system. They have worked upon refining chemical, biological and nuclear warheads, to deliver the kind of horrific devastation that we had feared would be visited upon us, or upon Israel, during the Gulf War. More than seventy years after Nazi Germany developed the V-2 – the world's first long-range guided ballistic missile – its derivatives are out there, and being perfected into ever more devastating weapons systems.

As just one example, North Korea's Hwasong-6 ballistic mis-sile is a derivative of the Soviet R-17 Elbrus – the same missile system from which Saddam Hussein developed his Scuds. The Hwasong-6 carries the NATO reporting name 'Scud'. Similar weapons systems have proliferated in Iran, Syria and Yemen, amongst other countries, with North Korea being the main exporter of such lethal technology. North Korea also produces mobile launchers for its Scud missile systems, and for its ICBMs, which are reportedly the world's largest road-mobile ICBMs and potentially the largest liquid-fuelled missiles anywhere.

Hunting for the Scuds and their derivatives may be far from over, but fortunately, as Saddam discovered in 1991, we are up to the challenge.

With regards to the careers of all those who served on the Bravo Three Zero patrol after the events portrayed in this book, suffice to say all are doing well, having enjoyed fine periods of service in the military, and all have managed to put some water back into the well, as we like to say – doing good in the world.

ACKNOWLEDGEMENTS

We could not have written this book without the help of the following people, and please forgive us for any individuals we may have inadvertently forgotten, and to those we cannot acknowledge by name, due to security reasons.

Our good friend, military and intelligence veteran Paul Hughes, deserves a very special mention, without whom this book would never have seen the light of day. Huge thanks to Nickie Robinson, for always providing clarity; to Nick Tulip, for your friendship and support; to Jamie McGinlay, for cooking up a lot of laughs along the way; to Mark Mel Georgia and Jay Ward, for offering help when it was most needed; to Derren Robertson - 'The Governor'; to Ken Hollings, for influence more than you can know; to Luca Gorlero - my Dubai family; to Derek Gamblin - forever a blade; to Brian Thornton - my right hand man; to Stephen Raisbeck, for watching my back.

Our gratitude is extended to our literary agent, Gordon Wise, of Curtis Brown, for steadfastly helping bring this project to fruition, and to all at our fantastic publisher, Quercus, for the same, including, but not limited to: Charlotte Fry, Hannah Robinson,

Bethan Ferguson, Ben Brock, Fiona Murphy and Jon Butler. Our editor, Richard Milner, deserves very special mention, for his constancy, inspiration and fortitude, as does Luke Speed, our film agent at Curtis Brown.

Our superlative and long-standing publicist, Sophie Ransom, also deserves special mention, as it is always a pleasure to work with such a steady pair of hands and a sharp and incisive mind, as possessed by such a true professional.

Thanks also to Julie Davies, for your research and diligence concerning the story as portrayed in these pages. We are also indebted to those authors who have previously written about some of the topics dealt with in this book and whose work has helped inform the writing; we have included a full bibliography.

Thank you also to Paul and Anne Sherratt, who read the MS of this book in draft form, and provided your incisive and insightful comments, as always, and not to mention picking up a plethora of typos.

Huge thanks to the real Phillip Jeans, for the very generous donation to the charity Supporting Wounded Veterans, who do such wonderful work with wounded veterans affairs on all levels. Huge thanks also to the real Jim Dickson, whose wife entered Jim into a raffle for an author's promise, without telling him, and all to support the excellent WWII museum in Northern Ireland, War Years Remembered, run by curator and owner David McCallion and a team of dedicated volunteers, which houses amongst other wartime memorabilia WWII SAS commander Colonel Blair 'Paddy' Mayne's private family collection.

Enormous gratitude is also extended to Sensei Ben Mills, of the Wimborne-based Bushido Wado-Ryu Karate Club, whose inspiration, leadership, rigorous training and occasional beastings have proved such a welcome antidote to sitting at the desk, punching the keyboard. Your classes have kept the author(s) both focused and inspired, and helped keep them relatively sane during yet another punishing research and writing schedule. Every path starts with a first step. Thank you.

The first author, Des Powell, would also like to thank his family for their help and understanding during the lengthy and at times stressful period of writing this book, namely 'The Acorns' – Jake, Sam and Jessica, for staying strong as always, and especially during your early years when Dad was away travelling the world.

Thanks are due also to Eva and the ever-patient David, Damien Jr and Sianna, for not resenting Dad (Damien Lewis) spending too much of his time locked away . . . again . . . writing . . . again.

BIBLIOGRAPHY

The Real Bravo Two Zero, Michael Asher, Weidenfeld & Nicolson, 2011

Storm Command, General Sir Peter de la Billière, Motivate Publishing, 1992

Soldier Five, Mike Coburn, Mainstream Publishing, 2004

Victor Two, Peter 'Yorky' Crossland, Bloomsbury, 1996

Bravo Two Zero, Andy McNab, Corgi Books, 1993

Immediate Action, Andy McNab, Corgi Books, 1995

Eye of the Storm, Peter Radcliffe, Michael O'Mara Books, 2019

The History Of The SAS, Chris Ryan, Coronet, 2019

The One That Got Away, Chris Ryan, Century, 1995

Sabre Squadron, Cameron Spence, Michael Joseph, 1997

INDEX